Cold War Exile

Cold War Exile

The Unclosed Case of Maurice Halperin

Don S. Kirschner

University of Missouri Press
Columbia and London

Library of Congress Cataloging-in-Publication Data

Kirschner, Don S.
    Cold War exile : the unclosed case of Maurice Halperin / Don S. Kirschner.
        p.   cm.
    Includes index.
    ISBN 0-8262-0989-0
    1. Halperin, Maurice, 1906–   . 2. College teachers—United States—
Biography. 3. Academic freedom—United States. 4. World War, 1939–1945—
Secret service. 5. Cold War. I. Title.
LA2317.H36A3   1995
378.1′2′092—dc20
[B]   94-44129
                                                                              CIP

∞™ This paper meets the requirements of the American National Standard for
Permanence of Paper for Printed Library Materials, Z39.48, 1984.

Text Design: Rhonda Miller
Jacket Design: Stephanie Foley
Typesetter: BOOKCOMP
Printer and Binder: Thomson-Shore, Inc.
Typefaces: Gill Sans and Times

For Tony and Elena

Contents

Acknowledgments

I have been most fortunate in the assistance I have received with this project along the way. A President's Research Grant from Simon Fraser University financed my research trips to Oklahoma University and to the National Archives in Washington. Halperin's children, Judith and David, both contributed important information and have been supportive from the beginning. Barnett Kalikow very generously turned over to me a bundle of material that he had already gathered on Halperin's life. Hayden Peake shared his extensive knowledge of Elizabeth Bentley with me, and sent me copies of all congressional hearings in which Halperin's name was mentioned, as well as a copy of the relevant sections of Bentley's 1945 deposition to the FBI. Woodrow Borah, Ernest Blaustein, Hubert Gibbs, Solomon Lipp, William Newman, and Nathaniel Weyl offered their recollections of different periods in Halperin's life. I was also assisted in various important ways by John Taylor of the National Archives in Washington, and by Joseph Boskin, David Bushnell, Alberto Ciria, Robin Fisher, Saul Gamoran, Barry Katz, Kathleen Kilgore, Stanley Kutler, Robert Lamphere, Elizabeth McCrank, Ortrud Newton, Karl Peter, Jim Ross, Arthur J. Schlesinger, Jr., Hari Sharma, John Silber, Penny Spagnolo, Joe Walwick, and Lauren Wispe.

Woodrow Borah, David and Maurice Halperin, Solomon Lipp, Arthur Schlesinger, Jr., and Nathaniel Weyl all granted me permission to quote from their various communications with me.

Three of my colleagues merit special commendation. Ronald Newton guided me through some of the mysteries of Latin American affairs and served patiently (and often) as a sounding board to my ruminations on the project. Richard Debo translated a key document for me from a recent Soviet military journal. Michael Fellman put his own work aside to give the manuscript a thorough going-over. Predictably, his comments added both clarity and subtlety to the finished product.

I owe something beyond gratitude to Maurice Halperin. Quite apart from the taped interviews, he has been cooperative throughout and gracious enough to remain silent in most cases where my judgments did not flatter him, although in a few instances I think I heard him grinding his teeth. It has been a bonus for me that he is such delightful company.

As always, my wife, Teresa, brought a keen professional eye to my work and her buoyant spirit to my sometimes dour disposition. The professional eye helped; the buoyant spirit was essential.

Cold War Exile

Introduction

For years several of us—professors at the university—had badgered Maurice Halperin to write his memoirs. We did not know his life in detail, but what we did know suggested that it was a life like few ordinary Americans in our century have experienced. One day, a few years ago, I was having lunch with Maurice, and I asked the obligatory, "Why don't you write your memoirs, Maurice?" Apparently I caught him in the right mood, because within a few weeks the two of us were at it. Maurice's role was to reminisce on tape and to provide me with relevant memorabilia and materials—everything from photographs of his parents to his ten-year FBI file. My job was to provide continuity and context, and to do the writing.

My original scheme for the book was to tell the life story of a political refugee from mid-century America. Before long, however, I began to realize that there were implications in this story that suggested something more complicated. Eventually I defined the project in terms of three interrelated themes.

The dominant one was simply Halperin's life, which is a remarkable tale in its own right. Like a picaresque novel, it is made up of loosely connected adventures in which the hero engages a series of rogues in combat, emerging from each encounter bloodied but unvanquished, and ready to ride off to the next adventure. The reader, of course, should feel free to reverse the roles of hero and rogues in any or all of these encounters.

Halperin left his native Boston when he was twenty years old, taught school in a small town very deep in the heart of Texas, earned a master's degree at Oklahoma University, and completed his doctorate at the University of Paris, all by the time he was twenty-five. Ten years later he was fired from his professorial position at Oklahoma

1

University just in time to join the fabled Office of Strategic Services (OSS) on the eve of the Japanese attack on Pearl Harbor. After the war he was successively a lobbyist at the UN for the emerging state of Israel and the head of an academic department at Boston University.

Then he got caught up in the rapids of history, and his life spun out of control. In 1953, at high tide of what is commonly known as the "McCarthy Era," he was publicly accused of having committed espionage for the Soviet Union during the war. Convinced that no good could come of this situation in the prevailing political climate, Halperin chose to expatriate himself to Mexico, where he spent the next five years, before moving on to Moscow for three years during the "Khrushchev thaw." In 1962 he took advantage of an open-ended invitation from Che Guevara and moved to Havana, where he spent the next six years as a guest and employee of the Cuban government. Finally, in 1968, he joined the faculty of Simon Fraser University in Vancouver and has resided in Canada ever since.

In the most general sense, this is the story of a second-generation American Jewish intellectual who responded to the rise of fascism by moving into the political left, and spending many years there before coming to the conclusion that the Soviet Union was a lie and that the reality of socialism would always betray its promise. But that story has been told a thousand times. What makes Halperin different is how he experienced the journey. Very few American leftists ever actually saw the Soviet Union, relatively few got a really good look at Cuba after its revolution, and almost none of them experienced both Russia and Cuba in any serious way. Halperin lived and worked in Moscow for three years and in Castro's Cuba for six. He is unique.

The second theme is a cracking good spy mystery that grows from the charge of espionage made against Halperin shortly after the end of the Second World War. His accuser was a woman named Elizabeth Bentley, who had served as a courier for the Soviet Union throughout the war before turning herself in to the FBI in 1945. The mystery springs from the fact that she had no evidence to back up her testimony against Halperin or any of the other several dozen people she accused of wartime espionage. Halperin admits having known her briefly, but he flatly denies passing along or discussing any classified information with her. Clearly one of them is lying, but which one is it? The answer to this question is important far beyond Bentley and Halperin, for the whole jerry-built apparatus of the domestic Cold War rests in part upon her credibility.

The solution to the Halperin-Bentley mystery, then, is important not only for the light it sheds on Halperin's life, but for what it might tell us about some of the deeper historical currents of the postwar years. Ordinarily it is the historical context that helps us understand the behavior of an individual. In this case, it is the behavior of an individual—two individuals actually—that might help us understand the historical context.

The third theme involves the solution to our mystery and raises important questions about the nature of historical knowledge. How do we historians "know" things? Specifically, how do we know things in the absence of documentary evidence? The answer, in brief, is that we explore whatever indirect evidence is available, we weigh the possibilities that arise from this evidence, we choose what appears the most likely from among them, and then we do our best to make a persuasive argument for it. To put it less delicately, we often fly by the seat of our pants and deal with blurred probabilities.

That is what I propose to do with the mystery at hand. Since I have two conflicting accounts with no way to verify either, I intend to discuss the behavior, ideals, motives and characters of the principals involved. I shall try to make a best-case argument for both Bentley and Halperin, raising questions about their credibility and asking why either one might have lied; and then, having laid out the evidence, and having discussed a few alternative possibilities, I shall invite you, the reader, to be the historian. I shall ask *you* to consider the evidence and the theories, to weigh the probabilities, and then to solve the mystery on your own terms. Finally, I shall offer my own thoughts about the mystery.

A few words of caution are in order. This book is addressed to the general reader, which should explain to the specialist why I seem at times to be discussing the obvious. It should also explain the absence of scholarly apparatus. Where I think it is useful or necessary, I have included citations to specific sources. Otherwise I have chosen not to burden the reader with the lengthy bibliographies and complex scholarly debates on such subjects as Communism in the 1930s or McCarthyism in the 1950s. I have appended a general Note on Sources to the end of the book.

Finally I want to call the reader's attention to a device I have used extensively. Throughout the book there are passages—some of them quite lengthy—that are in italics and set off from the text. These are passages taken verbatim from interviews that were taped from late 1988 to early 1991. Almost all of them are from Halperin himself. My purpose is to try to convey to the reader a sense of the man through the words and rhythms of his own reminiscences. Occasionally I edited the text very slightly for purposes of compression or clarity, but I tampered as little as possible with the cadences, and in no case have I altered the meaning or intent of what was said. Halperin himself reviewed the entire manuscript and did not alter a word in any of these quotations.

1

Perspectives

_____

On a morning late in March 1953, Maurice Halperin appeared before a closed session of the Senate Internal Security Subcommittee (SISS). It was at the peak of that phenomenon known to us today as "McCarthyism." This particular committee was chaired by Senator William Jenner of Indiana, but it was engaged in the same type of investigations as Senator McCarthy's Operations Subcommittee, though with a bit less hoopla and a bit more responsibility. A bit. Halperin's first session with the committee lasted only minutes. He was asked a few questions about his political beliefs and affiliations and about subversive acts he was alleged to have committed while he was with the Office of Strategic Services (OSS) during the war. He refused to answer the questions on the grounds that Congress had no right to invade his conscience and no right to force him to bear witness against himself, citing the First and Fifth Amendments, respectively. Halperin was released with the understanding that he would reappear before the committee that afternoon to answer essentially the same questions in an open session.

The second bout turned out to be rather more grueling. Committee Counsel Robert Morris first asked a series of questions that delved into Halperin's educational and occupational history in considerable detail, and then he got down to the matter at hand. He asked Halperin if he had been a member of the Communist party when he appeared before the committee that morning. The two men sparred verbally for a few minutes, then Halperin asserted that the committee had no right to inquire into his politics and that, as a teacher, he had a special obligation to protect academic freedom, which was threatened by the

5

question. Eventually, he again used the First and Fifth Amendments to justify his refusal to answer the question.

That exchange set the tone for the remainder of Halperin's testimony. Morris fired off a barrage of questions about Halperin's politics at various times of his life, about the politics of some of his acquaintances, and about the allegation that he had committed espionage in conjunction with Elizabeth Bentley, a onetime courier for the Soviet underground in the United States. To each of these questions he responded with his Bill-of-Rights defense. He made a general denial of having committed any crimes, including espionage, but he refused to answer any specific questions about espionage.[1] The session dragged on with neither party budging. Morris asked question after question, and Halperin avoided answer after answer, invoking the First and Fifth Amendments repeatedly.[2] He intoned "I refuse to answer that question, sir, for the same reason" so often that it began to sound like an incantation.

At the end of the session, Halperin received permission to enter a statement into the record on the meaning of these amendments. In it, he asserted that any teacher who yielded before congressional pressure to discuss his beliefs and affiliations, and those of his friends, "has given up his freedom of thought and conscience; he has conceded that the state has the power to investigate his mind and, by inescapable inference, to control it." He went on to address the Fifth Amendment, which "was born in the struggle of religious dissenters resisting tyrannical attempts by the state to punish non-conformism" and which continues to serve as a safeguard against "tyrannical prosecutions" such as those latent in the abuse of power by congressional committees.

The Boston press the next morning paid little attention to this stirring defense of the Bill of Rights. It focused instead on the fact, as one tabloid put it, that Halperin had not denied that he had committed treason. What came across in the coverage was that Halperin did not

---

1. I shall discuss some of the implications of answering and not answering such questions in a later chapter.

2. The committee refused to accept the First Amendment as grounds for silence, but it did accept the Fifth.

deny being a Communist, did not deny that he had had many friends and acquaintances in Washington who were Communists, and did not deny that he had committed espionage. In the eyes of many he was, in the parlance of the era, a "Fifth Amendment Communist," although in fairness to the Boston press, that term did not appear in the accounts of his session with the Jenner Committee. Eight months later Halperin was living in Mexico, a refugee from the politics of his country.

Before we shed tears for the plight of a man persecuted for his beliefs, perhaps for beliefs he did not even hold, it is necessary to emphasize that the real issue here was not what Halperin believed, or which political party he supported, or what his friends' affiliations were. It was espionage, and as Earl Latham caustically observes about Halperin's First Amendment declaration, "It is hard to imagine that wartime espionage is one of the truths that the great teacher Socrates died to maintain."[3]

Actually, the Jenner Committee entered the investigation sweepstakes rather late in the game. The first serious postwar congressional probe into Communism began in 1947, when the House Committee on Un-American Activities (HUAC)[4] inquired into the beliefs and affiliations of ten Hollywood figures, mostly writers. The "Hollywood Ten," as they came to be known, did not take kindly to the inquiry, and they responded to the questions with a collective loud and nasty attack on the integrity and patriotism of the committee. Asserting that the First Amendment protected them from such an assault on their beliefs, they refused to answer the committee's questions. Unfortunately, they ignored the advice of some of their lawyers and refused to employ the Fifth Amendment to justify their silence. As a consequence, they were found guilty of contempt of Congress and sentenced to substantial periods of confinement in federal "correctional institutions."

3. Earl Latham, *The Communist Controversy in Washington: From the New Deal to McCarthy* (Cambridge: Harvard University Press, 1966), 202.

4. The correct acronym for this committee is thus HCUA, but the committee is commonly known as HUAC (pronounced HUGH-ack), perhaps because it is difficult to pronounce HCUA without sneezing. Some people feel that the acronym HUAC is itself political—that it has a derisive connotation. Absolutely none is intended in this book.

With this sensational beginning, the issue of domestic Communism entered into the nation's postwar political debate. The following year the issue took on much darker implications with the testimony of two former couriers for the Soviet underground apparatus in the United States. Whittaker Chambers produced substantial evidence that implicated Alger Hiss, a rising young State Department official, in prewar espionage. Elizabeth Bentley, while she produced no evidence at all, made allegations of wartime espionage against several dozen federal employees. One of her subjects was Maurice Halperin. Thus the McCarthy era began before anyone outside of Wisconsin had ever heard of Senator Joseph McCarthy.

Halperin was a devoted family man with a charming, lively wife and two lovely children. He was open, relaxed, and affable, an altogether pleasant and normal man who enjoyed good food, good wine, good cigars, and good conversation. Bentley had identified him as an accomplice in 1945, and his name had surfaced in that connection once or twice since then, but nothing came of her accusations until the Jenner Committee took up his case in 1953. Now, having stood accused before the nation and presenting no defense, he was living as a political exile in a foreign land. How had it come to this?

Maurice Halperin was born in Boston in 1906. His parents were Jews who had come to America a few years earlier from Gritsev, a town in the western Ukraine near the Polish border. His father's family had been small merchants, and his maternal grandfather had been a bookkeeper. Thus, on both sides of the family, work with the mind prevailed over work with the hands. Halperin's parents had been sweethearts in the *shtetl* (ghetto) back in the old country, but, as was often the case with emigrants from southern and eastern Europe, the man came over first to establish himself before sending for his wife or fiancée.

The senior Halperin became the owner of a cigar and notions store. It was the kind of mom-and-pop operation that filled the neighborhoods of that era. This is not to romanticize the running of a small business. Working from early in the morning till late at night six or seven days a week is no picnic. But seventy- or eighty-hour work-weeks were not uncommon at the time, and the store at least served, much as the farm had served traditionally, as a means of integrating the family, holding it together, and giving it meaning, and it freed its owners from the tyranny of factory regimentation. The store did not make the Halperins wealthy, but it provided them with a modest income that shielded them from the economic insecurity that blighted the lives of many immigrants at the time. All things considered, Boston was good to the Halperins.

The language of the household in the early years was Yiddish, but by the time Maurice was in his teens it was perhaps two-thirds English. The secret language, the language the parents spoke when they did not want the children to know, for instance, that Dorothy next door was sleeping with the milkman while her husband was away at work, was Russian. On the whole, the general framework of their lives was not much different from that of many other East-European Jews at the time.

In some respects, however, the Halperins were quite different from many immigrants of the same background. The father was a man of broad learning and eclectic interests—he had gone beyond the basic Jewish education he had received in Russia and was self-taught, but none the less learned for that. In the old country he had begun to translate Shakespeare from Russian into Hebrew, and he continued to read voraciously in the New World, where he discovered, among others, Thoreau and Emerson. Even more unusual in an immigrant home, Halperin's mother was also educated and a reader. So young Maurice grew up in a home where books were read, music was heard, and art was appreciated. That sort of thing stamps itself on a child; it provides a reference point. In most cases it rubs off on the child. Sometimes it rubs the wrong way, and the child rejects it forcefully, which is an act of affirmation in its own right. Either way, it leaves its imprint. In Maurice's case, culture rubbed off and played a major role in shaping his life.

HALPERIN: One of my earliest recollections was having visited the Boston Museum of Art. This [experience] was a traumatic one. We were in the section in which the Greek statues were displayed—enormous

white figures. I was a little shaver and suddenly I found myself alone.
Lost my father. And I remember the terror of being among these great
big figures, you know, white figures, all alone. I began to cry and he
showed up. This past summer I went back to the same collection. I
had my brother and sister-in-law with me and I explained the reason
I wanted to go to this particular spot. While we were at it, a very
interesting thing. There was a bust, the head of someone identified
as Hercules. I looked at this and I said, "Oh, my God, that's Fidel
Castro!" Perfect image. Castro has a classical Greek face. I showed
this to the others there, and I said, "Yes, this is the spitting image of
Fidel Castro." Amazing, you know. Of course, it was a young Castro,
the Castro that I knew twenty years ago. Well, it's an example of how
the present and the past interlock.

The presence of books in the household, and of people who read
them, encouraged Maurice to read from an early age. More than that,
they gave a certain direction to his reading because they reflected the
broadly humanistic orientation of the father, which had grown out of
the cultural renaissance of East-European Jewry in the late nineteenth
century. Politically this was expressed as a kind of humanistic socialism. (Marxist literature, which was unknown to the father, was absent
from the household.) Morally it was expressed as a broad tolerance
for the opinions and commitments of others, and for the acceptance
of all sorts of people in proportion to their own humanity. Religiously
it meant that Halperin's father was a non-observant Jew, that is, a
man who was steeped in Jewish lore and history, and who commonly
observed the religious holidays as a means of honoring his cultural
identity without particularly honoring God.

These were the values that nurtured the young Halperin. His Jewishness was impressed upon him, but, he says, "from a secular point
of view." Thus the Jewish holidays were often celebrated in a secular
fashion. Halperin remembers one Passover that was attended by some
friends of the family who were also secular Jews, along with a few
Gentiles, and a still relatively unknown black singer named Roland
Hayes, who was to become perhaps the first major black concert artist
in the nation. To welcome a black to a social occasion before World

War I, at a time when Woodrow Wilson was busy resegregating government jobs in Washington, was indeed remarkable, but it underscores the broad humanism of the Halperin household that played such a large role in the socialization of young Maurice.

It was at about this time that Halperin began his musical education. His violin teacher was a young man recently over from Gritsev and badly in need of pupils. He was also a cousin of Jascha Heifetz, then a young prodigy at the start of his career. Coincidentally, Halperin's father had known Heifetz's father when they were boys back in Gritsev. As a result, Halperin's father was invited to the Heifetz suite at the Copley Plaza after the prodigy's concert in Boston.

HALPERIN: First of all, going to the Copley Plaza would be like going to the Presidential Suite of the Waldorf Astoria. It was something, you know, going into this luxury thing, and he came back with some very interesting stories about how difficult a boy Jascha was. Jascha was then a minor so the old man still had control of him. I don't remember the details, but my impression was that this boy—this marvelous player—was an ornery s. o. b. Well, you know, years later we found out more about the character of Heifetz. Somewhere around 1930 he came to Oklahoma City and gave a concert. Naturally Edith and I were there. Afterwards we lined up in the dressing room area to shake his hand. And when I came to him I put out my hand and said something about "I was a pupil of your cousin Gerber, and my father knew your father, and so forth." His face was absolutely like a block of granite; there was no expression. He seemed a little bit almost not human.

The violin lessons began when Maurice was eight, and after a few years it became clear that he had more ability than Gerber could handle. So he moved up to another teacher and proceeded to use up that one in a few years as well. Eventually he ended up with a teacher who sat directly behind the Concertmaster of the Boston Symphony. Maurice proceeded to try the man's patience by not practicing, a common affliction of adolescent male music students. Had he stayed with the instrument, Halperin thinks he could have had a career in music— not as a soloist perhaps, but as a member of a first-rate symphony orchestra. It was not to be. The battle of wills between teacher and pupil was a standoff, and a standoff in that situation is a victory for the student. Halperin put his violin down when he was nearly finished with high school, and didn't touch it for another twenty years.

A different perspective on the socialization of the youngster was provided by the father's politics. While not a political activist in any sense, he did vote, and his vote went regularly to Eugene Debs, the perennial Socialist candidate for the presidency early in the century. It went to Debs, that is, until 1916, when world affairs forced him to reconsider and vote for Woodrow Wilson. That was the campaign in which Wilson ran as peacekeeper, hammering away at his success in keeping the nation out of war with Germany. As it happened, this was very important in the Halperin household. The Halperins were pro-German at the time, because Germany was at war with Russia, and anyone who was an enemy of the tsar was a friend of all Russian Jews. Of course, it helped that Debs was not the Socialist candidate that year, but Debs was not really the issue; the fate of the tsar was the issue, and it was discussed passionately by the Halperins' circle of friends.

The intensity of these discussions impressed itself on ten-year-old Maurice, who expressed his own commitment by fervently admiring the German army, playing soldier with replicas of its helmets, and worshipping his hero, the kaiser. When the tsar was overthrown early in 1917 the Halperin circle could then in good conscience swing behind the increasingly belligerent Wilson, and behind the nation when it finally did go to war with Germany. That was fine with Maurice, who had no trouble turning on the kaiser and becoming "a very great American patriot."

The Russian revolution itself became a hot topic in the Halperin circle during the next few years. There were perhaps a half-dozen families of similar background in this group, and they debated long and hard about the matter. Some of them rejected Communism, and argued that the only solution for Russian Jews was Zionism. Others felt that the Communists should be given a chance. Halperin's father was in this second group. Zionism, at least at that time, was not considered a realistic solution by very many Jews. But Communism, well, who could say? The values proclaimed by the Bolsheviks were certainly consistent with the humanistic commitments of the father, and more than that, the Bolsheviks had firmly and explicitly rejected anti-Semitism. In fact, they made it illegal. It was all so new and promising. Give them a chance. That, too, impressed the boy.

The Halperins lived in a modest working-class neighborhood in Boston. Ethnically it was a neighborhood in transition from Jewish to Italian with a sprinkling of Irish. It was there that Maurice first learned about anti-Semitism as something other than an abstract topic of conversation at home. In particular, he remembers an Italian boy at school when he was perhaps ten years old, the class bully who regularly picked on him. One day Maurice decided he had had enough. He was going to put a stop to this or die trying. So when the bully pushed him, Maurice pushed back, and in an instant, as happens with schoolboys, they were scheduled to meet in the yard after school. "So right at the end of school there we were out in the playground and the kids formed a ring and we started to fight. I don't think it lasted more than two, three minutes. I knocked the hell out of him." It was the first time Maurice had ever fought in his life, and his victory startled him.

Unfortunately, it was only temporary. The bully demanded a re-match and Maurice could not back away from it. So they met again after school, and this time the ring was enormous, the whole school. "Well, the thing barely started when I was hit from the rear, from the side, from the top, from the bottom; it was a massacre. Understand? It was a massacre." Fortunately, Maurice had a close friend at school who was Italian. This boy too was the son of a merchant and, more important at the moment, he was big. The friend waded in, pulled Maurice out from under, and sent him running like hell for home. Perhaps it was a case of class ties being stronger than ethnic ties, although the lesson that Maurice drew from the fracas was simply not to let himself get pushed around, and also not to take on more than he could handle. In any case, bloody and only slightly bowed, Maurice had made his point. Neither the bully nor anyone else at the school bothered him again.

It is interesting that in some very free-wheeling, taped monologues, Halperin's only recollection of his primary school years was of these two fights. Obviously they made a very heavy impression on him. He learned from them that being a Jew was not only what you were, but what you did as well, and that what you did could be painful. He also learned that there was a time to fight and a time to duck.

Finishing primary school after the war, Halperin entered the Boston Latin school in 1919. Boston Latin was a remarkable institution, a public school with a difference. Unlike other schools, Latin did not draw from a neighborhood district; it drew from the entire city. Admission, though necessarily limited, was not terribly difficult, but survival was another story, because standards were high and the competition stiff. The school was unique because it offered the sort of classical education that was otherwise available only at the elite and very expensive private schools in the East, the sort of education that almost guaranteed entry into Harvard in those days. And Maurice was already thinking of Harvard as one possibility for the future. After all, he says with mock seriousness, "The ambition for Harvard was natural [because it] was the closest university on the subway."

At Latin, Halperin was subjected to the rigors and discipline of a classical education in which the curriculum was laid out with virtually no room for "electives." Greek and Latin, math, physics, and history, but only ancient history. The emphasis, quite in contrast to modern pedagogical thinking, was skewed heavily toward drill and rote memory. On the whole, Halperin found it a positive experience. It was hard to swallow at times, but it was extremely effective on its own terms. And it did get him into Harvard, just a short subway ride away.

At that, Harvard was not his first choice. In high school he had romantic notions about the joys of open spaces, of vast expanses of land, trees, water—of almost anything that did not smack of the more congested ambience of the Boston he had grown up in. It was a reflex of that fantasy that led Maurice to choose the Naval Academy at Annapolis as his university. The trouble was that you didn't choose the Academy; it chose you. And it did so only on the recommendation of your Congressman or Senator, and even that was no guarantee. Maurice's father had a friend who knew that very patrician Bostonian, Senator Henry Cabot Lodge, but Lodge informed them that he had already chosen someone for the current year, and would be willing to recommend Maurice the following year. Maurice wanted to get on with his life, however, and made it known that he preferred not to wait for the appointment.

Halperin entered Harvard in 1923, and by taking an annual overload of courses managed to finish in 1926, although he is still listed with his original class in the yearbook of 1927. He had done very well in languages at Latin School, and at Harvard he directed this ability toward a major in Romance languages, with emphasis on French literature. As a consequence of his immersion in the humanism and rationalism of the French Renaissance and Enlightenment, the values he had already absorbed at home were broadened and deepened. It was another important shaping factor in his life.

At Harvard he also renewed his interest in music, though not with the violin. Instead he auditioned for the Glee Club, which was really a first-rate choral group, and was accepted as a second tenor.

HALPERIN: The last year I was there we performed the Brahms Requiem with the Boston Symphony Orchestra with Koussevitsky conducting. I still remember this was sort of the highlight of my whole Harvard experience, including Voltaire, Rousseau, and Montaigne, you know. We had our choral conductor, Archibald Davidson, who was considered to be outstanding. Well, he rehearsed us for, I don't know, weeks or months, and then the final rehearsals were with Koussevitsky. And I still remember the difference. You've heard the word charisma? Hypnotism! It exists. I was transfixed to the extent that somewhere in the Requiem the Second Tenors have to sing a high C, which I had never reached before, never. I would just sort of gargle when I got there, you know, never reached it. With Koussevitsky it came out clear as a bell. It was fantastic; it was hypnotism.

Years later Halperin's son was studying cello with a member of the Boston Symphony, and had a lesson the day after Koussevitsky died.

HALPERIN: So David comes out of the lesson and he says, "You know what, Dad? I told the teacher how sorry I was that Koussevitsky died.

*He said, 'Sorry! Why it's the best thing that ever happened; why that
s.o.b.; why that tyrant! You know, I was just waiting for him to croak.' "*

MORAL: when hypnotism fails, terror too can produce beautiful
music.

It was also at Harvard that Halperin was introduced to some of the
nuances of social class in America. Every year the *Comité France-
Amérique* held a competition to determine the outstanding student of
French at the university. The award, purely honorific, was a medal.
Halperin was a French major, so he decided to enter the competition
in his second year at Harvard. Each contestant presented an oral essay
of about twenty minutes in French. Contestants were judged on the
substance of the essay, the correctness of the French, and the quality
of their accents.

*HALPERIN: Now what is interesting about this is the fact that I was
not a member of the* Cercle Français—*the French Club—because I
wasn't invited to be a member. At Harvard you got into the clubs
only by invitation. Who were the members of the* Cercle Français?
*Well, they were people of a certain pedigree and a lot of snobbishness.
And these people, I discovered, were people who had lived in France
for periods, you know. Their parents were diplomats, or they would
vacation in France all summer. My vacation was in East Boston. Near
the docks.*

In the past, a member of the *Cercle* had always won the contest. The
contest was not exactly rigged; it was just understood how things were
supposed to end. But apparently nobody remembered to notify the
principal member of the jury that year, a visiting professor from France
who was unfamiliar with the nuances of Harvard's class structure. He
awarded the medal to Halperin, which, of course, was a breach of
the status quo that did nothing to endear Maurice to members of
the *Cercle*. As before, Halperin was not invited to join the club. As
before, Halperin and the members did not speak to one another. In
either language.

HALPERIN: I knew when I finished Harvard that I wanted to be a teacher of Romance languages and a researcher in a university. I had that, what shall I say, vocation in my mind. But I also wanted to do two things. I wanted to get married—there was this wonderful girl and I'll say this, you know, she was really a raving beauty, no question about it. A very lively, spirited kid. . . . Good athlete; she would win races; played basketball at Boston University. . . . But in those days things had to be done normally. You didn't cohabit. And also there was the question of making a living, you know. And then there was a really great urge to get away and see what it was like in the United States. And so I—we—decided that the first thing I was going to do was get a job, a teaching job.

Halperin was graduated cum laude in 1926. He was twenty and Edith was eighteen when they were married that summer. He had already sent out inquiries and took the first job that came along. It was in Ranger, Texas, a hundred miles or so west of Fort Worth, and a million miles from the boundaries of his mind. He had never heard of Ranger. For that matter, he had only barely heard of Texas. But there was a high school there, and a junior college, and they needed someone to teach French and Spanish as badly as Halperin needed a job. In that sense, at least, it was a match made in heaven. Of course he didn't know any Spanish, but he had studied some Italian at Harvard, and armed with that and a Spanish grammar he taught Spanish. Fortunately for his reputation, there were no Latinos in Ranger at the time.

And so Halperin, steeped in Jewish culture, toughened by a classical education at an elitist high school, broadened by a liberal education at an elitist university, newly married, and not yet eligible to vote, moved to a town of five thousand people in central Texas. He had never known anything like Ranger, and, in truth, Ranger had never known anything like Halperin.

The newlyweds took a room in a boarding house and set out to learn about another America. The house was run by a pair of aging sisters who were Christian Scientists, which was also something of an oddity in Ranger. This certainly did not hurt the Halperins, coming as they did from Boston, the home of the Mother Church. Actually, the boarding house turned out to be a significant part of their education. They had a new culinary experience, because the sisters were experts in classic American cooking—hot biscuits three times a day, chicken and gravy, the works—and they loved it.

They were also introduced to the role of sports in Texas culture. The Ranger football coach once drove Maurice and a few other people to Dallas to watch a Southern Methodist game. Football was nothing new to Halperin, but Texas football was.

HALPERIN: I got a full view of this thing, with the difference between football teams there and Harvard. There's something elegant about the Harvard football scene. Tradition. This was pretty rough and raw.

On a different occasion Maurice had a moment of glory in a baseball game between the faculty and students at Ranger. He had never played more than an occasional game of sandlot ball in Boston and found himself relegated to that graveyard of all inept sandlot ballplayers, right field, which was fine with him, since that's where the action usually was not. Maurice recalls that when he came to bat his knees were knocking, because the pitcher for the students, who later played for the Cleveland Indians, had a blazing fastball. The pitch came in, Maurice shut his eyes and swung, the ball and the bat coincidentally arrived at the same place at the same time, and Halperin was on first base with a single. It had something to do with the laws of physics, if not with the laws of probability, and it was one of his triumphant moments in Ranger.

Edith also learned about sports in Texas. She had been an excellent basketball player back in Boston and was hired as school librarian and coach of the girls' basketball team in Ranger. Now, while basketball was not as big in Texas as football, and girls' basketball was not as big as boys' basketball, it was still important because, along with all the other sports, it was the main focus of gambling locally. In those days, girls' basketball in the East—the game that Edith had learned—was not the same as boys' basketball. Guards were restricted to certain areas on offense, for instance, and dribbling was limited. It was not only a noncontact sport, it was almost nonmobile. In Ranger, girls and boys played basically by the same rules, as they do today everywhere. Unfortunately, Edith was trying to coach the Boston game she knew, while her players were trying to play the Texas game they knew. They lost every game, and the locals lost a lot of money betting on them.

It seemed that everything about Ranger was different. The climate was different—hotter and drier; the air was different—cleaner and fresher. And above all, the religion was different. In Boston the Halperins were part of a minority where Catholicism was dominant. Here they were a minority of two in the Bible Belt, where Fundamentalist Protestantism reigned. Curious and then intrigued, they went to church meetings from time to time.

HALPERIN: The Fundamentalist business there, and also the itinerant preachers. Fascinating! We used to go, Edith and I. It was like going to the theater. I remember particularly one preacher, Will Hogg. I remember that he set up a tent. Everybody went; we were there, sawdust on the ground, and Will Hogg began his preaching. It was theater, really, kind of like medieval theater. And he called for sinners to come up and repent, and I learned the meaning of "going up the sawdust trail." The thing is, this is something primitive. There was a question of alcohol and gambling and sinning. But it meant the first exercise in readjustment.

By the time the school year ended, the Halperins were learning, changing, broadening. They had come in order to find a different America, and they were finally beginning to absorb some of it. Now it was time to move on. Maurice wanted to get on with graduate school, and Edith had worn out her welcome as basketball coach. But it was not just a matter of going to grad school. Halperin was married now and also had to worry about making a living. He needed a teaching job as well. So he borrowed a typewriter and pecked out applications to seventy universities for admission and a teaching job. The Universities of Florida and Oklahoma were interested, but Oklahoma was the first one to make a concrete offer, and Halperin, in no position to negotiate, accepted at once. Some time later, he learned that he never would have received an offer if he had not spent that year in Texas first.

The chairman of his department figured that if this Bostonian could survive a year in Ranger, Texas, he would be able to adjust to Norman, Oklahoma. So in September 1927, the Halperins were off to widen their southwestern horizons at the University of Oklahoma.

It is worth emphasizing that this part of the country was only a few decades removed from the images we carry of the Wild West, and a world removed from today's Southwest. Oklahoma had only been a state for twenty years. Roads ranged from poor to nonexistent; radio and movies were only beginning to come into the cities and larger towns; the economy was generally polarized between the fabulous oil wealth of a few at the top and the hard-scrabble poverty of a mass of sharecroppers at the bottom; the significant Indian population was for the most part contained on reservations; and blacks existed in a rigidly segregated society. Oklahoma City was twenty miles from Norman, connected only by a thin ribbon of poor road running through empty prairie. To the south lay cotton country; to the north, wheat country. To an Easterner the sense of space was awesome.

But Norman was not really like the rest of the state. Its economy and its tone were dominated by the university. True, it was not Harvard; nor was it yet the football Mecca that it was to become in later years. Like the state, it was raw and new, having been launched not many years earlier as little more than a one-room school house. But it was a university, and the people connected with it were concerned with the things that usually engage university people—learning, teaching, and research in humanistic, scientific, and technological matters. To the Halperins, it was an oasis in a desert.

The chairman of the Modern Languages Department was typical of many of the faculty there. Roy Temple House was not a renowned scholar, but he was a man with broad literary interests who wrote book reviews for various literary journals as well as for *The Nation* magazine. These interests led House to found a journal of his own the year Maurice arrived. It was called *Books Abroad*, and it was published by the University of Oklahoma Press, which was founded at about the same time and run by Joseph Brandt, who was to play an important role in Halperin's life some years later. The idea of the journal was to publish reviews in English of foreign-language books. It filled a void for scholars who had an interest in the literary, political, and social publications of European nations. It also filled a void for European publishers, who were delighted to have their books publicized for an American audience. Halperin did his first publishing in the journal, brief reviews of literary works in French.

HALPERIN: The fact that House founded Books Abroad *just as I got there was a very important thing to me. First of all, he had books coming in from all over the world. Everybody and his uncle outside of the United States was looking for some recognition in an American journal, even though it was Norman, Oklahoma. They sent their best stuff. Big publishers. Part of the stuff that came in had very distinct Marxist orientations. This was the first time I got literature that had an explicitly Marxist analysis. It was fascinating, a new analytical approach, a new understanding of history. It didn't stir me into any action at all, but intellectually it broadened my vision, especially of the contemporary world. Among them, books dealing with the Russian Revolution, which I never would have found on the stands in Norman. An accident, but I think it played a real role in my future development.*

One review that he remembers in particular, because it too was to play a role in his life soon, was of a book of Polish fairy tales written in French by Suzanne Strowska, a Franco-Polish professor of literature at the University of Warsaw. Halperin and House found these tales so charming that they decided to translate them into English. Halperin did most of the translating, and House did most of the editorial work, including some necessary bowdlerization of a few rather crude peasant tales. One of the stories, for instance, told of a horse that farted every time it wanted to say something. House changed that to "the horse whisked its tail every time it wanted to say something." There was simply no way they could have published a faithful translation of that sentence in those days. When they were finished, they sent the book to a publishing house that bought it outright to publish as a lavishly illustrated coffee table book for Christmas. House and Halperin split the $500. Halperin's scholarly and economic horizons were widening.

So were his social horizons. For the first time he became aware of Jim Crow laws—the segregated South. Curiously, he has no recollection of it in Ranger. It must have existed there, he realizes, but he was so absorbed in his new duties that he simply never noticed it. He became aware of it in Norman, oddly enough, because of the very lack of blacks. The fact was that blacks were not permitted to spend the night in Norman. This was a concession to the students, many of whom were poor whites from the countryside who had to work their way through school and were quite willing to take any menial job available, precisely the kind that were usually reserved in the South for blacks. The last thing these students wanted was to have to compete with blacks for these jobs, so the city simply kept blacks out. Occasionally local middle-class citizens protested against this discrimination, not because they found it immoral, but because they found it expensive. Why should they pay low wages to white menials when they could pay even lower wages to black menials? They did not prevail, however, and Norman remained at the time an almost lily-white town. Maurice was struck by this strange amalgam of the cosmopolitan and the retrograde in Oklahoma. He was beginning to feel that it was much more the "real America" than Boston.

Meanwhile, he proceeded with his master's degree. He had mixed feelings about the department. Of the twenty or so faculty members in it, he remembers about half being quite competent, and the rest being clearly below par. Maurice did his work with one of the highly qualified men, Lewis Winfrey, a recent arrival from the University of Chicago. His thesis was on the development of the Tristan legend in English, in reality a work in comparative literature, since he had to trace the legend to its origins in medieval France. The training he received from Winfrey was so solid that he was able to publish one of his seminar papers in a major journal while he was still a graduate student, which anyone who has been through this process will recognize as a real achievement and an important bit of scholarly luggage to display.

By the spring of 1929 Maurice was writing his thesis, and had no doubts at all about his attraction to the life of the scholar. He wanted to be a university professor, which meant he had to go on for a Ph.D. But where? Oklahoma was out of the question because it had no doctoral program at the time. Harvard was a possibility, but Halperin had a better idea. He wanted to continue his work on the Tristan legend, so why not go to the cradle of it all? Why not go to the Sorbonne in Paris? For what he wanted it was the best and most prestigious place in the world. It was a bit impractical, of course. The University of Paris was not geared to finding jobs in the United States for its Ph.D.s. But, flushed with his acceptance at the Sorbonne, he set off with Edith for Paris without really looking beyond tomorrow. They had saved enough money from their earnings in Norman to last them a year if they lived like church mice. After that? Well, after that would have to take care of itself.

In September 1929, with American politicians and publicists aglow at the prospect of permanent prosperity, they sailed for Europe on the brand new pride of the Holland-America line, the *Staatendam*. In Paris they took a room five flights up in a residential hotel (bath and toilet down the hall), and plunged into their new life. Halperin felt as if he had been preparing for this since high school. He knew the language, he knew the culture, he knew the history; he almost knew Paris street by street. It seemed just like Boston to him, only more so. Oklahoma was a distant memory. He and Edith had left the Bible Belt in prohibition America and landed in the cultural capital of the Western world. It was irresistible.

One thing that struck them almost immediately was the role that ideas played in France, especially among the intelligentsia. It was not that American scholars were uninterested in ideas, but that ideas and life in America occupied separate categories, which permitted intellectuals to remain cool and politically disengaged if they chose, which most of them did in the 1920s. In France ideas and life were fused; they generated friction, heat, fire, explosions. To illustrate the difference, one might note that the American Revolution was, and still is, enshrined in a mythical past somewhere beyond the realm of debate. Even those Americans whose knowledge did not extend much beyond George Washington's hard winter at Valley Forge knew that the Revolution was a good thing. In Paris the intellectuals were still fighting the French Revolution, sometimes quite literally.

HALPERIN: There was going to be a thesis defense, which in France is a public affair. There is a special hall reserved in the Sorbonne for this. And word got around that this was going to be a very, very lively affair: a student was going to present a thesis dealing with the French Revolution, one in which he was going to support the Revolution, you know. And this was already a mature student, an instructor at some university in France, who had done some publishing. A major event. And so we made our way in. It was crowded, you know, and it didn't take long before the jury and professors were insulting one another back and forth with the candidate. And then a big hubbub and then fists began to fly, and the first thing I knew, Edith and I, we decided to get the hell out of there. It became a real riot. We got out and outside there were ambulances, the police—there was blood spilled, but we got away. Inconceivable, you know, an academic riot concerning ideas!

This passion for ideas as a combat zone spilled over into politics, and it intrigued Halperin. The sheer breadth of the political debate, and of the political press that expressed it, amazed him. Drawn especially by their egalitarian rhetoric, he was a regular reader of *Le Populaire*, the Socialist newspaper, and *L'Humanité*, the Communist paper. The very fact of their existence fascinated him. There was no significant political press in the States. In France it seemed that all the press was political. In the States the Socialist and Communist parties were on the far fringes of politics in the late 1920s. In France they were at the very heart of it.

Even more astounding to him was the *Action Française*. The Communist and Socialist parties did at least have feeble counterparts in the United States. But this was a royalist party—royalist!—led by a brilliant and learned reactionary who wanted to restore the *ancien régime*, who actually wanted to abolish the one hundred forty years since the storming of the Bastille. It was not simply that such a person existed—most Western societies make room for a certain number of cranks—but that he played a significant role in the political ferment of the era. In Paris he was not a crank; he was taken seriously. Maurice was learning that in addition to the similarities, there were also some serious differences between Boston and Paris.

While all of this played a major role in the continuing socialization of Halperin, it was not the purpose of his journey to Paris. He had come to get a Ph.D., or the French equivalent, so that he could get on with his life as a professor in America. In France there are two different doctorates given, the university doctorate and the state doctorate. Most foreign students choose the university doctorate, which takes two or three years; most French students choose the state doctorate, which may take four years or more, and is a requisite for them to teach in a French university. The university doctorate is considered a rough equivalent of the American Ph.D., although the requirements for these degrees in the two countries bear no resemblance to one another. Although Maurice had an opportunity to go for the state doctorate— an opportunity that few foreign students are given—he opted for the two-year university doctorate.

Unlike their American counterparts, students who enter a doctoral program in France are presumed to be well educated. This is because of the marked difference in the educational systems of the two countries. Comparatively speaking, American students are *shaped* through high school and *educated*, in the common meaning of that word, at university. This process continues right through graduate school. They are required to take courses for the master's degree and still more courses for the Ph.D., often as many as twenty for the Ph.D. alone. In some cases these courses are fairly large lecture courses, but more often they are small seminars or one-on-one tutorials with a professor. But they are required. At some point in the process the students are required to take examinations, often several written comprehensive exams covering different areas in their discipline. Every course is a potential hazard and the general exams can loom as a terrifying barrier.

In France—indeed in much of Europe—because education is so much more intensive from the very beginning, and because admission to university is so much more selective and elitist, course requirements and comprehensive exams do not exist at the doctoral level. The only real requirement is the dissertation, and the only real ordeal is the defense of that dissertation before a triumvirate of professors who, in some cases, are bent upon demonstrating just how incompetent the student is.

Maurice met with his adviser, Charles Cestre, when he arrived in France, and they settled on his dissertation topic, which was to be a broadening and deepening of the work he had done on the Tristan legend for his master's degree. During the next two years he sat in on an occasional lecture or course, especially when it involved some renowned professor, but he did so at his own choosing. This was common practice among the students.

On one occasion he enrolled in a course at the *Collège de France*, a curious but prestigious institution where one could take courses with outstanding professors at no charge and for no credit. This course related to his dissertation and was given by a famous scholar of medieval French literature.

HALPERIN: There were probably never more than ten people present and here was the top man in the field, you know, in the world. About ten people present. Among them one or two would invariably be what the French call clochards. *The tramps. They came in to get out of the cold. And they moved from room to room because when the course was over the attendant would lock the room. So they moved to where the next course was. . . . You couldn't do anything to them. They immediately fell asleep. Began to snore sometimes. Always smelled bad. Unshaved and so forth. So you had this tremendous contrast, you know, of the most refined scholarship in the world cohabiting with those who slept under the bridges.*

Otherwise Maurice turned his attention to his dissertation, which he finished in two years. In that time he remembers seeing his adviser twice. The grand climax was the defense. The dissertation defense in France is conducted by a panel of three scholars before as large an audience as choose to attend. In addition to your own adviser, who is supposed to defend you if necessary, the panel includes the *avocat du diable*, or devil's advocate, whose function, as Halperin characterizes it, is to "squash the hell out of you." If you are fortunate, the third member will be neutral. If not, he is liable to join the devil's advocate gleefully. Audience participation may range from scholarly questioning through light skirmishing to aggravated assault, depending upon the ideological or political implications of the dissertation. Fortunately, Halperin's thesis was somewhat arcane, as a result of which the audience was small and quite well behaved. When the defense was over Halperin received a *Mention Honorable*—not the best, but above average, and certainly admirable for a foreigner.

But Halperin's education in Paris was not only of the mind and spirit. It was of the senses as well. Now for the first time he was beginning to learn about food and drink. Coming from a Jewish home, and then from prohibition Oklahoma, he had a lot to learn about both. And where better to do it than in Paris?

HALPERIN: Suzanne Strowska had said, "When you come to Paris, be sure to see my father, Fortunat Strowski." He was one of the great luminaries at the Sorbonne at that time. So I went to see Strowski, who, of course, had heard about me. He was excited; his daughter was going to be published in the United States. He looked upon me as sent by heaven. And he was one of the star professors of the Sorbonne in French literature at the time. Strowski invited me to come to his apartment one evening. It was about a fifteen-minute walk from where we lived. And I came there. Well, here I am with the great man, you know, and he is delighted with me.

After we talked for a while about university affairs and my academic future, he said, "Let's go out and have a drink." At that time I would say he was a man of fifty odd. I was twenty odd. And we went to one of the cafés—a good café, the Select. One of the famous cafés, and it was right around the corner. He ordered pernod. I didn't know about pernod—don't forget I had come from prohibition America and knew nothing except bathtub gin and things of that sort. Pernod? Fine, okay. And we sipped pernod. I was sure it was not alcoholic. Doesn't taste like an alcoholic drink, you know. Has a slightly anise flavor.

As time went on I noticed he began talking about the problems he had with his daughters. He had something like four daughters and he couldn't marry them off. He didn't know that I was married and I think he had his eye on me as a possible candidate. Then we had another pernod and it began to seem to me that he was talking a little bit too freely, and his voice was receding a good deal. I was leaning closer and closer. Finally he said, "You know, I think maybe we had better go now." So we left. And what I remember was the sidewalk coming up to meet me. Strangest thing. I mean I had been somewhat intoxicated and sick back with the bathtub stuff. But this, I didn't know what was going on. Somehow I got onto the right street and Edith explained what had happened. She had come out to look for me and found me zigzagging on the street. She took me by the arm and took me home. Well, I'll tell you the fantastic thing about this pernod. I woke up in the morning—no hangover—absolutely clear.

As his education in the various forms and flavors of alcohol proceeded, Halperin was also learning how Parisians ate, and this was even more of a revelation to him. That aspect of his education was conducted in part by a man named Gluck, a regular at the Dôme, which was the center of Maurice's café life in Paris. Gluck was a retired insurance broker of some wealth and the first husband of Alma Gluck, a famous diva early in the century.

HALPERIN: Well, Gluck was interesting because he was the first gourmet I ever knew, and I mean a real gourmet. He also was somewhat of a gourmand, as his belly would indicate. And he would discourse on foods in a most fascinating way. He would discuss the question of chicken. What he said is that there is only one chicken that is fit to eat, and that is known as the Spanish Black. I had never heard of the Spanish Black. I had never heard of it before, and I have never heard of it since, you know. And he would discuss why the Spanish Black is so much better than the Rhode Island Red. This was fascinating to me. Then I remember one time he looked at his watch and said, "Oh, my, I am a little late. I am marinating a saddle of boar and I have got to go and turn it over." Saddle of boar. Amazing thing! He said, "Do you want to come with me?" "Sure," I said. Well, I left Edith at the Dôme sitting there with some friends and I went five minutes around the corner to his apartment, and I saw him work on the saddle of boar. And then he opened up the door of his bathroom, and over the bathtub he had strung up two or three lines of salami. There may have been thirty or forty salamis hanging there. And he explained this was this and that was that and so forth. Well, so I also became interested in food. Never got as serious as Gluck, but. . . .

Other horizons were being broadened at the same time. Halperin remembers in particular two women who used to come to the Dôme as part of the group. In their forties, they seemed almost like elderly ladies to the young Halperins—pleasant, convivial, well-educated, elderly ladies. It soon became apparent to one member of the group that this American couple did not really understand the relationship between the two women, so he took the Halperins aside and explained it to them. They were vaguely aware that such a thing as lesbianism existed, but it had never really intruded into their consciousness. It was an abstraction. It existed in books or "out there" somewhere. So they were startled—not dismayed, but startled—to discover that homosexuals existed in their own world, right there in their own circle, and that what these women chose to do with their private lives played no part in how they were judged in café life. The whole experience dovetailed perfectly with the easy-going tolerance that had characterized Maurice's upbringing.

All the while, Edith was keeping herself quite busy. When they arrived she began to take French lessons at the *Alliance Française*. There are two kinds of people who learn a foreign language. There is the person who is the perfectionist, who wants to make sure that the past perfect tense is used when the past perfect tense ought to be used, that the subjunctive mood is used when the subjunctive mood ought to be used, and, of course, that the pronunciation is as correct as possible. That person can often begin to communicate effectively after a year or two of immersion in the language. Until then, however, he is in trouble. By the time he laboriously puts together a proper sentence with the proper vocabulary, the proper tense, and the proper accent, the conversation has moved on. By the time he is ready to say his piece it is usually irrelevant, as a result of which he doesn't usually say anything. It is not uncommon for that person to remain nearly mute for the first year or two. His counterpart, and in some ways his nemesis, is the person who picks up a language very badly very quickly. The grammar is all wrong; gaps in the vocabulary are filled in with desperate gestures; and the accent is a catastrophe. But the person doesn't care. Uninhibited, with bad grammar, sparse vocabulary, and a grim accent, all this person does is communicate quite easily with the natives, while the purist is trying to figure out how to say it properly, and not saying it at all.

Edith was the second type. Nothing about her French was quite right, except the accent and the rhythm. The French can be very unpleasant with people like that, yet she communicated, and her manner was so cheerily infectious that not even the French objected. By the second year she was a full-time student, taking a course in French Civilization for foreigners, and excelling at it, as she did in her quiet way with everything.

At the end of the first year, Halperin was not certain that they had enough money to see them through the second year to complete his degree. So he decided to try his luck with Fortunat Strowski. Strowski had found out soon enough that Maurice was not a likely candidate for one of his daughters, but he had remained a good friend and counselor. Now it was time to find out if he could serve as something other than tutor to Halperin's blossoming sybaritic tendencies. Maurice went to him and explained the problem. Was there some way that Strowski could help? Strowski said, "Of course," and on the spot he wrote a letter to a New York–based foundation almost demanding that it give Halperin a fellowship. Halperin got the fellowship.

As it was, his income had been supplemented the first year by a windfall of a different sort. He was speaking to his adviser shortly after his arrival in Paris, and Cestre told him that the man who was supposed to teach that year in their American civilization program had not shown up, and how would Maurice like to have the job. It paid enough to cover the rent, and the experience buttered his ego because he was now a member of the faculty at the Sorbonne. In the status-conscious world of European universities he was deferred to as such, and that counted for something.

HALPERIN: I came to my lecture room and there was an anteroom for each lecture room, and when you arrived there was a flunky there to open the door for you. "Bonjour, Monsieur," right? He takes your umbrella and your rubbers—you know you always have an umbrella and rubbers in France in the winter—takes your overcoat, hangs it up. There is a great big mirror so that you can look at yourself to see how you will look when you get on the platform. I was still a kid in a way, you know. It was really something. I would walk from the anteroom right onto a platform and sit down. Well, there was a certain amount of dignity there. I was like a performer. There is a sense of special protocol with a professor there. In the States a professor means nothing special, usually. But there you have a degree of social eminence. You don't get it in salary but you do get it otherwise in respect. It was very nice.

It was a revelation to Halperin. In Oklahoma he had taught language at a basic level to some pretty raw American students. Here he was expected to handle a much more subtle subject with some far more sophisticated students. He loved it. There were about a dozen hardy regulars in the class, with perhaps that many more who came and went. The course would focus on one novel—the first year it was Willa Cather's *Death Comes to the Archbishop*—and then, by *explication du texte*, the class would study aspects of American culture through an intensive exploration of that novel. Led by Halperin, who would discuss the social background as they went along, they tore the novel apart almost word by word. The class was taught in English and the English of the students was impeccable—British English which they had learned in school and, many of them, in England itself.

The appointment was renewed for the second year, and if Halperin had wanted, it would have been renewed indefinitely into the future. But at the end of the second year he had his doctorate and Edith was pregnant. It was time to return to the States and build a life for themselves. They were even beginning to show signs of homesickness. It drove them to hunt out the only American restaurant in Paris a few times near the end so they could dive into a stack of hotcakes. In Paris of all places, a craving for hotcakes! It was, indeed, time to leave.

That could have posed a serious problem, because professors at the Sorbonne do not have ready access to American universities, and this access was a major factor in finding jobs for freshly minted doctorates.

But fate treated the Halperins with a gentle hand once again. Maurice had stayed in touch with some of the people in Norman, and he had mentioned in a letter to Roy Temple House that he was finally finishing his degree. It was just a chatty comment in a newsy letter, but to his surprise, House wrote back offering him a tenure-track job now that he had his doctorate. In the depression year of 1931, when American universities were beginning to cut costs by releasing faculty, that was an incredible stroke of luck.

Five years earlier, barely out of his teens, Maurice Halperin had set out for Ranger with his young bride. In many ways he had been an extremely provincial person. His window to the world was literature, but while the French classics influenced the way he was to think about things in the years to come, they did not particularly relate to the day-to-day world, and least of all to life in Ranger, Texas. He knew something of Jewish culture, and he knew something of Boston from the perspective of that culture. But even his years at Harvard had only moved him from one part of the Boston cloister to another, and while he was educated at Harvard, he never really entered into its larger culture. He had entered an outsider, and he remained an outsider there for the entire three years.

The Maurice Halperin who returned to the Southwest in 1931 was far different from the post-adolescent who had left Boston five years earlier. A year in a small Texas town and two more in Oklahoma had weaned him from his New England provincialism and introduced him to an America he hadn't even known existed. And it became a part of him. Two more years in Paris added a completely different dimension. Quite apart from the professional patina of his Sorbonne degree, he had become almost a *boulevardier*, a man about town. He was on speaking terms with saddle of boar and, rather more warily, with pernod; he was a seasoned participant in French café life and an eager student of French political culture. They didn't know about these things in Norman. For that matter, not too many people knew about them in Boston either. He returned to Norman a cosmopolite.

2

Oklahoma!

The Halperins left for Europe just before the stock market crash, and they returned to America just before the depression reached Europe. Thus, quite by accident they missed the first two years of the depression altogether. They returned to the United States shortly before the birth of their first child, Judith, and were shocked by the breadlines in Boston.

However, when the three Halperins arrived in Oklahoma, they found themselves living in comfort compared to the genteel poverty of their student years in Paris, and compared more immediately to the desperate squalor of depression Oklahoma. Maurice's starting salary was twenty-four hundred dollars, an almost indecent amount at a time when their house rented for eighteen dollars a month, eggs were two dozen for a quarter, guinea hen—not chicken, but the partridge-like guinea hen—could be bought for a pittance from local farmers, and desperate students were available to work for a song. Almost immediately the Halperins hired a young woman student to do housekeeping in return for room and board—no wages. They felt almost guilty living so well while millions of others were falling into misery and despair as the depression deepened.

For Maurice little adjustment was necessary. His job, colleagues, and environment were all familiar to him. He was now a young father, to be sure, but he was very much a family traditionalist, and in traditional homes, the burden of parenthood fell primarily on the mother.

For Edith things were more complicated. She was traditionalist enough to assume the job of homemaker with pleasure, but she was also modern enough to want to extend her life beyond the kitchen and nursery. Almost as soon as they arrived in Norman she became very active in the League of Women Voters. Eventually she became state secretary of that organization. By mid-decade she was involved in a day-care center for working mothers, a commitment that grew from another of the hard economic realities of the era. Workingmen could not find work, and sharecroppers were being blown off the land, but women often could find work in Norman as domestics, or could take in ironing and sewing at home. The day-care center was opened to give the working women time away from their children so that they might make enough money to feed their families and hold them together. Soon Edith became involved with some women who took it upon themselves to take food and clothing to a camp for transients in town, where the displaced "Okies" stopped over in their epic migration westward. All in all, Edith was engaged in some fairly high-profile activities in a culture that did not take kindly to women who did those sorts of things. She began to attract some unflattering attention in the basically southern town.

It was during the years in Oklahoma that Maurice first turned his attention to Latin America; at the same time, he began to drift leftward politically. The two developments were related in important ways. After the summer term of 1932, Maurice took his family for a vacation down to Saltillo, a town in northern Mexico a few hours below the border. He had intended to read *War and Peace* as a vacation project, but he was so intrigued by the town that he forgot all about the novel. What struck him in particular was how a boundary as puny as the Rio Grande could define two such hugely different cultures. From southern Texas to northern Mexico the climate was much the same; the topography was not dissimilar; even the people, with so many Mexicans in Texas, were not all that different. But these were two worlds with nothing in common. How could it be? Halperin's curiosity on this matter was one of the factors that sent him veering off in a new direction.

Two years later, he took the family down again, this time for an entire summer in Mexico City. Maurice plunged immediately into local affairs and was caught up in meetings and rallies that expressed the leftist ferment of Mexico City at that time. He remembers a Communist party rally in the main square of the city that drew thousands and thousands of people, and he was struck, as he had been in Paris, by the marked contrast with the politics of his own country, which had very little room for left-wing politics of any sort, even now in the depression. He was also struck by the intense hostility among Mexicans toward "Yankee imperialism" and toward Americans in general. He was learning about Latin America rapidly.

While he was down there he interviewed several writers, among them Mariano Azuela, who had written *Los de abajo*, one of the great classics of Latin American literature, many years earlier. In his younger years a revolutionary, he was now a doctor and politically a very conservative man. Halperin also interviewed others—poets, novelists, playwrights—and when he returned he wrote a long article for the *New York Times Book Review* on the state of literature in Mexico.

More important was an article he wrote for *Current History* late that year.[1] Halperin was still only a neophyte in his knowledge of Mexican politics and culture, but at the time, there was virtually no familiarity at all in the United States with Latin American affairs, so his limited expertise was in some demand. And this expertise was tilting clearly leftward, as one can see in the article. In it, Halperin dismissed the reforms of the Calles government since the mid-1920s as a demagogic hoax to hold insurgency at bay. Ten years of these reforms had left Mexico still "a semi-colonial country, chiefly an American economic dependency." And while national industry had grown, its benefits had "gone to a handful of capitalists, not to the masses, while the old system of large landholdings and its eternal adjunct, peonage, still persist[ed]." Writing soon after the 1934 election, he held little hope for real change from President-elect Lázaro Cárdenas, whom he dismissed as a representative of the left wing of the official party, which "believes in dispelling the crisis with bigger and better New

---

1. Maurice Halperin, "Under the Lid in Mexico," *Current History* (November 1934): 166–71.

Deals and for holding the masses as long as possible with an ever-deepening crimson oratory." The implication here is that the New Deal itself was something of a sham designed to hold off the roiling masses.

Halperin's survey of the opposition to the P.N.R. was revealing, especially in light of the near-universal distrust of the official election figures, according to which the P.N.R. had swamped the combined opposition by the unlikely margin of thirty to one. Surveying this opposition, he scorned the rightist candidate and simply dismissed the Socialist candidate. Instead, he saw the probable wave of the future in the Communist candidate and movement. Actually, the Communist party had been outlawed in 1929, but the government had permitted the Worker-Peasant Bloc—the party in another guise—to run a candidate, Hernán Laborde. Halperin foresaw the imminent "collapse of the present régime" and concluded that "through bitter experience the Mexican workers and peasants have learned the price of vague utopianism and misdirected terrorism and are now turning to a belief in other revolutionary ideas and methods."

The prognosis plainly anticipates a Communist resolution to Mexico's problems. Doubtless this reflects the views of various left-wing Mexican sources that influenced Halperin, and it is quite compatible with the line of the American Communist party at the time. But it was no accident that these were the sources that Halperin chose to heed, for his political views were being influenced just then by a remarkable man named Paul Snodgress, who was quietly wrenching him out of his political quietism.

Throughout the 1920s, and for a short while after Halperin's arrival in Oklahoma, this quietism muffled a kind of passive liberalism. Halperin had voted for Al Smith in 1928 because Smith was a Catholic who was being attacked for his religion. He was an underdog, and Halperin identified with him. By 1932 everything had changed. Halperin had been to Paris and had returned to a depression-ridden nation. He was still a liberal, but he was no longer passive. On one occasion, in the election campaign of that year, he went with some colleagues to a union hall in Oklahoma City to hear James Ford, the Communist party's candidate for vice president. He still knew next to nothing about the party, but he was impressed that they were running a black man and doubly impressed that the audience was a mixture of blacks and whites. This was Oklahoma in 1932, and that sort of thing was simply not done there.

HALPERIN: Oklahoma was a Jim Crow state back then. Black and white there, and Ford's message—I don't recall anything spectacular about it. It wasn't concerned with the overthrow of the government but with the rights of the poor. The message was unobjectionable as far as I recall it, you know. Clearly I knew that this candidate is not going to be elected and that the message was a kind that not too many people were going to accept fully at that particular time. In other words, I knew that this was a utopian little group here. Another thing that impressed me was the religious attachments that these people had to the cause that they were supporting. Religious almost in the literal sense because when they approved of something, they would shout "Amen!" As if they were in church. It was almost like an expression of Southern Pentecostal religion.

Halperin voted for Roosevelt in 1932, and after the inauguration, he felt the same surge of excitement that millions of others felt at the time. St. George was slaying the dragon. If, in fact, this modern-day St. George was chasing different dragons in different directions, Maurice didn't notice it at the time. Not many people did. What they did notice was movement again, and with movement there was hope, which had been the ultimate victim of the Hoover administration. There were also relief funds, and Maurice persuaded Roy Temple House to use some of those funds to employ Paul Snodgress on *Books Abroad.*

HALPERIN: It was an accident that we met. He and I were on the same fellowship, an American Field Service fellowship. We met in Paris. And I would say he was certainly one of the most remarkable people I've known. He died in the early 50s, a man of maybe fifty years old. He was an Arkansawyer, a real southerner. Not a migrant Arkansawyer. His family had lived there since way back. Paul was raised as a Roman Catholic. He studied for the priesthood and was selected to go and complete his studies at the North American college in the Vatican.

Probably a brilliant young priest coming up. At the last moment he was converted, I guess converted, to atheism. You know, from Roman Catholicism you don't go into Presbyterianism usually, right?

Well, somehow he got into the teaching of French at the University of Illinois. One of his sponsors there was Louis Cons, a notable French scholar who was an academic star at the time. So after the first semester Paul got disgusted with the whole business—the students, the teaching, the grades, what he considered the lack of seriousness—the whole business. And I think it was the mid-term exam of the second semester, he took the exam papers and burned them. He was just not going to accommodate human nature. He was a natural rebel. He had left the Catholic Church and now he was leaving the university. But he got the fellowship because Louis Cons stayed behind him. Louis Cons says, "Give him a fellowship," and he gets the fellowship.

Paul and Maurice became fast friends in Paris. They talked endlessly about philosophical problems. Marx played no role in these conversations. The two young men barely knew who he was. Instead, Maurice was impressed that Paul, this militant young atheist, read Thomas Aquinas for pleasure. In Latin. "You know," he would say, "this [Aquinas] is a remarkable man. I so much enjoy reading him." It had never occurred to Maurice that someone might read Aquinas for the sheer enjoyment of it.

HALPERIN: Paul was married to a very nice Arkansas girl who was working and supporting him at the time. I remember her name was Zonola. Then one day he was going to go to London to finish some research at the British Museum. We had a little party in his apartment. Well, Zonola was there and various other friends came. I met some really interesting people there. Two days later I ran into Paul in the street; he's supposed to be in London. So I said, "What's happened, Paul?" Half shamefacedly he said, "You know, I passed by a bookstore on the way to the railroad station, and I saw some things I just had to have." He'd spent his fare on the books. He came home broke! I don't know how many books he bought—a hundred, two hundred. He'd spent everything he had, the whole damned business. Well, that was Paul.

When Paul arrived in Norman, Zonola was no longer with him, and neither was Aquinas. Instead he had come upon Marx, whom he devoured as he had earlier devoured the Scholastic philosophers, and he had become a disciple. It was Paul who steered Maurice for the first time to the writings of Karl Marx.

HALPERIN: So I started reading Marx. I never became a systematic reader but I was very much interested. Marx made a tremendous impression and the impression had to do with maybe two or three things. One, his historical method seemed to throw a great searchlight on history. And number two, his critique of capitalism which I got not from Das Kapital, *which was just too much for me, but from essays and interpretations by other people. And of course his ethical concerns were expressed in such a convincing way. It was clear that I was dealing with a huge intellect. He was a giant.*

The logic of Marx's dialectical view of history and the essential humanism of his goals made Maurice feel for the first time that perhaps there was an alternative way of understanding the world and organizing society. Still, Marx's vision remained for him an ideal of what the world could be, and this didn't seem to have much to do with the day-to-day realities of the depression. He was able to divide his political thinking. Roosevelt was relevant to depression America; Marx was there for other places or future times.

As Maurice was beginning to discover the Left in his thinking and writing, not surprisingly, the Left was beginning to discover him. *Current History* was then published by the *New York Times* and had a wide readership, especially among the eastern intelligentsia. Moreover, Halperin's scathing summary of peonage in Mexico was quoted in a *Time* magazine cover story on Mexico shortly after his article appeared in *Current History*.[2] Obviously his analysis made an impression in the East, and before long he received an invitation from novelist Waldo Frank to join a group of people who were going to Cuba in the summer

2. *Time* (December 3, 1934): 21–2.

of 1935 to investigate reports of atrocities by Cuba's strongman, Batista, in connection with a long-term strike there. If Halperin could make it to New York and back, he was told, his expenses between New York and Havana would be paid.

Halperin was just beginning to teach the summer semester, but he had great admiration for Frank, whom he saw as "to the left, but in a broad sense."[3] So he went to House, his department chairman, showed him the letter, and got House's blessing to go: "You can't miss this opportunity."

HALPERIN: I left Edith and Judith in Boston, and when I got to New York there was a public meeting, a sort of send-off for our committee. I saw that Clifford Odets was one of the members of the committee.[4] Well, we met in a fairly shabby hall. There was a smell of something far Left about the whole thing. But there I was on the platform with ten, twelve, fifteen other people, and then there were important people who came to address the group who didn't go on the trip but who gave their support. Archibald McLeish, for example, Carlton Beals—a number of people who gave it a kind of aura of respectability in the middle of this shabbiness. When I got to the ship I went to my stateroom—supposed to be for two people—and there was something on the lower bunk to indicate that it was already taken. What was it? A copy of the Daily Worker. *So I could see that some element of the Communist party was involved in this thing.*

The committee turned out to be a mixed bag. In addition to Halperin and Odets, there was an American Legionnaire, who had gained stature on the Left by taking a leftish line in the Legion, and there were several

---

3. Like many artists and intellectuals early in the depression, Frank started out on the Left in a broad sense. That breadth narrowed as the decade lengthened. By mid-decade he was a reliable fellow traveler, although he apparently never joined the Communist party.

4. The Group Theater had produced Odets's play, *Waiting for Lefty,* the preceding year. Not only was it wildly popular on the Left, but it was a commercial success as well and remains something of a landmark in the American theater, though by now it is clearly a period piece.

trade union officials. Before long, Halperin noticed that every so often four or five members of the committee would disappear, and that they seemed to be directing things. Later it became clear to him that they formed a Communist party cell, but at the time he was only dimly aware of that.

The ship arrived in Havana at night, and the members of the committee were told that they would not be allowed to debark. After the regular tourists left the ship, the Cuban police came aboard, well armed, and lined up the committee.

HALPERIN: I recall one thing. We had two, I believe, black people in our group. And I was standing next to one of them as the police and functionaries came by and they began pushing and shoving the black man around. Instinctively I said, in Spanish of course, "Hey, quit that, that is not allowed." And you know, they stopped pushing him around. I had forgotten that incident completely until I met a member of the committee in Cuba years later. He greeted me like a hero and said, "You know, we practically fainted when you began defending that guy." I said, "Well, that was a normal thing to do." And he said, "No, no, that was an act of heroism." It wasn't at all. It was a biochemical reaction, is what it was.

By this time it was the middle of the night. The committee was herded onto a boat under armed guard and hustled across the harbor to an immigration detention station called Tiscornia. It was not a jail but a fairly comfortable, if spartan, compound. They spent the night there. They had been away from New York for two days. For the first time Halperin talked to Odets, whom he found to be arrogant and unpleasant, a person with no apparent human responses at all. While they were waiting, he received a cable from Tallulah Bankhead, who was then, to put it euphemistically, a very close friend of Odets, and who was one of the bawdiest personalities of the American theater. There was nothing of importance in the cable, but it was addressed to Pisscornia. From Bankhead this was not an error, and it helped relieve the tension of the night.

Except for the side trip to Tiscornia, the committee might as well not have gotten off the ship. Without ever getting into Havana they were herded onto a tourist vessel the next morning and returned to New York, where they were greeted as heroes by the Left. Odets wrote stirringly of the incident in the *New Masses*, and the eastern press made quite a noise about it.

In fact, the noise was heard all the way back in Oklahoma, as a result of which Halperin was invited to see the president of the university upon his return to Norman. Roy House accompanied him to the president's office, and together they explained that Halperin had been invited by Waldo Frank, that he was not aware of the sponsorship of the expedition, and that he had cleared it with House before leaving. The president, who cared more about the publicity than the politics of the venture, cautioned Halperin about the importance of public relations, and then waved the matter off. But it was not the last that Maurice was to hear about the trip.

By 1936 Halperin was moving more consciously toward the orbit of the Communist party, and by 1937 was, by his own description, a fellow traveler, although he is quick to point out that there were different kinds of fellow travelers, and that his attraction to the party was issue oriented rather than ideological. That raises some questions. What was there about the Communist party that attracted this middle-class Boston liberal? Why did his leftward drift lead him toward the Communist rather than the Socialist party? And in more general terms, since Halperin's political journey was by no means unique, how did the Communist party of the 1930s manage to attract so many liberals who were by no stretch of the imagination revolutionaries? There is an extensive literature that deals with these questions,[5] but a brief review of the issue is necessary at this point.

In the liberal ascendancy of the 1930s, and especially by mid-decade, there were two areas of supreme importance. First of all,

---

5. The best survey of the Communist party in the 1930s is Harvey Klehr, *The Heyday of American Communism* (New York: Basic Books, 1984). Insights into the Communist *experience* in that era can be found in Vivian Gornick, *The Romance of American Communism* (New York: Basic Books, 1977). In addition, there is a large and growing body of memoirs dealing with these questions.

liberals desired to humanize the social system with a network of policies that would protect the individual from the consequences of economic insecurity. Second, except for a significant minority among them who preferred to remain aloof from European politics, liberals wished to confront the threat of fascist expansionism with an interventionist foreign policy geared toward collective security. They were at least partially satisfied by the social legislation of 1935, although the social program was still unfinished in their eyes. They were much less satisfied with Roosevelt's timid foreign policy, and their frustration grew in the next few years as Congress passed legislation designed to prevent the president from taking independent action in the various political and military crises that were occurring in Europe and Asia.

At first, the Communists held this liberal agenda in contempt. And why not, since the prospects for radicalism in the United States were never brighter than during the presidential campaign of 1932, when the prospects for the nation were never dimmer. In Germany, faced with a similar economic catastrophe, and a general election at the same time as the Americans, nearly 40 percent of the voters supported either the Socialist or the Communist party, and another third supported the Nazis. This meant that seven out of every ten German voters rejected the political economy of the Weimar Republic.

In the United States there was no real counterpart to the Nazi party as a political threat on the Right. On the Left stood the Socialists and the Communists. By 1932 the Socialists were a well established party of democratic socialism. The Communists, on the other hand, had had a shaky existence since they broke away from the Socialist party after the Bolshevik revolution. In the early 1920s they went underground, and when they finally surfaced, they sounded to most Americans as if they were speaking in tongues. The "Third Period," launched later in the decade, proclaimed the imminent collapse of capitalism; it was trumpeted in the rhetoric of class war and revolution, and in the arcane language of Marxist sectarianism and intramural eye gouging; on the whole, it simply didn't describe the world that most Americans perceived.

The rhetoric did not change early in the depression, but the realities did, and the Communists began to gain an audience. Still, with more than ten million people unemployed at election time, their candidate for president did not even draw 100,000 votes in the 1932 election. The Communists had attracted only two-tenths of 1 percent of the voters at the very depth of the depression. Moreover, for every Communist vote there were nine Socialist votes. If, as their rhetoric insisted, the capitalist order was ready to topple, the Communists were in no position to give the final push, let alone to build the new order. Not much changed in the Communist outlook for the next few years. Wall Street bankers remained the archfiends, and Franklin Roosevelt, a fascist or "social fascist," remained their stooge. The party made some gains in the unions, but most people continued to tune out.

That began to change in the summer of 1935. By then Soviet leaders were thoroughly alarmed at the apparent unwillingness of France and Britain to do anything about German expansionism. So Moscow issued a call for Communists everywhere to make common cause with all people and parties of good will, by which the Soviets meant any party or organization that would support their goal of collective international action against the new order in Germany. The "Popular Front" was born. In France this meant that the Communists cooperated with the Socialists. But who was there to cooperate with in the United States? The Republicans were, on the whole, opposed to an interventionist foreign policy, and the Socialists seemed scarcely worth trifling with. The only alternative, then, was to rally internationalist sentiment in the Democratic party, which meant all-out support for Roosevelt and the New Deal. Suddenly yesterday's enemies were today's allies. It was the first of several bewildering reversals of Communist party policy in the next several years that were dictated by the imperatives of Soviet foreign policy.

That explains why the Communist party made peace with liberals, but it doesn't explain why so many liberals accepted this embrace from the Communists. If the best chance to broaden their support on certain issues lay in moving left, why didn't they seek out the Socialists, who at least shared a commitment to democratic procedures, in contrast to dictatorial Russia?

Unfortunately that alternative was closed off by the Socialists themselves, who were busy exploring various paths toward self-destruction at the time. It was not so much a party in the 1930s as an ill-digested mix of groups divided by ideology, policy, and personalities. At various times in the decade there were Christian Socialists, non-Marxist gradualists, moderate Marxists, harder-line Marxists, and Trotskyists struggling to control the Socialist party. While the Popular Front moved the Communists rightward, the Socialists, with factions shuffling dizzyingly in and out of the party, moved leftward. It was a development that cost them many old friends without winning them many new ones.

The finishing touch was applied by party leader Norman Thomas, when the issue of collective security came to the fore, near the end of the decade. For Thomas and his followers, war was simply the clash of expanding capitalist nations in the international arena; it was an inevitable by-product of imperialism. They saw little difference between imperialist Germany, on the one hand, and imperialist Britain and France, on the other. Therefore, their objective was to keep the United States out of the impending European war among these imperialist nations. Now, this might have been good Leninism, but Leninism was bad politics at the time, because it sealed the Socialists off from the Left, the center, and the Right. After the outbreak of war in Europe, Thomas was embarrassed to find himself arguing alongside archconservatives and rabid anti-Semites in his efforts to hold America aloof from the European conflict.[6]

The future for the squabbling Socialists was already bleak in 1936, when Thomas got less than one-quarter of the votes he had received in 1932. Four years later, insisting that the United States avoid any commitment to a war in which Germany had already overrun western Europe, he presided over the collapse of his party, losing almost half of his pitiful 1936 vote total. Some measure of the party's futility is visible in the fact that it barely finished ahead of the Prohibitionist

6. By that time, of course, the Communists were also very cozy with the non-radical isolationists, which made it a strange ménage indeed. The Socialist party in this era is discussed in Frank A. Warren, *An Alternative Vision: The Socialist Party in the 1930s* (Bloomington: Indiana University Press, 1974). An assessment of Norman Thomas as "political actor" can be found in Bernard K. Johnpoll, *Norman Thomas and the Decline of American Socialism* (Chicago: Quadrangle Books, 1970).

party in the 1940 election. Riven by internal discord, contemptuous of an enormously popular president, and rigid in its opposition to a foreign policy that was rapidly gaining support in the nation, the Socialist party rendered itself ridiculous in the eyes of most liberals.

Until late 1939 the Communists stood in sharp contrast to this. For one thing, nobody was ever in doubt about where the party stood on a given issue at a particular time. Internal discord was never a problem because of "party discipline," which meant basically that party members were not permitted to oppose the party line once it had been laid down in Moscow. Their choice was to follow it or get out. If the party line dictated that today you embrace the people whom you had vilified only yesterday, you did it as if yesterday had never happened. Unlike the Socialists, the Communists allowed no divisive infighting—at least none that was visible to the public. So when the official line changed to proclaim the Popular Front in 1935, members shifted like a flock of birds swerving in unison from one direction to another.

When the Communists abandoned the radical analysis and rhetoric of the Third Period, they were barely distinguishable from the advanced liberals of the Democratic party. They worked selflessly to help organize the new CIO unions in the mass-production industries. They were far ahead of the Democratic party on what was called in those days "Negro equality." Their support of social welfare measures was also unexceptionable to liberals and well in front of the Democratic party. And on matters of foreign policy they seemed to be the only organized group of any consequence that was demanding action to stop Nazi expansionism. If they were too strident and confrontational for the taste of many genteel liberals, they at least worked tirelessly for all the liberal causes, and that was what counted in the end.

Of course, there was still the question of the party's ties to the Soviet Union. In spite of efforts to muffle their radicalism, the Communists left no doubt that they saw the Soviet Union as the model for the future development of the United States. Here was a potential area of conflict in the Popular Front, because few liberals had illusions about the implications of a Stalin-style dictatorship in the United States. They solved this problem by rigidly separating the political and economic spheres in the Soviet Union, which permitted them to praise the economic developments even as they ignored or condemned the political. The purge trials of the late 1930s troubled many liberals, but the charges and countercharges were so confusing that it was difficult to know what the truth was, especially with so many of the accused confessing their guilt.

Many liberals preferred instead to focus on the new Soviet constitution and to assume that the rhetoric of this humane document expressed the reality of the Soviet Union. Far more of them admired Soviet economic planning and cradle-to-grave social welfare. Indeed they had the same goals for the United States, although without the large-scale socialization of property that characterized Soviet socialism. Moreover the Soviet experiment—and it was often called just that—was still young. It had only been fifteen years since the triumph of the revolution, and the world could not be remade overnight. Who could tell? Maybe the Communists were right; maybe Stalin's harsh dictatorship would yield to a more benign form in time.

For those Americans who wanted to go beyond liberalism without quite joining the party, there were the values and goals, as well as the analytical tools, of Karl Marx. In the context of the Great Depression it did not seem outrageous to analyze political and economic problems in class terms. It did not seem out of line, for example, to see a class struggle in the great battles that took place in those years between capital and labor in the mass-production industries. Those who were troubled by certain similarities in the political structures of Nazism and Communism could at least find comfort in the differences in values. They could overlook means for ends. The goals of Marxism were framed in the language of the Enlightenment, which spoke in universal terms of brotherhood, of freedom, of equality, and of the fullest development of the individual's potential as a human being. And the appeal was always to human reason. On these terms, it made contact with American values that were also a legacy of the Enlightenment.

The question of property ownership could have been a divisive issue, but the party kept attention focused on the vast areas of concurrence. Nazism, in contrast, spoke a language that made no contact at all with the core values of America. It spoke of blood, of soil, of fatherland; it condemned representative government; and it flaunted its commitment to unreason and violence. To liberals, it smelled of death, and it horrified them.

The final element in this situation was, of course, the Nazi approach to race. Although all the implications of Nazi racism were not yet clear, two elements stood out from the beginning: fervent Aryanism and ferocious anti-Semitism. Many liberals were not without their own prejudices, but this talk of the supremacy of Aryan blood seemed a little silly to most of them, and the ranting over a world Jewish conspiracy seemed completely beyond reason. Non-Jewish liberals saw Nazi racism as ugly and indefensible; Jews perceived it as a mortal threat. If Jews moved disproportionately toward the Communist party from 1935 to 1940, it was primarily because the Communist party seemed to be the only organization demanding that the United States stand up to the Nazis on the world stage. That this was a reflex of Soviet foreign policy was irrelevant to them. If anything, it made the Soviet Union more attractive to many Jews than it would otherwise have been. They already recognized that resistance to Nazism was a matter of survival.

Thus the Communist party, so recently estranged from American society and politics, now moved consciously toward the mainstream. Yesterday FDR had been a front for Wall Street; today he was a heroic leader. Yesterday the New Deal had been the road to fascism; today it was the road to social and economic equality. Yesterday the Communist party had been the vanguard of revolution; today it was an expression of twentieth-century Americanism. And it worked. Thousands joined the party in the next few years, and for every one who joined, there were a dozen who trailed closely behind, and for every follower, there were ten, fifty, a hundred who signed petitions supporting the party's position on foreign affairs. It was the first clear manifestation of one of the great paradoxes of American politics: the Communist party grows in inverse proportion to its apparent radicalism. In this case, the radicalism was muted and the party grew.

A word of caution is in order here. It is important not to exaggerate the size or influence of the party in the 1930s. Membership never reached one hundred thousand, and most of that was concentrated in a handful of eastern cities. New York City alone often had one-third of the party members. Moreover, Communist influence was limited primarily to issues that were within the pale of respectability. But the party had spruced up its image, and it had become at least tolerable to many who had previously held it in contempt.

Maurice Halperin made his political commitment on these terms in the 1930s. He was not interested in a socialist revolution in the United States, which he considered unlikely in the foreseeable future because of the conservative nature of the American people, and perhaps even unnecessary because of the reformism of the Democratic party. Anyhow, the party had put revolution in storage for the time being, and was generally supporting New Deal reformism. Halperin's interest was in pressuring a divided Democratic party into taking a strong position against the rising forces of European fascism, and to him that meant supporting the Communist party on foreign policy matters. Those were the terms on which Communists and liberals began to rub elbows during the Popular Front period.

Halperin had returned from France a political noncombatant and then had had his liberal sensibilities aroused by the depression and engaged by Roosevelt. After that he moved gradually leftward until by 1936 he was a fellow traveler. Yet all the while he remained an ardent supporter of the New Deal. It is necessary to emphasize this last fact to an audience unfamiliar with the political currents of the 1930s. Halperin and thousands like him saw nothing anomalous in supporting the Democratic party and the Communist party at the same time, because they were acting on specific issues of the day, and not on ideology or the promise of a socialist utopia rising out of the rubble of a collapsed capitalist order.

Halperin's political journey can actually be traced, and in some ways verified, in his publications during the era. His first essays were brief reviews published in *Books Abroad* even before he left Oklahoma for Paris in the late 1920s, and they reveal no political or ideological stance at all. His first significant publication with a point of view was his 1934 essay on the Mexican political scene. This was the essay that brought him to the attention of the eastern radicals who organized the Cuban adventure of 1935.

A 1936 article in *Current History* praised the Cárdenas regime in Mexico for following "the middle way, the path that leads to liberal capitalism." The essay is more radical than this fragment suggests, however, because of the way it handles stereotypes drawn from the radical literature of the era: the illiterate peasant who lives in squalor on his "acre or two of mediocre land"; the exploited worker whose "chief problem is how to get sufficient food"; the small-business man on the make who is buffeted about by contradictory economic forces; and foreign capital, which siphons off earnings to the mother country that could otherwise be used to expand Mexico's pathetic infrastructure and raise wages (thereby increasing purchasing power).[7]

This temperate radicalism is reflected in another essay on Mexico that he published a few months later. In it he contrasts the conservative peasants of Morelos with the radical peasants of Vera Cruz and explains the difference in terms of their respective relationship to the land. In Morelos the peasants are petty landowners. As one of them said, "We each have our own piece of earth, we want to work it in our own individual way and pass it on to our children." In Vera Cruz, on the other hand, they own no land at all. They are trapped in a system of feudal land tenure, and peasants "who own no land can hardly be expected to entertain great respect for private property."[8]

Halperin clearly sympathizes with the agrarian reforms of the Cárdenas regime. How radical these reforms were, however, depended upon one's perspective. Some of them, for instance, aimed at the expropriation of giant landholdings, but not at the collectivization of the property expropriated. From the point of view of laissez-faire capitalism, this was radical surgery; from that of Marxism, it was little more than a band-aid. The goal was to distribute the land to an impoverished peasantry in the form of small private holdings. It was a

7. Maurice Halperin, "Mexico the Incredible," *Current History* (November 1936): 47–52. This is not to comment on the accuracy of the analysis, only on the nature and tone of the stereotypes employed.

8. Halperin, "Inside Mexico," *Current History* (February 1937): 83–87.

vision of government-assisted petty agrarian entrepreneurship that was congenial to American populism and not to the forced collectivization of Russian agriculture that was taking place at the time.

Thus we see a clear shift in Halperin's analysis between 1934 and 1937, and it is probably no coincidence that it parallels a similar shift in the party line in those very years. The 1934 article had decidedly radical implications that were fairly consistent with Third Period orthodoxy, while the later articles had a populist tone that would not have offended the gentler sensibilities of the Popular Front.

Stronger medicine than this populism is only rarely hinted at, but it does occasionally surface. In reviewing a book on the history of racism, Halperin concludes that racism in the modern world serves an "extremely important purpose: it distracts attention from the class struggle and bolsters up chauvinism." In other words, it is an aberration that deflects historical forces from their true purpose.[9] In a review for *Books Abroad* during the late 1930s, he mildly implies approval of a book that takes a Marxist position on its subject. In others, where he might have indicated approval of a Marxist analysis or a Communist tract, he does not even hint at an ideological stance. Perhaps the most surprising example of this neutrality occurs in his review of a book by Georgi Dimitrov. It was Dimitrov who had announced the arrival of the Popular Front in a speech before the Communist International (Comintern) in 1935, and his book consisted primarily of the two key speeches he made in that Moscow summer. Considering the impact of the Popular Front position on Halperin's own thinking, it is surprising that he was content simply to describe this book without appraising it.[10]

9. Halperin, review of *Races—Mythe et Vérité*, by Théodore Balk, *Books Abroad* (winter 1936): 50. I remember vividly a conversation with a Marxist friend in graduate school, who said to me in despair, "You know, Kirsch, I've got nineteenth-century Europe all doped out Marxistically except for one thing. It's that goddam nationalism. It keeps intruding." Intruding! Such non-rational (goddam) forces as racism and nationalism do indeed intrude into what we might wistfully wish were tidy, rational, even symmetrical historical events and processes.

10. Halperin, review of *Pour Vaincre le fascisme*, by G. Dimitrov, *Books Abroad* (autumn 1937): 447.

Beginning in the fall of 1937, Halperin gives us another angle on his thinking, for it was at that time that he became a regular contributor to the University of Oklahoma's newspaper, the *Oklahoma Daily*. In October the paper launched a column known as the "Faculty Forum," which ran daily essays by faculty members, who wrote on everything from student behavior to world affairs. Halperin's weekly contribution leaned more toward world affairs than student behavior.

These articles were not written in a vacuum, but in a world where fascist aggression was accelerating in the face of apparent indifference on the part of the Western powers while conservative forces in Congress were regrouping to bring the New Deal's liberal reformism to a halt. In the preceding eighteen months alone, Italy had completed its conquest of Ethiopia; Germany had reoccupied the Rhineland in violation of the Versailles Treaty; Germany and Italy had come to the aid of Franco's rebels in Spain, where the German air force had virtually bombed the undefended Basque town of Guernica to rubble; and Japan had provoked a war with China that was accompanied by horrifying atrocities then considered shocking by the rest of the world.

Only a few weeks before Halperin's first article, Roosevelt had thrilled the interventionist community when he finally spoke out clearly against fascist expansionism in his famous "quarantine-the-aggressor" speech in Chicago. In the same period, however, Roosevelt had suffered his first serious defeat, when his ill-advised proposal to "pack" the Supreme Court with liberal justices raised an issue that finally gave his opponents in both parties an opportunity to unite against him. These issues—reaction at home and fascism abroad—dominated Halperin's contributions to the "Faculty Forum" in the two years that he wrote for it.

Thus, in the fall of 1937, he attacked Franco as a liar, condemned the "wholesale murder" committed by the Japanese in China as "unspeakably bestial," and cautioned that "Latin America . . . is today teeming with fascist intrigue," paying special attention to what he felt was a critical situation in Brazil.[11] He expressed his concern about

11. These articles appeared on October 6, 13, and 27, respectively, in the *Oklahoma Daily*.

the resurgence of domestic conservatism by implying that Wall Street itself had triggered the most recent stock market collapse in order to embarrass Roosevelt and discredit the Securities and Exchange Commission.[12]

All of these stands were consistent with fellow traveling and with the more militant liberalism of the era. Phrased somewhat differently, perhaps, they could even have been written by a Communist of the Popular Front era. But a column he wrote in 1938 reveals the anguish of a fellow traveler who was unable to follow the party line on the Moscow purge trials blindly yet was unwilling to abandon the need for collective action with the Soviet Union against Nazi Germany.

Begun in 1936, these trials gave Stalin a pretext to eliminate virtually all opposition, real or imagined, to his primacy in the party and the nation. At first sight, of course, the charges seemed to be absurd. To believe in the guilt of the defendants, as Harvey Klehr observes, one would have to believe that Stalin's foe, the extreme leftist radical Leon Trotsky, "had somehow united left-wing Zinovievites, right-wing Bukharinites, and disgruntled Stalinites with his own followers and then plotted with both Nazi Germany and Imperial Japan to overthrow the Soviet regime and install capitalism."[13] Nevertheless, the party faithful did believe in the guilt of the defendants, because, improbable as it seems, the accusations were usually confirmed by the accused at public trials. To try to get to the bottom of this strange situation, a group of prominent and reputable Americans, headed by John Dewey, investigated the affair, heard Trotsky's testimony in Mexico, and then exonerated him, thereby casting severe doubts on the whole trial process.

Halperin did not know quite what to make of it all. Because he had great respect for Dewey's integrity, he entertained some doubts about the validity and meaning of these trials. Yet there were those confessions. Whom to believe? In the end, he was inclined to accept the Soviet version, but wherever the truth lay, he was above all bent on seeing that the trials did not divert attention from the single

12. Ibid., November 3, 1937.
13. Klehr, *Heydey,* 358.

towering issue of the day, the threat of fascist expansionism. And on that issue the Soviet Union's position was impeccable and unyielding. So Halperin put aside his concerns about the trials and continued to support the Soviet Union on the basis of its foreign policy.

His column on the trials reflected this position. He cited coverage in the *New York Times* to support his conviction that "the accusations made against the condemned, and supported by their confessions, are essentially true." It seemed probable, he continued, that the accused were either trying to steer the Soviet Union into the fascist camp or force it "to resume its crusade of world-wide and thorogoing [*sic*] communism." He was not in any way troubled by the obvious incongruity of these alternatives, because that is what the "evidence" in the trials suggested. Either course, to the Right or to the Left, would threaten world peace and American security, and for that reason, if for no other, one had to support the Russians. "As long as Stalin keeps his communism and his firing squads within the borders of the Soviet Union," Halperin said, "and [as] long as he prefers to have friendly relations with the democratic rather than the fascist countries, he is less to be feared than his opponents." When we make such decisions, he concluded, "we must above all consider the well-being of our own democracy and the protection of our national interests."[14]

This was hardly a ringing endorsement of Stalinism. It is certainly not the sort of rhetoric that a "true believer" would have used, or that the party would have let a member get away with. Basically, Halperin was saying that in an imperfect world it is sometimes necessary to choose what may be the lesser of evils to protect one's own self-interest. On those terms he continued to follow the party line on foreign affairs.

A much greater test of his loyalty and his credulity came in the late summer of 1939 with the Stalin-Hitler Pact. Far more than the purge trials, the Stalin-Hitler Pact sent shock waves through the leftist

14. Halperin, "Faculty Forum," *Oklahoma Daily*, March 23, 1938. Only recently, several high-level party members, including the legendary old Bolshevik Nikolai Bukharin, had been convicted of such crimes as sabotage and plotting the restoration of capitalism.

community. For Socialists and Trotskyists, of course, it merely confirmed Stalin's treachery and the American Communist party's toadying posture before the demands of Moscow. For Communists and fellow travelers, it was the jolt of the decade. Many of them had been drawn toward the party in the first place by the need for the Western democracies to stand united with the Soviet Union against Nazi expansionism and fascist principles. Now, when the party line finally crystallized after the outbreak of hostilities, they were told that this was only a war among imperialistic powers, that Germany and Italy, on the one hand, and France and Britain, on the other, were Tweedledum and Tweedledee. They were asked to believe the line of the despised Socialist party that they had been fighting bitterly for the past four years. The Communist party was to begin working just as feverishly to keep America neutral as it had, before September, to get America involved. That was the position; members had to accept it or leave. Many left, with public announcements of their bitter disgust.

Halperin made no public announcements. Indeed, what is surprising, in view of the forum he had in his weekly column on public affairs, was his complete silence on the issue. He neither parroted the new party line nor attacked it. Of course, he was not quiescent. He attacked the prewar version of HUAC; he attacked the university's proposal to charge tuition; he wrote on the growing threat from right-wing elements in Mexico. His populist radicalism was still intact, but in the remaining months of 1939, he wrote not a word on the war in Europe and the shocking pact that had made it possible. By 1940 he had discontinued his column altogether. Was Halperin's silence on this crucial issue due to despair? After all, he had invested an enormous amount of himself in the Popular Front only to see it abandoned. Was he simply stunned mute by the new international realities? We shall return to this question later.

It is worth noting that his silence also extended to the Russian grab of Eastern Poland in September 1939, and to the Russian invasion of Finland less than three months later. Both of these acts occurred while he was still writing his column. The opportunity for public comment was still there, but he remained mute. Perhaps he had soured on the Soviet Union because it no longer represented the best hope for anti-fascism, but his silence on Soviet behavior in the late summer and autumn of 1939 is astonishing. He did not attempt to justify Soviet actions as, for instance, the *Daily Worker* did, but neither did he condemn them. His general posture—or lack of one—in these months is curious indeed.

Meanwhile, he had become increasingly involved in local affairs at the university and in the community. He was appalled, for instance, at the array of forces in Oklahoma that opposed Roosevelt's effort to bring the Supreme Court to heel with his Court-packing plan. The press, the oil interests, even most of the state Democratic party were ranged against the president. To make his voice heard on this issue, Halperin joined a handful of faculty members in signing a petition supporting the plan. It was not much, but it put him on record against the most powerful interests in the state. He struck again the following year, when he gave lectures around town in defense of the Mexican government's action in expropriating American oil properties. At the same time, he spoke out frequently against the growing menace of fascism. He countered the lectures of occasional pro-Nazis who visited the university, and he defied the Oklahoma establishment by sympathizing openly with the Loyalist forces in the Spanish Civil War.

Still, war in Spain was a remote issue in Norman, Oklahoma. Closer to home, and much closer to the bone, was the great migration westward of thousands of Oklahomans forced off the land by drought and the modernization of agriculture. The plight of the wretched "Okies" was dramatically presented by John Steinbeck in his moving novel *The Grapes of Wrath*. Halperin knew about the reality behind the fiction. The migrants, uprooted and trapped between hunger and despair, were not even permitted to spend the night in Norman, except for their consignment to the transient camp in town. Edith and some of the faculty wives regularly and quite visibly took food and clothing out to this squalid encampment, while Maurice lectured around the state to middle-class audiences, insisting on the accuracy of Steinbeck's novel. Prudence never having been one of Halperin's virtues, he was rather noisily committing himself in local, national, and international affairs to positions that were well to the left of what was safe in the Sooner State.

He also committed himself to an economic investment that soon returned to haunt him. Halperin thinks it was around 1938 when he saw an announcement in the *New York Times* that the Chase Manhattan Bank was about to market some Soviet bonds in North America at 7 percent interest, which was more than double the going rate in the country at the time. Partly because he found the investment ideologically attractive, and partly because he liked the numbers, he invested several hundred dollars he had earned from his articles in these bonds. In retrospect, the whole situation seems marvelously ironic: the Soviet Union was employing the Rockefeller bank to entice private investors with a spectacularly high interest rate in order to raise capital for Communist economic development. At the time, however, Halperin saw no irony in the situation. As he explains it, it was simply a combination of "greed and a good cause." How could it miss?

When the Nazi-Soviet Pact was signed, he reappraised the ideological side of his investment and decided to sell the bonds.

HALPERIN: I decided after the [Nazi-Soviet] *Pact . . . it was '39, right? I decided I had better get the hell out and sell these bonds. For two reasons: one, I didn't want to lose money; two, I didn't want to support these people now. And so I wrote and asked the Chase people to cash my bonds. The money for the bonds—a receipt—was sent to my bank with instructions to pay me the money. The banker got alarmed and went to the FBI, to the President* [of the University] *and everything. . . . Of course, it was considered not ethical for a banker to do this sort of thing. But the only explanation they had was that I was on the payroll of the Soviet Union, that I was a spy. I mean these people were so stupid, you know, to think that if I were a spy. . . . Would I be doing it so that it would come to the bank?*

There were no immediate repercussions from Halperin's venture into speculative capitalism, but there were other signs that the climate was becoming less hospitable to people suspected of lurking on the Left. In the fall of 1940, there was the trial of Robert Wood, the chairman of the Oklahoma Communist party. When Wood was indicted under the state's criminal syndicalism act, the temperature of Oklahoma politics rose rapidly. Soviet aggression in Poland and Finland made Communists a better target than ever for local politicians, and the syndicalism act made an equally inviting target for radicals and civil libertarians. It was an omen of what was to come a decade later. Eventually Wood was convicted and sentenced to ten years in prison (his sentence was later overturned on appeal) for advocating the violent overthrow of the government.

But the conviction of Wood was only the local expression of a wider mood at the time that was embodied in the "investigative" activities of Martin Dies, the chairman of HUAC. Inspired by the Dies committee, several state legislatures set up their own "little Dies committees," and endowed them with investigative powers that amounted to unrestricted fishing licenses. Several people in Norman and a few in Oklahoma City, mostly liberals and a sprinkling of radicals, were alarmed at this development, in general, and incensed at the sentencing of Wood, in particular. Realizing that Wood's sentence had been imposed not for what he did, but for what he was alleged to have said, and sensing that civil liberties in Oklahoma were under attack, they met in late October 1940, to organize the Oklahoma Federation for Constitutional Rights.[15] Needless to say, Maurice was on the executive committee.

That fall, there were a few warnings of danger ahead, including a speech in Oklahoma City by Martin Dies and an attack on the federation by the governor, but the trouble did not really begin until January, when state senator Paul Stewart introduced a bill to keep parties that advocated violence off the ballot in Oklahoma. The federation immediately objected, sending Halperin and another member to argue against the bill on civil libertarian grounds. Now the battle was joined. By the end of the month the state senate had turned its committee on privileges into a little Dies Committee, and authorized it to conduct "a sweeping investigation of all state educational institutions and public pay rolls in a search for advocates of subversive doctrines." Accompanied by a "burst of flag waving oratory," the senate was nearly unanimous in agreeing that "all subversive influences should

15. The following account is taken from the *Oklahoma Daily*, which was the university's student newspaper; the *Daily Oklahoman* of Oklahoma City; the *Tulsa Daily World*; and the *Norman Transcript*.

be exposed and the enemies of the American form of government exterminated." According to the *Daily Oklahoman*, by the end of January, Stewart was taking dead aim at the Oklahoma Federation for Constitutional Rights.

At this time, university president Bizzell revealed that the FBI had been quietly searching out alleged Communist activities on campus since May. Bizzell endorsed the investigation, and at the same time he gave a vote of confidence in his faculty, which he felt certain was "as conservative as any other faculty in the country."

In early February, the committee launched its investigation by issuing subpoenas for a few of the state's leading Communists, along with the entire executive of the federation. The committee kicked off its hearings with its star witness, Robert Wood, and proceeded to embarrass itself even in the eyes of the conservative press. According to the *Tulsa Daily World*, "It isn't much of a secret that Robert Wood . . . 'held his own' while testifying." Some of the senators were beginning to back away because of adverse publicity in the local and national press, it said. The *Daily Oklahoman* observed that "Robert Wood . . . came out of the examination with a better showing than the senators expected. Those thinking the senators would . . . make him admit he took his orders from Moscow were fooled. . . ." Stewart, unembarrassed, continued to press the investigation.

Among the things that alarmed many of the senators were the first faint stirrings of civil rights sentiments in Jim Crow Oklahoma. Three university students in the gallery who "applauded remarks of Witness Roscoe Dunjee, editor of a Negro newspaper here," were promptly served subpoenas and compelled to testify before the committee about various of their beliefs. John B. Thompson, a southerner of good family who was now a Protestant minister in Norman and a member of the federation, was asked by Stewart, "You are aware there is a racial question?" "Yes, indeed I am," he replied. He was then asked, "Do you believe in social equality?" Thompson answered, "We would never agree on that question, Senator."[16]

---

16. Excerpts from a few of the hearings, especially those of John Thompson and Maurice Halperin, were carried in the *Oklahoma Daily*.

Halperin testified before the committee on February 19, and the nature and sequence of the questions are illuminating. After discovering where he was born, raised, and educated, the senators interrogated him rather closely about his parents, their origins, their religion, and their "political faith." Question: "Are you of the Jewish faith?" Halperin: "Yes." Question: "Do you attend church regularly?" Halperin: "Usually. Although sometimes it is inconvenient to drive to Oklahoma City." Question: "What branches of the church are there?" Halperin explained. One can only speculate what all this had to do with the political subversion the committee members were trying to expose. The committee established that Maurice was a member of the Oklahoma Federation for Constitutional Rights, and then asked, "Do you know any Communists?" ("Not that I know of. However, I don't go around asking people if they are Communists.") "Have you attended any meetings of the Communist party?" ("No.") "Have you read any Communist books?" ("I have read a little. About as much as the ordinary educated person would read.") "Do you believe in the Russian cause?" ("No, I don't, frankly.") Other questions established that he was a member of the American Federation of Teachers of the AFL, that he belonged to the Modern Languages Association and the Harvard Club of Oklahoma, that he belonged to no peace organizations, that he was not a conscientious objector, and that he had registered for the draft.

Up to that point Halperin's testimony had been exemplary. He had testified under oath that he was not a Communist and had answered all other questions in a straightforward manner. He had been compliant without being either obsequious or confrontational. In this respect he differed considerably from John Thompson, whose demeanor before the committee was much more prickly, and who, in addition, was national head of the American Peace Mobilization, a Communist front organization pressing the party line that the war was an imperialist conflict on both sides, and therefore no business of the United States.[17]

17. According to Earl Latham, the American Peace Mobilization was formed in June 1940, when the Communist party directed its followers to establish peace

But then the committee's line of questioning took a different turn which suggests that it had done its homework, perhaps assisted by the FBI. Committee members questioned Halperin closely about his involvement in the trip to Cuba that had taken place more than five years earlier, and his replies were more than a bit disingenuous. Asked about the purpose of the trip, he said that it was "to study the culture, the civilization and the political situation in Cuba (in three weeks!)." Asked if they had been arrested, he replied that they had been "detained," and explained that the authorities "preferred we did not land because the situation there was rather tense. They feared for our safety." The only apparent threat to their safety, of course, was from the authorities who were "detaining" them. Asked who went along on the trip, Halperin could remember the name only of Clifford Odets and described the others as "lawyers, trade unionists, an economist or two . . . a pretty wide representation of professions and occupations."

Whatever he might have known before he set out for Cuba, he was very aware, by the time he returned, of a small clique of party members who were giving direction to the entire endeavor. Had he

---

organizations throughout the country. "The result was the creation of the American Peace Mobilization, which launched a fake pacifist movement." Immediately after Germany attacked Russia in June 1941, "the American Peace Mobilization changed its name to the American People's Mobilization, [and] what had been a war of imperialist aggression immediately became a people's war." See Latham, *Communist Controversy*, 155. In his history of the Communist party during the war, Maurice Isserman, who is far less hostile to the party than many historians, says that the American Peace Mobilization "never attracted significant non-Communist support." *Which Side Were You On?* (Middletown, Conn.: Wesleyan University Press, 1982), 64. In fact, how one responded to Communist party initiatives during the period of the Stalin-Hitler Pact is a fairly reliable test for what one believed. One could make common cause with the Communists before the pact or during the war in the name of anti-fascism, without being particularly sympathetic with the party or the Soviet Union. But those who followed the party pirouette of 1939 did so for the single reason that they were willing to follow wherever the party led them. Thompson was, if not a party member, operating within strict doctrinal boundaries laid out by the party, and surely he knew it. Of course, this does not absolve the Oklahoma legislature from the reprehensible policy it was pursuing at the time in trying to shut down dissent on the campus and in the state.

anticipated this line of questioning, he would probably have assumed that the committee had been fully informed of the trip by the FBI, and might then have scored some points by discussing the political drift of the group openly. But he was not asked about it and he did not volunteer anything about it.

The hearings seemed to fizzle out soon thereafter, but the committee did not betray its mission. Seven weeks later it issued its report and made several recommendations. First of all, it recommended that the university separate itself from the School of Religion, a meaningless recommendation because the school was privately funded and had no administrative connection with the university anyhow, although its courses were accepted for credit. It also declared that John B. Thompson was a "bad influence" on the students, because of his affiliation with the American Peace Mobilization, another gratuitous comment, since Thompson had no connection with the university. It described the Oklahoma Federation for Constitutional Rights as a "subversive group" with a "fellow-traveler spirit." And without offering either argument or evidence, it recommended that Halperin be fired for the good of the university. He was the only professor among the several in the federation singled out for this honor.

Furious with these procedures, the federation pointed out that there was a complete disjuncture between the evidence the committee had received, including the federation's minutes, and the conclusions it had come to. At a loss to explain it any other way, it charged that "the selection of one professor who has played a less prominent part in the activities of the federation than several other professors . . . smacks of religious and racial intolerance and is alarmingly close to the program of the Ku Klux Klan, which publicly supported the work of this senate committee."

The likelihood is that the committee chose Maurice simply because he was such an irresistible target. He was a high-profile nuisance for the political establishment of the state. He was outspoken on all of the controversial issues of the day, and inevitably he was on the wrong side of the controversy. The fact that he was a Jew—and it is clear from the hearing that this was a significant factor for the committee— was only the icing on the cake. There were still pockets of agrarian radicalism in Oklahoma that might have supported a liberal activist, but that radicalism was often cinched in a Bible-belt religion that was not particularly concerned with the civil liberties of a fellow-traveling, Jewish professor, even if he was not fellow traveling at the moment.

After the committee issued its report the situation deteriorated rapidly for Halperin. He was called before the Board of Regents and interrogated once again. It was during this session that the matter of the Soviet bond came up. Although matters of this sort are supposed to be kept confidential by banking personnel, the information had somehow found its way to the Board. Members were obviously more interested in finding out that Halperin had owned the bond than they were in learning that he had sold it in anger after the Nazi-Soviet Pact was signed. The regents asked him why he had bought the bond and he replied, "It's very simple—it's a good investment. How many of you gentlemen have been earning 7% on your investments?" The regents laughed, and after the meeting they recommended that Halperin be fired.

A group of students, meanwhile, hastily circulated a petition defending the professor as a good teacher and a loyal American. Unmoved by the five hundred signatures they gathered in just a few days, the acting chairman of the department for the summer session notified Halperin that there was no place for him to teach in the summer term, although he always taught in alternate summers and it was his turn in 1941. Halperin hastily put out some feelers and found a job teaching at the University of Florida for the summer. While he was in Gainesville he learned that he had been fired.

Or so it seemed at first. As it happened, however, the president who wanted him fired—William Bizzell—was retiring just at that time, and the man named to replace him was Joseph Brandt, who had founded the University of Oklahoma Press several years earlier, and was a personal friend of Maurice. Brandt informed the regents that he would not accept the position if Halperin were fired, because the dismissal would be a flagrant violation of accepted procedures in such matters. His position was strengthened when the regents learned that the American Association of University Professors had taken an interest in the case. No doubt they were looking for a way out of the humiliating publicity that would follow from firing a professor "for the good of the university" when they were not able to tell why it would be for the good of the university to fire him, except that the professor had once owned a Soviet bond that he had recently sold as an anti-Soviet gesture.

Then, while Brandt and the regents were negotiating, the situation took a different turn. Early in the year, well before his position at Oklahoma was threatened, Halperin had learned that the Pan-American Union had recently inaugurated a program for exchange professors in various areas of Latin American studies. So he applied to teach in the coming year at the University of Haiti, a position for which he was well qualified by his training in French language and literature. At around the same time that he learned he had been fired from the university, he was notified that the State Department had selected him as the exchange professor to Haiti. Unaware of Brandt's negotiations with the regents, Halperin finished a lazy summer session at the University of Florida and returned to New England certain of two things: he had been fired from the University of Oklahoma; he was about to embark on an exciting adventure in the fascinating country of Haiti. As things turned out, he was wrong on both counts. Only one of his expectations was borne out: he never saw Oklahoma again.

3

From Cap and Gown to Pick and Shovel

Late in the summer of 1941, Halperin was informed that his departure for Haiti was being held up for the time being because of the growing tension over American ships in international waters. To pass the time pleasantly while they waited, Maurice and Edith took the children and headed off to the little coastal resort town of Nahant, where they had been married years earlier. It was perhaps even better known as the home of the Lodge family estate. The Lodges and the Halperins.

Over the years, Halperin had moved gradually from his original field of French literature into Latin American affairs, with an emphasis on Mexican politics. His most recent publication, an article on Mexican foreign policy, had been published that summer in the prestigious journal *Foreign Affairs*,[1] and that, no doubt, played a role in the events that now sent his life veering off in an entirely new and unexpected direction.

While he was marking time in Nahant, he received a phone call from William Langer, whom Halperin knew to be a highly regarded professor of history at Harvard University. What he did not know was that Langer had recently joined the Office of Coordinator of Information (COI) in Washington as head of the Research and Analysis Branch (R&A). Langer explained that the COI was doing some interesting

1. Maurice Halperin, "Mexico Shifts Her Foreign Policy," *Foreign Affairs* (October 1940): 207–21.

and useful work gathering and evaluating information relating to the war, and he wanted to know if Maurice would be interested in joining its Latin America Division. Halperin was flattered but explained that he already had a commitment to the State Department to teach in Haiti for the year. Langer said, "Don't do anything until I get back to you." When he called back, he said, "I have your release from the State Department." Out of the blue, Halperin had been given a job with the agency that was the forerunner of the OSS, which, in turn, was the forerunner of the CIA.

It was not by accident that Langer came upon Halperin. Maurice had passed through Washington earlier that summer to clear up some business about Haiti with the State Department, and while there he had looked up an old friend and former colleague from Norman, Warren Thornthwaite, a climatologist who was working with the Department of Agriculture. Halperin told his friend about his problems at the university. Thornthwaite later spoke to a friend, Preston James, a University of Michigan geographer who was in charge of the Latin America Division of COI. James spoke to Langer; Langer made the appropriate phone calls; and Halperin was invited to Washington. This American version of the British "old-boy network" was used to handle recruitment (and dismissal) in the OSS throughout the war.

By now it was October. Classes were already under way in Norman, and president-designate Brandt was finally able to work out a compromise with the regents. Halperin would be reinstated retroactive to the date of his dismissal and would then be given a leave of absence, with full pay, for the entire academic year, at the end of which he would resign from the university. Halperin's reputation (and income) would be spared; the university would remain in good standing with the AAUP; the regents would be rid of a troublemaker; and Brandt would be able to accept his job in good conscience. The compromise left everyone satisfied, but no one more than Halperin, who could finally join the battle against fascism and, in the bargain, collect two full incomes—more than six thousand dollars—for the coming year. In 1941 that was a princely sum.

It is one of the miracles of Halperin's life that he seemed to flourish in the rubble of his disasters—"the intervention of the supernatural," he calls it, sardonically. His brother, Teddy, did not set his sights that high for an explanation. When Maurice landed in Canada after leaving Cuba years later, Teddy was the New England representative of the Jewish Theological Seminary. He appraised his brother's career in language that owed more to the East Boston docks of his youth than to the seminary. "You know, Maur," he said, "every time you fall into a barrel of shit you come out with a handful of diamonds."

The Halperins settled in Riverdale, Maryland, where they rented a large, somewhat run-down house on some sprawling, somewhat run-down acreage with fruit orchards. The "Scourge of Norman" was about to become the "Squire of Riverdale," a gentleman farmer in a lazy, semirural, Jim Crow ambience. He was also about to become very active in the affairs of a nation at war, for he had barely settled in when the Japanese bombed Pearl Harbor and transformed the European war into a world war.

Only a few days after the attack on Pearl Harbor, Halperin was summoned to the office of John Wiley, a career diplomat who was then acting as an adviser to the head of COI, William Donovan. When he arrived, he found Wiley waiting, along with Vincenzo "Jim" Petrullo, an anthropologist who was serving as Preston James's chief assistant in the Latin America Division. Washington was in disarray, the Pacific fleet was a shambles, and nobody knew where the Japanese were or what they might do next. It even seemed possible that they might attack North America through Mexico. Donovan wanted to know what to expect from the Mexicans if this were to happen, so he arranged for Petrullo and Halperin to go down to Mexico, assess the situation there, and see if effective resistance, including guerrilla warfare if necessary, could be organized in the event of such an attack.

With a wad of unvouchered funds (a hallmark of Donovan's administration of the OSS throughout the war) the pair took off immediately for Mexico City. Once there, they reported to the American embassy, to the complete surprise of the staff there. The whole transaction had been conducted without either the permission or the knowledge of the State Department, and embassy personnel were furious at this breach of protocol.

Petrullo and Halperin spent the next several days quizzing embassy staff, poring over local newspapers, and contacting various Mexican power brokers, including leaders of the Communist party. By then, the diplomats had reason to be alarmed at what they could only interpret as an investigation. This was no longer simply a breach of protocol, but a show of no confidence in the embassy, and thus, implicitly, in the State Department itself. Not surprisingly, the State Department raised hell in Washington and managed to get the pair of sleuths recalled, but not before they had formed a very unflattering opinion of the American embassy in Mexico. On the other hand, it was just in time to provide Petrullo and Halperin with a lively diversion on the way back.

HALPERIN: There was an interesting thing that happened on the trip back. We were on a sleeper plane and we changed at a border town, I forget which. I noticed a big commotion on the American side of the border. There were cameras and people, pictures flashing. I didn't know what this was about. And there was a woman who was making a lot of noise. She's saying, "Listen, I've gotta go! Leave me alone." She had to go to the toilet, of course. And then I asked, "Who is it?" It was Paulette Goddard. She had been in Mexico. She was on a plane with me. I mean, I could later say I had spent the night with Paulette Goddard. She was a big [movie] star then. Also, she had a companion there, and I think that was the main interest. Some man was with her. A scandal or something, huh?

After spending the night with Paulette Goddard, Halperin found his meeting with General Donovan the next morning a sobering experience. Wild Bill Donovan was a legend. A charismatic combat officer who had won the Congressional Medal of Honor in World War I, Donovan retained his contacts with the military after the war, dabbled in New York politics, grew slightly rich as a Wall Street lawyer, and managed to stay in the public eye between wars. He was one of those people who drew the spotlight to himself without apparent effort. Now here he was pumping Halperin, who was just off the plane, for everything about the situation in Mexico. Before Halperin even had a chance to get home, Donovan had him write a report summarizing his impressions of the situation there. A day or two later he called Halperin into his office.

HALPERIN: Donovan said, "I'm very much impressed with your re-port. I'm going to send it to the White House immediately." And then he said something about, "Well, you've been a brave soldier." And I'm wondering, "brave soldier?" What's he talking about? "And if you ever get into trouble, remember that you've got one of the top lawyers of Wall Street to defend you."

Halperin had no idea what Donovan was talking about. He had been asked to report on certain conditions in Mexico, and he had done so. Still an innocent in Washington, he was not yet aware of the rhetoric of duplicity, let alone the bloodletting that often characterized bureaucratic in-fighting in the capital. All he did was describe the situation as he saw it. Of course that was the problem. It was how he saw it that could get him into trouble in the future. In his report, for example, he observed that "our information-gathering services in Mexico are quite inadequate to cover the present situation," without realizing that the FBI was involved in the information gathering. For emphasis, he added that the military attaché was "alarmed by the mechanical inadequacy" of these services and thus "especially welcomed our presence in Mexico and suggested that an organization such as Colonel Donovan's should constantly maintain field agents in Mexico" for intelligence purposes that were too sensitive for the embassy to perform.

To Halperin this was a straightforward assessment of the deplorable status of American intelligence-gathering potential in Mexico at the time. What he did not know was that this evaluation plunged him squarely into the middle of a bitter jurisdictional struggle between Donovan and J. Edgar Hoover over whose agency was going to control intelligence work in Latin America. Shrewd as he was, Donovan might very well have seen this "objective" evaluation by an outsider as a useful weapon in his battle with Hoover.

Having taken his shot at "our information-gathering services," Halperin then turned his attention to the embassy and the State Department itself, and here he must have known full well what he was doing. "The Embassy," he said,

> seems to be handicapped . . . by the temperament of many members of the staff [who] still have not adjusted their attitudes to the new situation. They maintain their personal connections with the Mexican upper-crust, without realizing that most of that upper-crust is consciously or unconsciously allied with Hitler.
>
> In the second place, I recognize the same lack of awareness within the State Department itself. I wonder whether the State Department is fully convinced of the gravity of the situation in Mexico. I have seen evidence to indicate that the State Department believes that it can "play ball" with the Sinarquistas [a right-wing, pro-clerical movement of considerable importance in Mexico at the time].

As Halperin saw it, the State Department hoped to control the *Sinarquistas* while the *Sinarquistas* suppressed the trade union and agrarian movements. He called this "a continuation of the tactic and mental outlook which for years has guided our policy toward Japan, and with such disastrous results."[2]

In just a few paragraphs Halperin had managed to insult agents for the FBI (though not by name) as incompetents, to accuse embassy personnel of playing footsie with proto-Nazis in Mexico, and to attack the State Department for concentrating more on suppressing the Mexican masses than on winning the war. "Brave soldier," indeed!

HALPERIN: To go on just a little bit there, James was furious—Preston James—when he heard that we had been sent to Mexico without his permission. He's the Chief of the Division. And he had a suspicion that Petrullo was the one who had engineered this thing. And so, shortly after we got back Petrullo was moved out somewhere; disappears. Some-

---

2. *Memorandum to the President*, from William J. Donovan, December 23, 1941, personal secretary's file, container 163, folder 2, Franklin D. Roosevelt Library, Hyde Park, New York. The memorandum cited here is actually a cover letter from Donovan to the president that says, "I am sending you the report of Mr. Maurice Halperin, who has just made an examination for us in Mexico. I am sending it just as it came to me." The remainder is Halperin's twelve-page memorandum to Donovan, dated December 22, 1941. I am grateful to Barnett Kalikow for sending me a copy of the memo.

body gave him a job somewhere, you know. The usual thing; you trade people around; you don't fire people. I did it when I was the boss there; I used to trade people, send them off. They sometimes thought they got a promotion. The main thing is to get them out of the office. James realized it wasn't my fault. Apparently he discovered that Petrullo had something to do with instigating it. He became convinced that I was innocent and he recommended my appointment as Assistant Chief. I entered in October and I would say that by January I was Assistant Chief.

In another year James himself was out. Although a competent scholar, he was an ineffective administrator, and as the division's activities and personnel expanded, his administrative shortcomings became a liability. His fatal error was becoming involved in a rather messy extramarital affair. Donovan had no problem with leftists in his organization as long as they produced, but scandal was something else. And so James, too, was "traded around." By early 1943 Halperin was head of the Latin America Division.

The OSS evokes images of derring-do, of courageous Americans parachuting behind enemy lines to fight with partisans against the Nazis in the "last good war." There was that, but there was more. Broadly speaking, there were two branches of the OSS. One was concerned with operational activities in the various theaters of war, and is the one we know best for its paramilitary activities. The other was immersed in research activities of all sorts into the affairs of enemies, allies, and neutrals. In the agency itself, the agents of the operational bunch were known as the "Cloak and Dagger" boys, the research analysts as the "Pick and Shovel" crew—romance and drudgery, respectively. It was an in-house joke, but the imagery effectively sums up the aura that surrounded each branch.

The Research and Analysis (R&A) Branch included both geographical and functional sections.[3] Among the functional sections, for

3. Barry Katz, *Foreign Intelligence: Research and Analysis in the Office of Strategic Services, 1942–1945* (Cambridge: Harvard University Press, 1989). See especially chapter 1. See also Robin W. Winks, *Cloak and Gown: Scholars in the Secret War, 1939–1961* (New York: Quill/William Morris, 1987), chapter 2.

instance, there was an Economic Division that dealt with economic problems anywhere in the world. And among the geographical sections there was a Far East Division that handled research in that expansive part of the world. The Latin America Division was a geographical section that explored and reported on anything in Latin America that appeared to bear on the war. These activities were centered primarily, though not exclusively, on Mexico and Brazil, the two most committed allies; on Argentina, a nonbelligerent that leaned toward Germany (much as the United States had been a nonbelligerent that leaned toward England before Pearl Harbor); and on Bolivia and Chile. Activities of the division were limited to research and analysis because Donovan had lost the jurisdictional struggle with Hoover over covert activities in Latin America. His agents were not supposed to operate there.

HALPERIN: Apparently Roosevelt considered it prudent, in his relations with Hoover, to turn over the Western Hemisphere to him. Donovan basically never accepted it. He never paid much attention to it. He actually had some secret agents that he was using down there. I know about it because Donovan introduced me to one of his agents. He came to discuss matters. He would get some political orientation. . . . Mysterious fellow. Never learned who he really was. And there were others, I'm sure.

Bureaucracies, as we all know, are intended to function like well-oiled machines. Their aim is efficiency, and on paper, at least, they are as tidy as well-designed blueprints. The human element, alas, tends to mess them up. Consequently, there were not only interagency tensions with the FBI and other intelligence agencies, but squabbles within the OSS as well. Some of these were personal, some jurisdictional. Woodrow Borah recalls that

> There was a high percentage of Harvard-Yale-Princeton people in there. I will admit that [these] people really shocked me. They really meant business. They would cut each other's throat. They'd be perfectly friendly, smiling. They played football in their spare time if they could. And they'd knife each other without a moment's hesitation. A Harvard

man would knife another Harvard man, his own bosom pal, for a little advantage. I came from California and I was really startled by it.

From time to time one of these pleasantries would be committed by a type of bureaucratic predator commonly known as an "Empire Builder." There were Empire Builders in R&A, for instance, who would have welcomed the demise of the Latin America Division altogether. As far as they were concerned, the division was not really engaged in significant work. Immersed in the backwater of the war, it did not justify its existence in the larger scheme of things, yet it employed dozens of researchers, plus the requisite support staff. The predators coveted the money the division received, money they believed would make a richer contribution to the war effort if it were in their divisions. They saw their chance when Preston James was shuffled out of R&A, and the inexperienced Halperin took over. His first act as chief was to go before the committee that loosely watched over the general operations of the OSS and fight for the very survival of the division.

HALPERIN: Donovan was, in a sense, a kind of loose cannon. He was officially attached to the Joint Chiefs of Staff, but there was no-body there watching over him or controlling him. He had loads of unvouchered funds. I guess he, himself, created this committee of "no-tables," some in uniform and some civilians, to oversee his operations. So I was summoned to talk to this committee about the Latin America business, whether we should stay in business or not. Very eminent people there. I don't remember the names, but you could say almost the cream of Wall Street. It was quite an experience to be with these people—a pedagogue from out on the high prairies suddenly having to talk with these people.

Halperin's task was to persuade these cautious guardians of the public interest that Latin America was an important political battle-ground, even though it was not in any way a military battleground. He pointed out that he had perhaps the most competent group of Latin Americanists in the entire country and that what they needed was access to a wide variety of Latin American sources, such as newspapers, rather than the "secret" information being sent to them by the FBI, or the Office of Naval Intelligence, or Military Intelligence, little of which was of much value. If these newspapers were sent up by airmail, they would reach R&A within two or three days of publication and would be invaluable. By Halperin's calculations, the whole process would cost tens of thousands of dollars every few months. In those days that was a lot of money to ask bankers to come up with for research into marginal areas of the Western Hemisphere while battles were being fought and people killed in Europe and Asia.

Yet he succeeded. Not only did Halperin come out of the meeting with his division intact, but the division's funding was greatly expanded. Somewhat filled with himself, he went home that night and told his wife that he might have missed his calling. If he could beat that much money out of these Wall Street moguls, he said half-seriously, maybe he should try something more daring than teaching after the war. "You forget one thing," said Edith caustically. "It wasn't their money." So much for Halperin the tycoon.

By the time the war was over, R&A had the finest collection of historians, economists, political scientists, and sociologists in the country. No university even came close. The roster numbered dozens of academic all-stars, including such luminaries as William Langer, Ralph Bunche, Gordon Craig, Felix Gilbert, Wassily Leontieff, Walt Whitman Rostow, Carl Schorske, and Arthur Schlesinger, Jr.

The Latin America Division corralled its share as well. Halperin's chief research assistant was Woodrow Borah, who became one of the nation's preeminent Latin American historians after the war. Borah, an impeccable stylist with a nimble mind, never hesitated to engage Halperin in combat over anything from the wording of a sentence to the shaping of a project, and he won his share of these tussles. Then there was the brilliant Karl Deutsch, an intellectual jack-of-all-trades who had emigrated from Czechoslovakia a few years earlier, and who was to become a renowned Ivy League political scientist after the war. Halperin recalls that Deutsch suffered from an affliction that hobbled many Central European scholars working in America at the time—a chronic inability to say clearly in five pages what he could totally obscure in ten. Halperin struggled with Deutsch over his circumlocutions throughout the war; he emerged undefeated from these battles. Complementing Borah and Deutsch intellectually was Alexander Lesser, who was, in Borah's words, "a highly irascible and erratic, and very distinguished anthropologist." Beyond these three top scholars was a remarkably competent team of in-house intellectuals with a shared commitment to put in as much overtime as necessary and a shared belief in the importance of their research into this neglected theater of the war.

Recruitment into this fraternity was not done through civil service channels nor was it bound by normal bureaucratic conventions or regulations. It was accomplished through the old-boy network mentioned above.

HALPERIN: Always by somebody you knew. Somebody knew somebody else. That was the only way. Borah was at Princeton and James wanted to have a historian and he got him. Karl Deutsch? A friend of mine at M.I.T. got in touch with me and said, "Here is a very able young man. He's a Czech refugee with a brilliant mind. Maybe you could take him on." He came to see me and we had a conversation, a half-hour or so. Obviously this was a find, though he had had no direct experience with Latin America before. But he was a trained political scientist, a historian. . . . Some of these people had already been inducted into the army, and it was fairly easy to get them attached to the OSS. You simply put in a request.

The division was responsible for tracking and analyzing developments in Latin America that might have a bearing on American interests in the war. This it did in regular "situation reports," as well as in special reports, when those were deemed desirable. A situation report presented a digest of important developments in Latin America, country by country. A special report ordinarily focused on some specific development, movement, or trend in one or more of the Latin nations. Some of them packed an impressive amount of research and reflection into surprisingly brief papers that were characterized by a lean prose of great clarity. For all the scholars at work on them, the mark of the pedant was rarely visible. One would be surprised even to find the word *pedant* in one of them.

One example of these special studies was a report on the *Sinarquista* movement in Mexico, which had emerged in response to the official anti-clericalism of the Mexican government in the 1930s. Running to 150 pages of single-spaced text, followed by a few dozen more pages of appendices, the report was really a book on the subject, beginning with the historical and social roots of *Sinarquismo*, and continuing through its rise, its aims, and its relevance to the war. *Sinarquismo* was a pro-clerical mass movement with roots in the peasantry and leadership in a Church hierarchy that was traditionally a supporter of the old order. The report found the origins of the movement in the class relationships of a volatile nation and, more specifically, in the effort "to evolve a modern democratic nation out of an essentially feudal agricultural society."[4]

The Latin Americanists of R&A assembled this report because they were convinced that the *Sinarquistas* were connected with the Nazis and with the fascist *Falange* in Spain. It was an indigenous movement, but it employed the techniques and slogans of the European Right, and was spreading what amounted to Nazi propaganda in Mexico. Specifically, Halperin's crew felt that the right-wing, clerical populism of this movement was a potential source of political instability in Mexico, and the last thing America needed at that time was political instability on its southern border.

---

4. "The Sinarquista Movement in Mexico," record group 59, R&A report no. 843, June 1943. All R&A materials cited in this chapter are in the National Archives in Washington, D. C. Woodrow Borah says that he learned after the war that State Department personnel had actually encouraged the Sinarquistas to organize in the 1930s, with a view toward building an effective opposition to the radical Cárdenas regime. This squares with what Halperin encountered among embassy personnel in Mexico City during his quick tour there for Donovan at the end of 1941. Taped interview with Woodrow Borah, August 27, 1989. But Arthur Schlesinger, Jr., has his doubts. "Cordell Hull's State Department had no experience in or taste for covert action," he says, "and Josephus Daniels, FDR's ambassador till November 1941, would never have tolerated such activity in the Mexico City embassy." Arthur Schlesinger, Jr., letter to author, August 14, 1991.

There was little that R&A could do about a hostile movement in a foreign country, but it occurred to Halperin's staff that the *Sinarquistas* might be connected, through their own Church officials, to the Catholic hierarchy in America, and they might even be getting support from them. Therefore, with Donovan's knowledge and approval, R&A began to intercept and read the mail of a few key American Catholic officials, including Cardinal Spellman of New York. This meant that Donovan, a New York Catholic, had approved mail intercepts of his spiritual leader and personal friend, Cardinal Spellman. Donovan cautioned Halperin that this was a delicate matter, but he said that he would back him if trouble ever came of it.

In the end, nothing much did come of the intercepts. They proved that Spellman was in contact with the *Sinarquistas*, and that he was sympathetic to their cause, but not that the American hierarchy was helping them in any concrete way. Donovan's response to the situation proved something else; from a position on the Republican Right, Donovan was operating on the same principle as Halperin from the fellow-traveling Left: the paramount task was to win the war, and anything that contributed to that end was justifiable. For Donovan it was a commitment that rendered all other matters secondary for the duration, and no doubt played a major role in the fierce dedication that hirelings of all ideological persuasions in the OSS felt for him. To this day Halperin, the Jewish leftist, will not hear a bad word about Donovan, the conservative Catholic.

HALPERIN: You know, it was an accident that I ever met him, the accident of going to Mexico. As a result he knew who I was, whereas he didn't know anybody else at that level. So I had an opportunity to know him personally, as well as know what was going on. I also, from time to time, would attend a meeting with Donovan and the Division chiefs of R&A, maybe once a year. It was interesting for me to watch Donovan operating among these academics, including Langer. They were all very respectable academics, more respectable than I was. They were from Harvard and Yale and I was from Oklahoma. I was kind of an outsider from the whole damn business. Donovan was so much more alert, so much quicker. The intelligence, the ability to grasp a situation rapidly, analyze it correctly, and throw light on it in a brilliant way compared to the rest of us there. He just stood out as an extraordinary individual. As a matter of fact, it once occurred to me that Donovan was the kind of a guy who could ride on two horses, one leg on one horse, the other leg on the other horse, and the horses going at different speeds, and he'd stay on both horses.

Another of the major projects undertaken by the division was a study of anti-Semitism in Latin America. The study was launched after Halperin persuaded State Department officials that the subject was important. State obliged by making a formal request that the OSS conduct such a study, whereupon the division's scholars set about to mine materials in the National Archives on the subject. And that was not all.

HALPERIN: There was a big collection of Nazi posters somewhere in the OSS that we got hold of. Some outfit had been using it. I guess there was one outfit that was working on disinformation or something. And so we got a lot of very fine poster material, cartoons and so forth. We also followed the publications of the Spanish Falange and Mussolini, and we put together a nice report. The importance of this during the war was the need to combat this thing. Anti-Semitism was a useful weapon that the Nazis were using in Latin America.

The book-length report was the first formal study of the subject, and it illustrates the methods used by the division—a combination of the views of its leaders, a heavy dose of research by trained scholars, and a bit of plain old luck.

Another of the special assignments of the division was to compile a catalog of factories in Latin America. Lest this seem to the reader just one more ho-hum report, we should pause for a moment and consider what was actually involved in this project: a catalog listing, as far as possible, every factory in all of Latin America. To compile the catalog, researchers pored over business and engineering publications from many years past to find out what and where the factories were, when they were built, and even, if possible, what the construction plans were. It was a giant project that took nearly two years, of time stolen often from other projects, to complete.

This catalog of factories helps to explain the staggering workload undertaken by the division. At the outset of the war, the division had perhaps fifteen people without too much to do, and with no precedent or idea at all of how to do it. The work, the experience, and the personnel all expanded rapidly during the war. When it ended, there were some fifty analysts and at least five secretaries working for Halperin. Fired by a sense of mission, the personnel drove themselves to the limit and sometimes beyond. It was not uncommon for Halperin, Borah, and others to work through the weekend and, often enough, around the clock. Borah says,

> They kept demanding more work, and finally we reached a point where we couldn't give it any more. I remember many nights when we worked through the night. And it's no fun at two or three in the morning to have women start cracking because they're so exhausted that they would just go into hysteria. And this happened.

Geographically, Mexico was the closest Latin American country to the United States, and it continued to draw the attention of Halperin's crew throughout the war. Politically, however, it was Argentina that worried the Americans most. Economically the most diverse and developed country in Latin America, Argentina had a large and prosperous population of German immigrants and increasingly important economic ties to Germany since Hitler's rise to power.

When war broke out, Argentina remained neutral but made no secret of its sympathy for Germany. In strategic terms this meant that Germany had a friendly base of operations in the Western Hemisphere. The United States had never been pleased at the prospect of a European presence in Latin America, and German activities in Argentina during the war raised American apprehension to new heights. For one thing, the Germans were able to use Argentina as a base for gathering information from all over the continent. For another, the Germans were able to coordinate intelligence there about shipping from various Latin American ports. German U-boats were active and effective in the South Atlantic, and they were affecting the war effort. In addition, Argentina was serving as a center for the dissemination of German propaganda throughout Latin America.

Halperin's thinking was also affected by another factor, one that bore on the possible shape of the postwar world.

HALPERIN: There was a discussion going on, even in the early period, in high American circles, about which I was aware, concerning the final objective, the goals, of the war. In a sense, you might say that in addition to the declared war there was an internal war going on. What it amounted to was that there were elements who were arguing that it would be bad to defeat the Nazis totally, that at some point the Nazis could be turned around, incorporated in the real war that had to be fought—the destruction of the Soviet Union. To me this was a matter of considerable interest. Should there be an "arrangement," not an unconditional surrender, this would leave intact the Nazi apparatus in the Western hemisphere. And that represented a continuing danger to the interests of the United States. If nothing else, economic interests. Latin America would become, instead of an area over which the U.S. had hegemony, the Germans would have hegemony.

With all of these factors in mind, and with the outcome of the war still very much in doubt, Halperin wrote a memo in 1942 suggesting that some thought be given to a full-scale military invasion of Argentina. The memo was sent up the line to the Joint Chiefs of Staff, who approved it and ordered a preliminary survey.

HALPERIN: In the preparation for an invasion, as I recall it, there are three phases: one was [to get] the basic geographic and economic facts outlined—the question of harbors, of electric power stations, you might say the infrastructure along with geographical features. This was the first phase. And so a team was drawn up of OSS, ONI [Office of Naval Intelligence] and G–2 [Army intelligence]. OSS was placed in charge, which means that I was in charge of this team. Incidentally, I had a simulated military rank of brigadier general. [This was to give Halperin seniority over the military personnel on the project, which included navy captains and army colonels.] *Well, we worked hard and fast, day and night, and we got out the report. I had never participated in anything like this, but we had the right people. We had the geographers, we had the cartographers, you know, we had everything we wanted. ONI supplied certain things; G–2 supplied other things. We had a nice picture there. And the report was accepted as adequate.*

The report was adequate, all right, but the timing was off. By the time it reached the Joint Chiefs in 1943, the German army had suffered its debacle at Stalingrad, and the whole tide of war had changed. It seemed clear now that the Allies would triumph, and the recent Casablanca Conference had affirmed in no uncertain terms that a negotiated surrender was unacceptable. The war in Europe would end only with the unconditional surrender of Germany. Because the immediate German threat in Argentina was apparently eliminated for the foreseeable future, and because further work on the plan would undoubtedly strain the always-sensitive relations between the United States and Latin America, Admiral Leahy, head of the Joint Chiefs, sent word down to cancel the remainder of the project.[5]

There are implications in this project that are worth contemplating. Although the OSS carried out operations of various sorts and sizes in Europe, what was planned here was on a different level altogether. It envisioned nothing less than a full-scale invasion of what might, when it happened, still be a neutral South American nation—unfriendly, perhaps, but technically neutral. To appreciate the gravity and magnitude of such a plan, one might recall that the war began in 1939 with a well-planned German invasion of a neutral nation. At the same time, it is best not to get carried away with the analogy. The invasion of

5. Neither Halperin's original memo nor the first-phase report was available at the National Archives when I worked there in October 1989. However, archives personnel told me that they had just accessioned six thousand linear feet—a huge amount—of recently declassified OSS material and that there was still much more that remained classified. Unfortunately, scholars were not being allowed into these materials because they were not yet indexed. Worse still, funding for such projects as indexing had been slashed drastically during the 1980s, and archives personnel felt that prospects for increased funding in the foreseeable future were bleak.

Poland took place in a Europe at peace. The American plan for an invasion of Argentina was conceived only as a contingency in a life-and-death struggle, and was cancelled as soon as it was clear that there was no longer a need for it.

Still, when one takes the postwar CIA to task for covert operations against nonbelligerents in the Cold War, it might be well to remember that the precedent was set by the CIA's parent agency during World War II. If one can justify such a policy to win a life-and-death struggle, one is only an easy step away from justifying it to prevent a life-and-death struggle, and from there only one more easy step away from justifying it to eliminate the potential ally of a hostile nation, or simply because it is "in the national interest."

This means there is nothing intrinsically wrong with attacking a neutral nation. It is a judgment call that rests in a purely situational ethic. The deed cannot be separated from the circumstances. One does not ask whether the action is right or wrong according to some abstract ethic, but only whether or not it is justifiable at that moment.

Halperin explains his position by citing Lord Keynes's response to a journalist who had criticized him for reversing his position on some issue. Annoyed by the upstart, Keynes replied, "When my information changes, my views change. What do you do, sir?" This has always been Halperin's instinctive attitude toward things, in contrast, for instance, to the "true believer," who will not budge from his position, but instead will bend the information to fit it, if necessary, so that it does not upset his preconceptions. Thus, Halperin nowadays looks back on the Cold War essentially from an American perspective, but not even in retrospect does he look with favor upon such covert and overt operations as those against Guatemala in the mid-1950s and the Dominican Republic in the mid-1960s, although they are in some ways descendants of the plan to invade Argentina. "When the CIA intervened in Guatemala there was no urgency comparable in any way at all," he says. Moreover, he feels that American interventions in Latin America have always been counterproductive, yet he was willing to countenance an invasion of Argentina during the war because the situation warranted it. The information had changed.

The comforting thing about a situational ethic is its flexibility. When Halperin was called before the Senate Internal Security Subcommittee in 1953 he stood on his Fifth Amendment right not to testify, and, in addition, presented a resounding affirmation of the First Amendment's protection of free speech. A decade earlier, however, the Bill of Rights did not stand in the way of Halperin's fishing expedition in Cardinal Spellman's mail, although not even tortured reasoning could suggest that the cardinal was giving aid and comfort to the enemy. From Halperin's perspective the information had changed. Of course, we all employ this convenience from time to time.

After the invasion project was quietly folded, the volatile political developments in Argentina continued to play an important role in the reports, one of which related how the Castillo government tried to cling to power in the face of rising opposition by manipulating legal forms in some quite imaginative ways. When the women in one pro-Allied organization began to wear V's—Churchill's symbol for victory—on their sweaters and jackets, for instance, "the Department of Public Health suddenly noticed an alarming increase in the spread of venereal disease. Thereupon, purely for purposes of hygienic control, the government decreed that all women infected by venereal disease be required to wear a 'V' on their outer clothing."

Finally, in June 1943, the Castillo government was overthrown by an army coup led by General Ramírez. Although uncertain about just where the new government was going, the division had little doubt about where it was coming from. The purpose of the coup, said the report, was "to ensure the continued control" of the present governing oligarchy of aristocrats and military men.[6] In the next two years the situation reports traced the triumph of a military junta in the government and the emergence of Juan Perón as a leading figure in the junta. Changes in government, however, did not appear to signify changes in government policy. The division continued to challenge the foreign-policy commitments of the military junta, and had no

6. "The Argentine Revolt," record group 59, Latin America Division, situation summary no. 8, R&A no. 1399, June 26, 1943, in the National Archives. The tale about the women and their sweaters appears on page 10 of this report.

doubt that pro-Axis sentiments continued to dominate the government of Argentina.

Not until early 1945, when there was no longer any doubt about the outcome of the war, did the Argentine government turn clearly against the Axis. Finally, under increasing pressure from the United States, Argentina declared war against Germany and Japan at the end of March, as the war in Europe was drawing to a close. By that time, however, the fate of Argentina was becoming a bone of contention in the American State Department, and reflected the internal squabble at State over what to do with Germany when the war was over. One faction expressed the views of such people as Henry Morgenthau and aimed to impose a harsh settlement upon Argentina. This faction probably reflected the same sort of thinking that had impelled Halperin to suggest the Argentine invasion more than two years earlier: the ties between Germany and Argentina were strong, and it would make no sense to punish Germany after the war without destroying her base of operations in the New World as well. Therefore, Argentina also must be cauterized. The other faction was led by Nelson Rockefeller, who was under secretary of state for Latin American Affairs at the time and was willing to accept the political status quo in Argentina in order to get on with business as usual.

The OSS was drawn into this fracas when Rockefeller resigned as under secretary in August and was succeeded by Spruille Braden, recently the ambassador to Argentina and one of the State Department's hard-liners. Braden aimed for nothing less than reshaping Argentine politics by toppling the military junta and its candidate in the forthcoming election, Juan Perón. Toward that end he authorized the Latin America Division to dig up whatever it could to discredit the regime's activities during and since the war. Braden would then time the release of this information to coincide with the election in February. Angered by the revelations about the junta's pro-Nazi activities and general fascist tendencies, the Argentine electorate would then presumably reject Perón's bid for the presidency, cast out his fellow military rascals, and finally bring democracy to Argentina.

Halperin's crew shared Braden's hostility toward the junta and set about the task with relish. The only serious challenge in the assignment was the time limit. The research itself was relatively easy, since Braden was only asking the division to produce information that it had been gathering for nearly four years. It was primarily a matter of sifting through the old material, digging out whatever additional dirt existed for recent months, and putting it all together in the most damaging way possible.

The resulting "Blue Book" was a savage, 131-page indictment of the Argentine government's activities during and since the war. The chapter headings effectively summarize the substance of the book: "Argentine-Nazi Efforts to Subvert the Governments of Neighboring Countries;" "Argentine-Nazi Political and Social Collaboration;" "Argentine Preservation of Nazi Economic Power." Nor was there anything vague about these allegations. Each chapter was virtually a catalog of names, dates, and acts that appeared to document the charges fully. The final 30 pages of the Blue Book were given over to the present government, and argued not only that the Nazi influence was still strong, but also that "the totalitarian machine in Argentina is a partnership of German Nazi interests with a powerful coalition of active Argentine totalitarian elements, both military and civilian."[7] The "Nazi-Fascist Character" and "totalitarian program" of the current regime were revealed in police terrorism against democratic opposition groups, in the corporative organization and "totalitarian control" of labor, the "perversion of the educational system," and the effective control of the press, which was "intimidated," and subjected to "abuse," "repressive policies," and "mob violence." This was not the language of a sober, scholarly study; it was the language of a tract. And it was exactly what Braden had ordered.

The Blue Book was released in February 1946, and proved to be an explosive document in the Argentine election. Unfortunately the explosion went off in Braden's face, for he had not counted on the power in Latin America of Yankee-bashing. Perón simply took the Blue Book, waved it in front of the electorate and proclaimed that it was a flagrant

7. *Consultation among the American Republics with Respect to the Argentine Situation: Memorandum of the United States Government* (Washington, D. C., February 1946), 104.

example of American intervention in Argentina's domestic affairs, which it was, of course. On February 24, Perón was elected president of Argentina.

In the desperate circumstances of the war, and the often frenzied conditions of the Latin America Division, it was not difficult to slip into a Manichean mentality, to see the world only in terms of good guys and bad guys—*us* and *them*. There didn't seem to be a middle ground. That worked reasonably well with Argentina, because her "neutrality" really did tip toward Germany, and because there really were ties between influential Argentinians and influential Nazis. It was less successful six months later when the division had to analyze the Bolivian revolt of December 1943, and it led Halperin unexpectedly into a nasty confrontation with a young R&A editor named Arthur Schlesinger, Jr.

The Bolivian revolt was one of those affairs that sometimes confound American policymakers, because it did not conform to the more familiar Western models of revolution. The coup was effected primarily by a coalition of two major factions. One of these was the *Radepa*, an army group that probably had ties to the Argentine military, and perhaps tilted toward the Axis. The *Radepa* produced the leader of the new government, Major Guadalberto Villarroel. The other, and surely the more important and intriguing of the two, was the *Movimiento Nacionalista Revolucionario*, or MNR as it was commonly known.

The MNR had been formed two years earlier by a group of young intellectuals led by Víctor Paz Estenssoro, who was to become a towering political figure for the next forty years in Bolivia, and eventually its president. The movement was sympathetic to the tin miners, who were the dominant group in the Bolivian work force; it supported a program of strong social reform; it had pronounced nationalist sentiments; and, at least at the outset, it was tinged with a rather immoderate tone of anti-Semitism. Central to almost any Latin American nationalism, of course, is a heavy dose of anti-Americanism, and it was this anti-Americanism, along with the anti-Semitism and the *Radepa's* coziness with elements in Argentina, that alarmed the Latin America Division.

The overthrown Peñaranda regime had been friendly to American interests in Bolivia, and had posed no threat to the Allied cause. The Villarroel regime, with its intense anti-American nationalism, was something else again. Although it was not at all clear that this regime would support the Axis, it did seem fairly obvious that it would not extend itself for the Allies. The matter was not simply academic nor was it primarily ideological. Bolivian tin was an important resource in the American war effort, and the Americans were not willing to see their access to it threatened. Nor were Halperin and his colleagues in the Latin America Division prepared to let Bolivia fall into the arms of Argentina's military junta, which they saw as a distinct possibility.

In all situations Halperin was driven by one basic imperative: he supported any person or cause that he believed might hasten total victory; he opposed any person or cause that he believed might retard total victory. That factor took precedence over any consideration of social reform or social reaction. It was, he notes, the same imperative that shaped State Department policy and, by the way, it was the same imperative that led the conservative Bill Donovan knowingly to employ Communists. Indeed, it was the rock upon which the OSS was founded. On those terms, Halperin and his crew had no reservations in their analysis of the situation. The Villarroel government was not for us, which meant that it was against us, and thus, had to be opposed.

HALPERIN: Maybe two months before Peñaranda was overthrown he was in Washington at a big reception. I was there and I remember the magnificent banquet we had. This was official red carpet treatment. And there's no question about it, he was 100% pro-U.S. So this man was overthrown, and you had to look at it very carefully to see what you were getting in return. We had been following the MNR in our division very carefully. We knew everything there was to be known about it. This movement consisted of a combination of populist reformers, anti-imperialists and out-and-out Nazis and anti-Semites. The anti-imperialism was anti-American, not anti-German imperialism. That's how I recall this thing forty or fifty years ago. And accordingly we submitted in our weekly report an analysis of the situation, the analysis being that the new government was hostile to the United States. It wasn't our business to propose what had to be done, but to explain what had happened: a political defeat for the United States in Bolivia at that time.

That, at least, was the substance of the report that Halperin submitted. But it was not the substance of the report that came out on the Bolivian coup. What appeared instead was a report that praised the MNR and suggested that the new government would stabilize the situation in Bolivia by eliminating social injustice. Halperin was astounded. The report contradicted not only the appraisal of his own division, but also similar appraisals reached independently by army intelligence, navy intelligence, and the State Department.

Furious, Halperin went to Langer's office to find out what was going on, and Langer told him that the report had apparently been prepared by Arthur Schlesinger, Jr., at that time a young editor in R&A.

HALPERIN: Well, I put it to him very straight. I said to him, "Bill, maybe you don't need a Latin America Division. If you have one man who can handle this, maybe you don't need us. You can save a lot of money, distribute the slots. . . . You've got a man who can handle a whole Division."

In effect, Halperin was telling Langer that he would resign unless the situation were corrected immediately. Although Halperin did not know it at the time, this put Langer in a difficult position, because Schlesinger's father was an eminent historian who had been a colleague and friend of Langer's at Harvard before Langer joined the OSS. Schlesinger, however, puts the matter in a somewhat different light. From the division's reports, from the general tone of Halperin's comments, and because "Halperin was the only section chief who kept the *[Daily] Worker* on his desk," he was convinced that Halperin was pushing the Communist party line.

SCHLESINGER: The showdown came over the MNR and Bolivia. The CP line was that this was a pro-Nazi putsch. I got a very different impression of what had happened from Larry Duggan in the State

Department and especially from Ernesto Galarza, a Latin American
with labor connections whom I had met through Gardner Jackson. As
I recall, Enrique Lozada either was already in Washington or soon
arrived as the ambassador from the new regime, and he was, I think,
another source.

In any event, I printed my own interpretation of the Bolivian revolu-
tion. Halperin protested to Bill Langer, the head of R&A. Langer told
me that I should use the reports from the Latin America desk or noth-
ing at all—a decision made not on the merits but on understandable
bureaucratic grounds.[8]

At that time Schlesinger was neither a prominent historian nor a
public figure. Halperin had no idea who he was and had never heard
of his father. Recalling the situation with some bitterness, Halperin
refers to Schlesinger as a "pasty-faced boy" and says, "I didn't know
that he was a knee-pants genius." When he found out that Schlesinger
had no expertise at all in Latin American affairs, he asked Borah to
find out what was going on. Where did this man get his information?
Borah dug up something very different from Duggan and Galarza. He
concluded that Schlesinger was taking his cue from a group of Italian
refugee socialists in New York. In their tracts, the Italians had made
numerous errors in Spanish, and Schlesinger's report made exactly
the same errors. As Borah puts it, "It was the old trick of finding
out copying by finding the errors that are copied." From time to time
professors sniff out plagiarized term papers the same way. Schlesinger
denies taking his cue from these people. He admits that he had "close
connections" with several "Italian anti-fascists," but says, "I cannot
remember that they had any strong views on Bolivia. Why should
they?"[9] Borah, however, stands firm.

Halperin took the Borah version in to Langer, and Langer no doubt
confronted Schlesinger with it. To settle the situation, Langer decided upon a compromise that left Halperin free to proceed as he
had, and left Schlesinger irate. Until then the various division chiefs

8. Arthur Schlesinger, Jr., letter to author, March 14, 1989.
9. Arthur Schlesinger, Jr., letter to author, August 14, 1991.

had prepared weekly summaries, which were then put together in a classified report for distribution in the OSS and for what Arthur Schlesinger calls "limited distribution outside the agency." Schlesinger edited this weekly report. Langer's Solomonic solution was to place Schlesinger and Halperin in separate spheres. In the future Latin America would publish its own reports separate from the other divisions, and Schlesinger would continue to edit the weekly report minus the Latin American material. Schlesinger would continue with his duties as editor; Halperin would be free of Schlesinger's interference; and presumably everyone would be happy. Schlesinger, however, took a dim view of this settlement, since it clipped his wings and left Halperin untouched. So he went storming into Halperin's office.

HALPERIN: [Langer effected] *a kind of compromise, at least to start with, but the nature of this compromise was such that it infuriated Schlesinger. And, lo and behold, shortly after that he came to see me in my office in a rage, literally in a rage, like a young child in a tantrum. And I kind of instinctively got up from my chair, as I recall, and I think he was smaller than I, but he was yelling at the top of his voice, and I told him to get out. He kept on yelling. I went over and, as I recall it, I grabbed him by the collar of his coat, turned him around, and shoved him out. Some gross indignity, the exact details of which I don't recall. There was no scuffle, no assault and battery. I just shoved him out.*

Schlesinger recalls "an exchange of sharp words," but says that "Halperin's account of grabbing me by the collar and shoving me out of his office is pure fantasy." Borah, though not a witness to the incident, remembers that Schlesinger "put on quite an act." Whatever happened was obviously unpleasant. Apparently the whole division was buzzing about it.[10]

---

10. Ibid. I mention these different accounts to illustrate one of the pitfalls of oral history when there is no record of the original incident to check against remembered accounts at a much later date. There is a significant difference, implied rather than spelled out, between the Halperin/Borah and the Schlesinger accounts of the Bolivian situation. For one thing, Borah's recollection does not actually verify Halperin's be-

Freed from Schlesinger's revisionism, the division pursued its anti-Villarroel and anti-MNR analysis, which, along with the developments in Argentina and elsewhere in Latin America, it saw as part of a growing "crisis in Western Hemisphere Relations." In an extraordinary "Political Intelligence Report" the division asserted that there was an emerging coalition between native and Axis forces aiming to prolong the war, and "to prepare, in case of defeat, a refuge for Axis funds and key personnel." Led by Nazis, and using the Spanish Falange to divide the Catholic Church, this coalition was centered in Argentina, had recently captured Bolivia, and now posed an immediate threat to the rest of the South American continent.

To that point the report was concerned primarily with description and analysis. Then it moved into the realm of prescription, concluding with a recommendation that the United States refuse to recognize the new Bolivian government; that it "overthrow . . . the Ramírez (Argentine) regime, with the use of economic sanctions if necessary"; that it send military aid to friendly governments; and that it press "the intensification of economic and political warfare against Axis interests and their native fascist allies" wherever necessary in Latin America.[11] Although no longer formulating plans for military intervention in South America, the division was still actively promoting political and economic meddling there. And it is clear that Halperin's people had more than mere diplomatic nonrecognition on their minds.

This report was only one among many that suggest that the Latin America Division frequently and flagrantly violated the guidelines laid down for R&A on how to write a report. Barry Katz discusses these

---

cause he did not witness the encounter. It is possible that Halperin himself was Borah's source originally. But there is quite a difference between Schlesinger's recollection of "sharp words" and Halperin's memory of grabbing an enraged Schlesinger and physically throwing him out of the office. I have no reason to doubt that each of the contestants remembers the incident exactly as he describes it, which does not add to my comfort.

11. "Political Intelligence Report No. 16," R&A 1306, record group 226, entry 56, box 1 (January 17, 1944). Compare this statement with Halperin's assertion that "it wasn't our business to propose what had to be done, but to explain what had happened."

guidelines in his recent study of R&A. They grew from some serious doubts entertained originally by the State Department and by the other intelligence agencies that any good could come from R&A. From their point of view, it was bad that this new agency was staffed by ivory-tower intellectuals, and even worse that many of these fuzzy-minded scholars held dangerous political views.

To combat these prejudices, R&A regulations insisted that all reports be stripped of ideological baggage—that they be strictly objective. The guardians of this mandate were to be lodged in a watchdog committee set up to screen reports for " 'stylistic misdemeanors' and outright 'crimes against objectivity.' "[12] Schlesinger, himself, was one of the chief editors and insisted that " 'in the writing of reports, one is expected to turn out thoroughly objective and neutral intelligence. . . . There should be no personal pronouns . . . and care should be taken about the use of color words such as 'reactionary,' progressive,' 'left or right.' "[13] Above all, the reports were "not to suggest, recommend, or in any way determine the strategy or the tactical decisions of the war."[14] Compare this directive with the discussion (above) of the "crisis in Western Hemisphere Relations."

This meant that R&A was working under two major injunctions. One, which was explicit and in writing, demanded that the reports be objective; the other, which was implicit but in the very raison d'être of the OSS, demanded that R&A support anything or anyone that would hasten victory, and oppose anything or anyone that might retard victory. The trouble was that these two orders were not really compatible. In a way they were actually contradictory, because the second injunction could easily exert a subtle psychological pressure to emphasize certain factors and suppress others.

12. Richard Hartshorne, "Style Sheet for Use in the Research and Analysis Branch," quoted in Katz, *Foreign Intelligence*, 16.

13. Ibid., 17. After the war, Schlesinger abandoned these constraints. His writing, always brilliant, has teemed with "color words," and his stance has been quite openly partisan.

14. "Functions of the Research and Analysis Branch," in Katz, *Foreign Intelligence*, 14.

Bolivia is a case in point. Halperin supported the conservative Peñaranda regime because it was pro-American, in contrast to the anti-American nationalism of the military clique and the social-reformist MNR. Schlesinger supported the MNR because he felt that it would serve American interests by providing stability, in contrast to the demonstrated instability of the Peñaranda government. The facts of the case might have been "objective," but which facts to choose and the arguments drawn from them were not. It was a matter of judgment, and judgments do not speak for themselves; they are made by people who operate from different perspectives and select facts that often point in different directions. You emphasize certain information and minimize or dismiss the rest. The difference between Halperin and Schlesinger (apart from temperament) was evident in which information each chose to emphasize and minimize.

The only thing we can say with certainty about the Bolivia situation is that the MNR remained in power and the Allies won the war, but this does not mean that the Allies won the war *because* the MNR remained in power; it does not mean that Schlesinger was right. The Allies would have won the war in more or less the same way and time no matter who governed Bolivia. Halperin might have thought he was being objective, but he was not. He was selecting the facts that supported his position, and he was minimizing those that did not. And in the bargain it is quite possible that he was distorting some of the realities in Latin America.

Again, Argentina and Bolivia serve to illustrate the point. Although it was unsavory at the outset and grew worse in time (my own judgment), and though some of its leaders did, indeed, have ties to important German economic, political, and military figures, the military junta in Argentina was not a "Nazi-fascist" regime; nor was Argentina merely a surrogate or pawn for the Nazis in the Western Hemisphere; nor was it ripe for Nazi pickings after the war. Still less was Bolivia about to fall into the Nazi-Argentina orbit after the MNR revolt, though there was indeed some anti-Semitism in the early stages of the movement, and though there were indeed some ties with the Argentine military. Yet the facts that were emphasized and the increasingly feverish rhetoric of the reports certainly gave the impression that Argentina and Bolivia were on the verge of falling to the Nazis.

There was nothing sinister about these reports. They were not the products of a few men cackling behind closed doors as they plotted to impose the Communist party line on American policy. More than anything, they were a simple reflex of the leftward-bent Latin America Division and of the Manichean mentality that guided the OSS in general.

Ordinarily this mentality did not dominate the reports, but simply remained in the background, powerful but unspoken. Once in a while, however, it was expressed in a blatant way. In a report on the Colombian presidential campaign of spring 1942, for instance, the division described the apparent foreign-policy vacillations of President Santos, and concluded that he was merely "a weak president, trying to steer a middle course in a situation where no middle course is possible."[15]

But of course there was a middle course, and Santos was steering it. For those nations actually fighting the war, policy decisions might well be limited by the single consideration of what was most likely to bring total victory as soon as possible. But Colombia was not fighting the war, and her policy grew from Colombian considerations, not from American needs. The United States, for example, was a market for her resources and Argentina was a source of her foodstuffs. Those two variables alone would be enough to warrant a cautious foreign policy, from the Colombian point of view. Thus, what the division saw as weakness appears, in a different perspective, to be prudence, and the middle course which seemed to the division to be impossible was not only possible, it was the policy in practice.

Halperin's thinking about Latin America was also nurtured by his general intellectual framework. His, like most people's, was composed of a loose cluster of values, beliefs, attitudes, and symbols that he brought to bear to try to make sense of the world around him. A major element of Halperin's belief system was the awareness that his

---

15. "The Presidential Campaign in Colombia," record group 59, coordinator of information, Latin America section, R&A report no. 264, March 27, 1942.

Jewishness made him just a little different from most other people, not only in his own eyes, but in theirs as well. This was probably impressed upon him the first day in school, when he discovered that the other children did not speak Yiddish. And if not then, he was certainly reminded of it in his confrontations with the schoolyard bully a few years later. It shaped the political discussions at home as he grew up, and later Edith was there to remind him of it whenever it threatened to fade from his active life. By the time he arrived in Washington, the sense of being Jewish played an important part in his life.

A second factor in the way he viewed the world was a strong commitment to the rational tradition. It had been an unspoken, indeed unconscious, factor in the frequent political discussions at home as he was growing up, and it became a conscious part of his intellectual equipment at Harvard and the Sorbonne where he was steeping himself in the tradition of the French Enlightenment. From this tradition he learned that human beings were perfectible, that their problems were finite, and that these problems could be solved through the rigorous application of reason.

Another factor was the apparently cataclysmic nature of his own times. Raised and educated in relative comfort and safety all the way through his student days in Paris, he was unprepared for the terrible impact of the Great Depression and the war that followed, even if he was not impoverished in the one or maimed in the other. No one of his generation emerged from those years unaffected.

All of these factors shaped his feelings about the Soviet Union and the Communist party. Although he says he was not submissive to either, as were many others of his age and circumstances, he was nevertheless sympathetic to their avowed goal of eliminating social inequality and economic insecurity so that each individual would be free to develop his or her human potential to the fullest. At least in terms of their professed rationalism and egalitarianism, the Soviets met Halperin on his own terms, and he wished them well in their own country. He says he was more reserved about the American Communist party's advocacy of socialism for the United States. He had nothing against the idea as a remote objective, but for the present he was still willing to settle for the modest promises and scattergun reforms of the New Deal. Where he clearly agreed with the Communist party was in its policy of worldwide opposition to fascism in all its guises. Toward that end the party was willing to subordinate everything else during the war, even its commitment to socialism and labor militancy. The only thing that really mattered was defeating the Nazis, and Halperin was in complete sympathy with that position.

That raises a crucial question about Halperin. Given the intensity of his commitment in this struggle between good and evil, and given the general congeniality that he felt toward the Soviet Union, is it possible that the allegations made about him were in fact valid? Schlesinger accused him of being a Communist and infusing his reports for R&A with the party line.[16] More devastating still were the later allegations of Elizabeth Bentley, who told the FBI in 1945 that Halperin had passed OSS and State Department documents along to her during the war. Did he use his position in the OSS to press the party line and, worse still, to commit espionage for the NKVD, in order to hasten victory and lay the groundwork, as he saw it, for a just and durable peace? Evidence that the Latin America Division consistently presented a position that was strikingly similar to the party line might raise quite reasonable doubts about Halperin's loyalty.

At first glance the problem seems simple enough. The *Daily Worker* faithfully carried the Communist party line. By comparing it with division reports on a few key issues, one should be able to detect at least the more obvious similarities that existed. What about Bolivia, for instance? The revolt there was what brought the issue to a head in R&A in the first place. Is the *Daily Worker*'s analysis visible in the Latin America Division's reports on that revolt and its aftermath?

From the outset the *Worker* opposed the revolt, and tilted its news stories accordingly. The day after the revolt it reported that Secretary of State Cordell Hull was "urged" by the Council for Pan-American Democracy not to recognize the new Bolivian regime. The telegram

---

16. Arthur Schlesinger, Jr., *A Thousand Days* (New York: Fawcett Premier Books, 1965), 162–63. It was apparently the move to Moscow that confirmed Schlesinger in his belief that Halperin "was indeed a member of the Communist Party."

from the council warned that "the coup is inimical to the interests of the United States and the United Nations, and may be a first attempt to extend the influence of the pro-Axis Ramírez regime." The telegram was signed by Frederick Vanderbilt Field, a member of the Communist party, which probably tells us all we need to know about the Council for Pan-American Democracy. By simply quoting an obscure source with an appealing name, the *Worker* managed to state the party line without appearing to editorialize.[17]

A day later, the *Worker* amplified the party's position, once again in the guise of reporting what other people said about the new Bolivian regime. Under the headline "Latin-Americans Charge Bolivia Coup is Fascist," the paper asserted that "the Bolivian coup is essentially military, achieved under predominant influence of the fascists of the National Revolutionary party (the MNR) and of the Lodge of young officers." Anyone but a party aficionado might have been puzzled by the article's emphasis on "the participation of Tristian [*sic*] Marof, long an international Trotzkyist provocateur in anti-allied agitation and in the coup d'etat." The faithful, however, had learned to believe from the Moscow trials a few years earlier that the Trotskyists were not the revolutionary Marxists they claimed to be, but were, in fact, virtually interchangeable with the Gestapo. They were not the Communist heirs of Lenin; they were the fascist allies of the Nazis. The party faithful were expected to take the appearance of a Trotskyist in this "fascist" coup as a matter of course. It is obvious, the article continued, that the MNR was mere "window-dressing" to hide the real nature of the regime. "Like the German fascists, they disguise the ultra-reactionary basis of the party with sweet-sounding words." The *Worker* dismissed the claim that the MNR was a true nationalist party "since it is serving Hitlerite interests in Bolivia." Nor was the recent Peñaranda regime much better. According to the *Worker*, it bore much of the responsibility for the revolt because it had represented "the worst elements in the Bolivian oligarchy . . . [and] had used the war to advance the profits of small privileged groups." The final element in this analysis was

17. *Daily Worker*, December 22, 1943.

the growing certainty that the revolt would play into the expansionist hands of fascist Argentina.[18]

Thus the line was laid down within two days of the revolt: the exploitative nature of the Peñaranda government had led to a coup by a political/military clique that shrouded its fascist nature in a cloak of revolutionary-nationalist rhetoric while it prepared to subvert the Allied war effort and make common cause with the pro-Nazi government of Argentina. Thereafter, the *Worker* developed and expanded upon this theme but did not vary it significantly. A few days later, for instance, James Allen, the paper's Latin American expert, claimed flatly that "the events in La Paz are part of a far reaching development—yes, a conspiracy—fanning out from Buenos Aires, the capital bridgehead of the German Nazis, the Italian fascists and the Spanish Falangists in the Americas."[19] The plot had thickened, but it was still basically the same plot. The Manichean mentality was triumphant.

The reports of the division on the Bolivian situation were more circumspect, and the rhetoric more guarded, but in their essentials they were not significantly different from the *Daily Worker*, except for the assessment of the role of Trotskyists, which played no part in the division reports. So, too, with Argentina. The *Daily Worker* and the Latin America Division had the same perception of the military regime there, but the *Worker* was more strident about it.

At first glance, then, there do seem to be striking similarities between the Communist party line and the Latin America Division reports on Bolivia and Argentina. The tone of the division reports was muted, perhaps because of the R&A mandate to avoid heated rhetoric, but the content would not have ruffled the editors of the *Daily Worker*. Still, the issue is not as clearly defined as it might seem. The fact is that the new Bolivian regime *was* more hostile to American interests than the Peñaranda government had been; its military elements *were* in touch with the Ramírez government of Argentina; there *were* anti-Semitic

18. Ibid., December 23, 1943.
19. Ibid., December 26, 1943.

overtones in the MNR. Much the same was true of Argentina. The Ramírez government was increasingly ruthless in its suppression of dissent, yet quite tolerant of the pro-Nazi sentiment in the nation; the colonels behind the regime were cozy with the German military; German economic influence in Argentina was considerable.

Once again, it is necessary to emphasize the Manichean mentality that dominated not only Communist party analyses, but American policy-making as well. It allowed no room for shades of gray. There could not be three positions on an issue, or five or ten. There could be only two. Any development, or process, or condition that was not friendly to the Allied cause was, by definition, hostile to it, and thus fascist, and thus essentially, or at least potentially, Nazi. It was all of a piece. And, of course, there was evidence in Bolivia, and especially in Argentina, of friendly relations with German and pro-German elements. As a result, the Latin America Division's analysis was confirmed by Army and Navy intelligence and by the State Department. The counsel that Lawrence Duggan gave to Arthur Schlesinger, Jr., informs us that there was significant dissent in some quarters, but it was dissent from a broadly shared consensus. If Halperin was following the party line on these issues, then so were the policymakers in the military and diplomatic establishments, and for that matter so was Donovan, whose guiding precept was to align himself with any policy or ally that would help defeat the Axis. Few people in authority had yet focused on what issues might divide the United States and the Soviet Union after the war; the overriding issue was what united them during the war, and that was a life-and-death struggle against a common enemy. That their analyses of some situations coincided should not be surprising and certainly does not justify an allegation that the Latin America Division was pressing the Communist party line.[20]

There was at least one situation, however, in which the division did parrot the party line, and only by an extraordinary intellectual contortion can it be explained as essential—or even relevant—to the

20. Still, caution is in order here, because it is difficult to say what might turn up when all of the R&A materials are made available for research.

war effort. This involved the *non*-Communist community of Left expatriates in Mexico during the war. Some of them were Trotskyists, some were ex-Trotskyists; some were social democrats, others were unaffiliated, with only vaguely leftish impulses. Some opposed what they felt to be an internecine war among imperialist powers; others supported the Allied cause. Some had even been Communist party members at one time. The only common denominator was that none of them were then in the party fold, which might explain why they were vilified by the Communist community in Mexico.

Again it is necessary to emphasize the tendency toward fratricide among the factions on the left in the 1930s and 1940s. Trotskyists and Stalinists viewed each other as apostates from the true principles of Marxist-Leninism, and the true believer hates no one more than the apostate. Because of their superior organization, superior international networking, and far superior numbers, the Stalinists held a large edge in this battle, and they used it to flay their opponents mercilessly.

Gustav Regler was one who discovered this, to his great discomfort. Regler was a noted German novelist who had joined the Communist party in the early 1930s before Hitler came to power. He was honored at the Moscow Writers' Congress of 1935 and returned the following year to arrange for the translation and publication of a book he was writing on Ignatius Loyola. In the autumn of 1936, he went to Spain, where he served as a commissar with the International Brigade until he was badly wounded in June 1937.

Regler's disillusion with the party and the Soviet Union began with the trials and executions of Zinoviev and Kamenev during his visit to Moscow in the summer of 1936. After that it progressed in stages, but at each stage he resisted, excusing the bad he saw in the name of the larger good it was doing—excusing the means for the end—until the Stalin-Hitler Pact, which he was not able to rationalize at all, because it rendered everything he had believed and done and nearly died for in the 1930s meaningless. By then it was clear to him that the means had become the end.

At that point, disillusioned with Marx, with revolution, with the Soviet Union, and with the Communist party, he would have been content to retire from politics into art. The party had other ideas, however. It began a campaign to discredit him while he was still in a French detention camp early in the war, and it stepped up the campaign after he arrived in Mexico in 1941, by which time he was being attacked alternately as a Nazi and a Trotskyist. Stunned by this, he confronted a former comrade in a Mexico City café and asked if anyone in the community really believed that he, "with sixteen Fascist shell-splinters in [his] body," could ever be a fascist. The reply was chilling:

> Of course not, but you have deserted us, and that is treachery. No pity can be shown to traitors. Your idealism is dangerous. It is not a matter of honesty or morality. In this battle all means are permitted. . . . We made you a hero in Spain, but not so that you might work out a philosophy of your own. . . . If you go on fighting against us we shall liquidate you—here in Mexico you're as good as liquidated already.[21]

But it was not enough that Regler be attacked in Mexico. Largely because of the reporting of Ernest Hemingway from Spain, he had become a hero to many people in the United States, so it was important that his reputation be destroyed there as well. The attack began in January 1942, with the *Daily Worker* citing Mexican sources that accused various resident "anarcho-Trotskyite gangsters" of betraying democracy in Spain and of adopting and even outdoing the arguments of Joseph Goebbels.[22] The *Worker* did not mention Regler by name until a few weeks later, when it reported that he had been "publicly branded as a Fifth Columnist and Axis agent by German anti-fascist refugees" in Mexico City.

The sequence of events is interesting here. First, according to the *Worker*, a group of "Mexican Congressmen" had included Regler's name on a list of Trotskyists whom they denounced as pro-Nazis. At that point a number of prominent American liberals and social-

21. Gustav Regler, *The Owl of Minerva*, trans. Norman Denny (New York: Farrar, Straus & Cudahy, 1959), 365–66.
22. *Daily Worker*, January 18, 1942. Implicitly and explicitly, the interchangeability of Trotskyism and Nazism was present in almost all of this reporting. "Anarcho-Trotskyism" was simply a bonus. The language of vilification in party organs is a wonder to behold.

ists, including Roger Baldwin, Bruce Bliven, A. J. Muste, Reinhold Niebuhr, Michael Straight, and Norman Thomas, sent an open letter to Mexico's president, and some cables to local papers, vigorously defending the "anti-fascist" credentials of these people. It was only after this material was printed in the Mexican press that "four German anti-Nazis" conveniently surfaced to denounce Regler. They had known him in the French detention camp, they said, and now made the timely revelation that he had been a "Nazi informer and stool pigeon" in the camp, where, among other things, he had aided a Nazi agent in identifying "ten anti-Nazis," which was the party's euphemism in this case for Communists.[23]

A few weeks later a *Worker* editorial again deftly interlaced Trotskyism and Nazism when it equated Britain's infamous Cliveden Set with the "small clique of professional Trotzkyites" in Mexico, and condemned their American defenders "who should know better than to permit their names to be used in support of a Fifth Column in Mexico behind the grotesque hypocrisies of an alleged 'persecution.'" Socialists? Revolutionaries? On the contrary. "In no fundamental way," said the editorial, "is their activity different from that of the Axis Fifth Column in Mexico and throughout the Americas." More than that, the editorial continued, "No important difference can be found between what they preach and the propaganda of the Falangistas and Sinarquistas, Hitler's most dangerous Fifth Column in the Western Hemisphere."[24] Only a primal cynic could write such trash; only a primal innocent could believe it.

The controversy entered into the Latin America Division's reports a few days later, except that the division did not present it as a controversy. In a report titled "Pro-Axis and Anti-Axis Forces in Mexico," the division observed that *"A group of foreign Trotskyites recently have come into the political picture"* [division's emphasis].[25] The report

23. Ibid., February 11, 1942.
24. Ibid., March 2, 1942.
25. One might note, by the way, that the followers of Trotsky called themselves Trotsky*ists* (and took some delight on occasion in referring to Communists as Stalinoids). Communists and their sympathizers, on the other hand, referred to Trotskyists

then named Regler, Victor Serge, Julian Gorkin, and Marceau Pivert as the culprits, noting that they had been "denounced by a committee of the Chamber of Deputies as undesirable aliens because of their pro-Axis activities." The report then went on to link the quartet with the American Socialist Labor party, "whose connections with the Gestapo were revealed when the United States Government recently prosecuted the leaders of the group in Minneapolis."[26]

The timing of these comments (though certainly not of the entire report) leaves one with little doubt that they were part of an orchestrated effort to destroy the individuals named. To indict them as a "Pro-Axis force" was nonsense, since they were neither pro-Axis nor a force. Serge had been a Left dissident in Russia, had somehow survived the purge trials in Moscow, and had barely gotten out with his life. After that he became a Trotskyist for a brief while, but he abandoned that commitment too when he recognized in Trotsky's thinking some of the elements that had produced Stalinism. He had dropped Trotskyism more than a year before these accusations. Julián Gorkín, a Spanish Trotskyist during the Civil War, had escaped to Mexico with his life after the defeat, and then had become part of a nonaligned socialist opposition, along with Pivert and Serge.[27]

The effort to tie these individuals in with the recently convicted Trotskyist leaders in Minneapolis is another stain on the report. The trial was a complicated affair, but it grew out of a labor controversy

---

as Trotsky*ites*, a term that they used as an epithet. Socialists, not surprisingly, vacillated between the two terms.

26. "Pro-Axis and Anti-Axis Forces in Mexico," coordinator of information, Latin America section, R&A report no. 8, March 5, 1942. The report undoubtedly meant to cite the Socialist Workers party, which was the political arm of Trotskyism in the United States, and not the Socialist Labor party.

27. Victor Serge, *Memoirs of a Revolutionary, 1901–1941*, trans. Peter Sedgwick (London: Oxford University Press, 1963), *passim*. An article in the *Sunday Worker* noted that Trotsky's journal "pretends to be opposed to the notorious Serge and his band," when in fact they were simply the spokesmen of two "Trotskyite branches." That they attacked each other in their respective journals was presumably part of an elaborate hoax designed to mystify the true "anti-Nazis." Thus, when evidence clearly contradicted the party line, it was simply turned inside out to confirm the party line. See "Mexican Gov't Cracks Down on 5th Column," *Sunday Worker*, January 25, 1942.

involving a Trotskyist-dominated Minneapolis local of the Teamsters Union. Several leaders of the Socialist Workers party were convicted, under the recently enacted Smith Act, of advocating the violent overthrow of the government. Communist party members praised this triumph of justice, although they would have reason to reconsider the implications of the Smith Act a decade later when their own leaders were imprisoned by it. What is particularly intriguing in the report is the claim that the trial "revealed" the Trotskyists to have been connected with the Gestapo. Such an allegation was indeed made at the trial, but it was never corroborated for the simple reason that it was as preposterous as similar claims made at the Moscow purge trials a few years earlier.

What was "revealed," instead, was the willingness of the Latin America Division, on this occasion at least, to ignore the distinction between political fact and political cynicism in the interest of "historical necessity." Perhaps they can be accused of nothing worse than misplaced credulity in believing the charges of "pro-Axis" activities by these people in Mexico, but it is really too much to believe that men of such learning and sophistication as those in the Latin America Division really believed the inanity about a connection between Minneapolis Trotskyists and the Gestapo. It suggests that Schlesinger was correct in his analysis of some of the material coming out of the division and about the politics of those who wrote it.

Of course, it is difficult to assign responsibility for this material. Halperin was by then assistant chief of the division, but could not have pushed anything through without at least the passive consent of Preston James, the chief. On the other hand, Halperin himself says that division reports were consensual. In the end it is difficult to believe that Halperin was not complicit in this shabby affair. It is even possible that he was the one who brought the "information" from Mexico. It first appeared in the *Worker* about a month after he returned from his post–Pearl Harbor visit to Mexico, where, by his own account, he had met with Communist party leaders. At the very least, he was part of the consensus that sent it out.

Still, this does not in any way impugn the division's reporting on Bolivia and Argentina. In retrospect, some of that material may seem hasty and oversimplified, but haste and oversimplicity were hazards built into the kind of work the division was doing. On the really important issues in Latin American affairs, the reports were usually reasonable and occasionally brilliant. And they were almost always in accord with the line being advanced by the other intelligence agencies and by the State Department. At the same time, one can begin to see how the division acquired the reputation it had around R&A.

The OSS experience proved to be invaluable for Halperin. First of all, it plugged him into a network of high-powered researchers in his field after ten years of near-isolation from scholarly activities in Latin American affairs. Second, it gave him quality experience in administration and decision making. Third, and most important of all, it trained him in a new way of approaching his field. Barry Katz discusses this development at some length in his study of R&A. It is a good example of how new circumstances can lead to a fresh way of looking at old material.

The mandate of R&A was to find out everything that was important about any place that was significant to the prosecution of the war, and to collate the information in ways that would be useful in military and political decision making. At first glance the assignment seems straightforward enough, but it is well to remember that few scholars in those days had been trained to address their subject in those terms. Historians were concerned with the particulars of a nation's past; sociologists were concerned with the generalizations about its current social processes; political scientists focused their attention on the workings of political institutions; experts in literature immersed themselves in fiction and poetry, and generally insulated their subject from contact with "public affairs"; and geographers often appeared not to be dealing with human affairs at all. Scholarship in the United States was compartmentalized, and it is a good bet that sentries stood guard at each compartment to protect it from the poaching of scholars in other disciplines.

R&A worked to batter down these barriers almost from the beginning. An early directive stated that traditional academic categories "had to be repudiated in favor of a collaborative and interdisciplinary practice based upon the principle that 'in connection with total war, the traditional distinctions between political, economic, and military data have become almost entirely blurred.' "[28] Certainly it worked that way with Halperin.

HALPERIN: My main specialization had been in literature and to some extent in politics. But here I was associated with geographers, historians, anthropologists, as well as political scientists and economists. And I had to dig into these fields. Four years I was there and it was really a post-graduate course. I came out of there quite a different person in terms of my understanding of these different fields of knowledge. And also training in interdisciplinary work, pulling it all together. As I look back at it, it made me quite a different person.

The division functioned effectively on those terms. Scholars from a variety of fields came at problems from different angles and produced smoothly integrated analyses. The lengthy report on Mexico's *Sinarquistas*, for instance, included discussions of their social and economic roots, of the church-state conflict in the nation, of the demographic and geographic characteristics of the movement, of its ideology, its use of media for propaganda purposes, it goals, and its ties with elements of the Axis nations. Had the plan to invade Argentina been allowed to proceed, it would have called on the expertise of oceanographers, geographers, economists, sociologists, and historians (as well as military experts, of course) to plot the landings, the drive off the beaches, the seizure of transportation networks and factories, and the utilization of "friendly" elements of the population in military operations and postwar "reconstruction."

This fusion of historical, cultural, social, and economic factors to explore a specific problem was characteristic of the Latin America Division and of R&A in general. Langer, for one, was convinced that "such members of the staff as may return to academic life will never be able to view their teaching or research in the narrow way which was

28. Katz, *Foreign Intelligence*, 16.

all too common."[29] He proved to be prophetic. R&A personnel were instrumental in the development of area studies programs at many American universities after the war. Not the least of those was the Latin American Regional Studies Department established at Boston University in 1949. Its director was Maurice Halperin.

29. Memo from Langer to Donovan, March 15, 1944, quoted in Katz, *Foreign Intelligence.*

4

Starting Out Again

For Halperin and his staff, the real war was with Germany; Latin America was a combat area in that war. They were scarcely concerned with Japan. The ties between the Latin nations and Japan, after all, were tenuous at best, and by any measure, Japan did not call forth the same sense of urgency and emotional commitment among these people that Germany did. Thus, when the war in Europe ended, the raison d'être of the Latin America Division almost disappeared. There were still important questions to answer about Latin America's postwar future, but the life-and-death struggle was over, and the passion was gone. What remained for the division was not much more than a mop-up operation, and then, hopefully, some planning for the post-war world.

Halperin had been thinking about that postwar world, and especially about the relations of the United States and Latin America in it. So he was quite prepared when he was invited to address an inter-American defense organization made up of military representatives from the various nations in the hemisphere. At the conference he presented a plan for the industrial development of Latin America in which the United States would play a major role through both public aid and private investment. It would signal a new stage in relations between the United States and Latin America that Halperin felt was infinitely preferable to the exploitation of the past. In the back of his mind, he even hoped that the government might employ the "machine" he had built in the OSS to administer this "New Deal" for Latin America. He talked with General Donovan about the idea, and Donovan said, "Why not approach some private firm like a bank?" He promised to bring it to the attention of the Wall Street investment giant Goldman and Sachs. The firm would have the right connections. Nothing came of this suggestion, however. Instead, Halperin's fantasy took shape as a plan for the United Fruit Company to use his people after the war in a development program for Central America that would be beneficial for the natives and profitable for the company. He submitted his scheme to the company, and he received a courteous reply which said, in effect, that the company was not in a position at that time to make such an investment. Thanks, but no thanks. His efforts to preserve his machine and employ it in constructive ways came to nothing.

In the spring of 1945, Donovan sent a delegation of OSS figures to the organizing conference of the United Nations in San Francisco. For Halperin, the journey only added a dash of cynicism to the frustration he was feeling.

HALPERIN: We were there for some contingency which never arose. One or two of our people got jobs as reporters. They took notes and then wrote up the summaries. So some of them got little odds-and-ends jobs of that sort, though not for extra pay, of course. I mean, they were around and they were needed, so they were assigned, you understand. I had no assignment; I did nothing. I waited and observed. And San Francisco is a very nice town in which to wait and observe. I went to gatherings and meetings and parties, and I met a lot of people. . . . I was on the gravy train.

Karl Deutsch was included because of his facility with languages, but for Halperin the journey was honorific, scarcely more than a reward for services rendered. Apart from his sybaritic activities in San Francisco, he did little except phone his family daily on the private OSS line.

While there, he did renew a friendship that he had struck up with a prominent Chilean political figure in Washington, an intellectual and bon vivant named Eduardo Cruz Coke,[1] who was the leader of the

1. It is well to remember that people in Hispanic countries carry the surnames of both parents. Hence the last name technically is not Coke, but Cruz Coke. Still, Hispanics will often be referred to by only one of their two last names.

Conservative party in Chile and the head of the Chilean delegation to the conference.

A year or so earlier in Washington, Cruz Coke had outlined a scheme that he wanted Maurice to bring to the attention of American authorities. Cruz Coke would use his considerable influence to have Chile declare war on the Axis. As one of the Allied powers, Chile would then attack the Japanese fleet. At that point the real cunning of his scheme would come into play. The key to it was the battle readiness of the Chilean navy, which consisted of a few antiquated frigates that could not have intimidated a fishing fleet. That was the beauty of the plan. The Japanese fleet had been gravely weakened by then, but it was strong enough to blow the Chilean navy out of the water. Every last vessel would be sunk, and the United States would then reward Chile's courageous stand against the Axis by giving her an entire new, gleaming, modern navy. Chilean lives would be lost in the adventure, of course, but *c'est la guerre*. After ascertaining that the man was not joking, Halperin dutifully sent the idea up to the appropriate authorities. History does not record their response.[2]

The American radical and the Chilean conservative met several times; they ate, they drank, and they discussed Spanish literature and Chilean wines. Occasionally their revels were interrupted briefly by politics. On one occasion the head of the Chilean Communist party asked Cruz Coke if he couldn't somehow arrange a meeting with Comrade Molotov, who was the head of the Soviet delegation to the conference. Cruz Coke complied and told Maurice that the Chilean Communist had almost fainted with ecstacy when introduced to this living Soviet legend.

When the conference ended, Halperin returned to Washington and reality. By mid-summer of 1945, doubts were growing about the future of the OSS. Donovan had planned to continue the agency into

---

2. Some years later the English made a movie called *The Mouse That Roared*, in which a small Alpine duchy decided to repair its shattered economy by declaring war on the United States. The United States would win, of course, and would then treat the duchy as it treated all its vanquished foes, by putting the duchy's economy on a healthy footing. Complications arose in the story when the United States surrendered. One wonders what might have happened to Cruz Coke's scheme if the Japanese fleet had surrendered to Chile.

the postwar world and institutionalize it as a permanent intelligence organization, something the United States had never had before. As long as Roosevelt was alive, Donovan had a friend in the White House who supported the idea. Harry Truman, however, was hostile to the plan. He strongly opposed the creation of what he felt would be a peacetime American Gestapo, and less than two months after the surrender of Japan he terminated the OSS by executive order. Its various branches and personnel were fragmented and scattered among several government agencies, but an exception was made for R&A, which went intact to the State Department in the fall of 1945.

It was soon clear that R&A would be accorded lower status there than it had enjoyed in the OSS. From its inception Donovan had recognized the value of R&A and the extraordinary collection of individuals in it. With an intuitive sensitivity to the fragile egos and volatile temperaments of scholars at war, he knew how to make his people feel important, and he knew enough to give them plenty of elbow room. They responded by working their heads off. In the State Department, however, these same individuals were treated, at best, like stepchildren—barely tolerated by many, and despised by the rest.

By early 1946, it was obvious that the political climate in Washington was changing. The Grand Alliance was coming apart on the international scene, and the wartime coalition of liberals, Communists, and fellow travelers was unraveling at home. Allegations were beginning to circulate in Congress about Reds in the OSS, and these dark rumors found their way into the State Department as well.[3] Sometime early in 1946, Halperin became aware that he was one of those being singled out as pro-Soviet, and, things being the way they were now in Washington, he knew that his days with the division were numbered. Since he had accumulated a huge backlog of leave time during the war, he decided to resign and consider his options for the future while

3. See Richard Harris Smith, *OSS: The Secret History of America's First Central Intelligence Agency* (Berkeley: University of California Press, 1972), 364–65. Although Halperin did not know it at the time, Bentley's charges were forwarded from Hoover through the Department of Justice to the State Department in early February. Halperin, among many others, was named in the letter.

he luxuriated in a lengthy vacation. He had given himself completely to a righteous cause and he felt that the outcome had justified the effort. He was disappointed by the sad epilogue at State, but it gave him the push he needed to get on with his life and, after four years of seventy-hour weeks, to get reacquainted with his family.

HALPERIN: Well, I talked to some of my colleagues about their respective universities, about what might be available. I was just beginning to poke around. Then—it must have been in the early summer—a friend of mine whom I had met at the Library of Congress, and he was somehow attached to us in terms of getting books—I'd kept contact with him for quite a while—came to me and said that a new organization was about to be established. It was called the American Jewish Conference. This was an ad hoc *organization composed of the leading Jewish organizations, like the Zionist Organization of America, the B'nai B'rith, the Hadassah, and various other groups that had combined to form this thing for the purpose of lobbying at the United Nations, working for compensation for the Jewish atrocities, and also participating in the strategies and plans for the creation of the state of Israel.*

In the summer of 1946, Halperin became the representative of the American Jewish Conference to the United Nations. Again he speaks jokingly of "the intervention of the supernatural." He didn't even have to hunt for the job. It just fell into his lap and at the same salary that he had had as a division chief with the OSS. The conference had official "observer" status at the UN, and Halperin, its lobbyist, was given the title of "Non-Governmental Organization Observer."

Maurice planned to find a place for his family in New York near Carnegie Hall. Around the corner would be nice, he thought. After fifteen years in the cultural wastelands of Oklahoma and Washington, he was ready to gorge himself on music. Heifetz! Horowitz! Whatever he wanted to hear and whenever he wanted to hear it! He was near tears at the prospect. That was what Maurice expected. What he found was a housing shortage that was intractable. He couldn't find a place near Carnegie Hall. He couldn't even find a decent place in Manhattan. He finally settled for an apartment in Brooklyn near Ebbets Field. Rather than the New York Philharmonic, he got the Brooklyn Dodgers. And such interest as Maurice had in baseball was not even in the National League. Where was the supernatural now that he needed it?

Nowadays Brooklyn is not a particularly significant topic of conversation, except perhaps in the New York area itself. In the 1940s, however, Brooklyn was a joke. Along with Peoria it was a staple in the repertoire of stand-up and radio comedians. Peoria symbolized "the sticks," by which these comedians meant a kind of rural idiocy that was found just about everywhere but New York and perhaps Chicago, Los Angeles, and San Francisco. It is more difficult to define just what Brooklyn represented, except to say that it stood almost as an urban counterpart to Peoria, and therefore evoked images of a lovable urban idiocy, and, of course, of lovable urban idiots. Brooklynites were losers and proud of it. References to Peoria or Brooklyn were generally good for a laugh in those days. No explanation was necessary.

Halperin had never been to Brooklyn, so, when he moved there with Edith and the children, he expected the worst. But Maurice and Edith had proven to be marvelously adaptable in the past. They were a couple who could build a rich life anywhere, because what they were as individuals and what they had with each other allowed them to thrive in any environment they inhabited. It was a trait that had served them well in the past, and it would serve them much better in the future. So Brooklyn proved to be a lovely place to live. They were an easy walk from the Brooklyn Museum of Art, and if it wasn't the Metropolitan, it did have its own attractions, and it was accessible. There was also Ebbetts Field, but that proved to be a bust. Maurice took David there one day—David was around ten at the time—but they left after seven innings because they were bored. It wasn't like watching the Red Sox. They were fond of Sheepshead Bay for the seafood, and they were delighted by Coney Island in the winter. A few of the hot dog stands remained open, the summer crowds were gone, and the salt air was bracing. Best of all, they were only a short subway ride from central Manhattan. Things went well there, and life was sweet.

One morning—Halperin does not remember when it was—things suddenly turned sour. He was startled to read in Drew Pearson's column that Maurice Halperin, recently of the OSS, was about to be indicted for espionage. Espionage! What was going on? What was the source of this allegation? The original source, of course, had to be Elizabeth Bentley, for it was she who brought Halperin's name to the attention of the FBI in the fall of 1945. But Bentley had not yet gone public and was far removed from Halperin's thoughts at the time. What Halperin did know was that Pearson was generally acknowledged to be Hoover's conduit to the public. When Hoover wanted something known, it found its way into Pearson's "Washington Merry-Go-'Round" column. It is difficult to say more than that, except that the information was leaked to Pearson for a purpose. But why? And more to the point, what was Halperin to do about it?

HALPERIN: Before I left the OSS I was told informally there had been an investigation about me. Investigations, when I had had a whole slew of Communists in and out of my office in connection with my job—meetings and so forth. And my background and everything. But I had no idea what this thing possibly could mean. I thought, well, I'll see Donovan. He worked on Wall Street by then. So I called him up and got an appointment right away. Went up to his office—Wall Street—nice office—and I told him. I said, "Here, have you seen this?" I showed him the column. No, he hadn't seen it. He said, "Well, I'll look into it. I'll see what I can do about it." Of course, Donovan and Drew Pearson were not friends. Drew Pearson had been Edgar Hoover's instrument. They'd been collaborating together. "I'll see what I can do," he said. "Do you have any ideas as to what's behind this?" "I haven't the slightest," I said. "It comes right out of the blue." And then he said, "Well, you keep in touch with me, but don't use the telephone."

Don't use the telephone? By this time the old spymaster was out of the intelligence business, but he knew how it worked. Obviously he assumed that Hoover had a tap on his phone. Given the years of bad blood between them, and the probability that he still maintained sensitive connections, he had ample reason to suspect that. In any case, Halperin sensed that Donovan would be of no help in the situation and did not keep in touch. It was the last he saw of Wild Bill Donovan. It was also the last he heard of espionage for a while. The issue faded from view, and he continued his life as before.

Before Halperin was hired by the American Jewish Conference he had been quite ignorant of Jewish organizational life. Indeed, before he came to Washington at the beginning of the war he had been skeptical of Zionism—not hostile to it, but skeptical. How could there be a Jewish state of Israel, after all, when there were so many Arabs living in Palestine? The attitude had been formed in his early years; his father was neutral on the subject of Zionism. By the time the war broke out, his attitude was changing.

HALPERIN: We began to learn of the atrocities before we knew about the whole extent of the Holocaust. And then with the Holocaust coming, there was no more question about it. Something had to be done, some place for these Jews; there was no other place. This is where they're oriented. Where else can they go? So my views changed. When I took the job it was not only a question of some place to go at the moment— how nice it is to work in New York—it was also a question of a feeling of importance with respect to the whole postwar settlement, with respect to Jewish reparations and the whole question of human rights.

He was taken on by the American Jewish Conference because of his experience in government and political affairs and because he knew people in important places. For a lobbyist these were basic credentials. He met Jewish leaders from the United States and the rest of the world, and he learned quickly. Among other things, he learned that important Zionists did not speak with one voice on the matter of Zionism. In the main office, for instance, there was a "Jabotinskyite," a member of a "revisionist" group that eventually produced some of Israel's leaders many years later, including Begin and Shamir. As far as Halperin was concerned, they were simply a bunch of right-wing terrorists, and he had no use for them. There were groups on the Left also—not only the social democrats who dominated the early years of Israel, but Communists as well. And there were orthodox religious groups, who keyed all political thought to religious convictions. Before this, Zionism had appeared as a monolith to Halperin. Now it seemed more like a melee. Since there was not yet an Israel, the kind of Israel that would emerge was a matter of towering importance.

In the midst of these jurisdictional battles, Halperin took up his job as official observer for the conference at the United Nations. Meetings in the early years of the UN were held at Lake Success on Long Island, an easy drive from where Halperin lived in Brooklyn. He spent most of his time either there or at the conference office in Manhattan. He helped prepare claims for reparations from the defeated nations, and he did various sorts of analytical and statistical work. On a couple of occasions, he made presentations on Jewish affairs to the UN's Commission for Human Rights, which was one of the privileges of his job as observer, and eventually these reports were published as UN documents. And, of course, he was rubbing shoulders with luminaries at the UN—not only Zionist dignitaries, but also such international giants as Eleanor Roosevelt.

One of Halperin's lobbying triumphs was to persuade the UN Information Bureau to include Hebrew as one of the languages in which it sent out broadcasts to the world. Among other things, this got his picture in *PM*, a somewhat left-wing New York tabloid owned by Marshall Field, a Chicago multimillionaire. He also spent much of his time putting Jewish leaders in touch with Latin American statesmen so that, when the time came, the Latin Americans would vote for the establishment of the state of Israel.

After Israel was established, the American Jewish Conference was disbanded, and Halperin joined the American Jewish Committee, which had kept its distance from the conference. From its founding early in the century by German Jews it had been primarily an assimilationist outfit, and it was therefore at best aloof from Zionism, if not actually hostile to it. By the late 1940s it had come around to support the new state, so that it was not much of an adjustment for Halperin to join it.

It is interesting to look back on the discussions I had with Maurice on these first few post-OSS years. Each of our sessions lasted about ninety minutes, the length of the tape we used. The discussions were free-form, and any subject might occupy any number of tapes. The four OSS years, for instance, were spun out over three tapes. The next three years occupy less than half of one tape. That seems to be a reasonable indication of the commitment that Halperin made to each of the "causes." When he speaks of the OSS, he is animated, his memory is acute, and details pour out with remarkable clarity and enthusiasm. When he speaks of the American Jewish *Conference*, his memory is more vague, chronology is blurred, and details are sparse. About the American Jewish *Committee* he is perfunctory. He spent perhaps five minutes on it, and he gave the impression that it really did not seem very important to him.

In fact, he gives the impression that the entire three years in New York were an interlude between two more significant periods in his life. It isn't that what he did in New York was unimportant, but that he played no role in creating it. He was an outsider called in to do a job. He did it and then went on his way with no particular sense of achievement. When he speaks of the Latin America Division of the OSS he refers to "my machine." He is proud of the part he played in putting it together, and he was reluctant to leave it. Something of the same zeal appears when he speaks of his tenure at Boston University, where he made the other major contribution of that period in his life.

As was usually the case with Halperin, he found his new job because he knew someone. Boston University had barely started a Latin American Regional Studies Department when its young founder left for another position. It was precisely at that time that such universities as Harvard and Columbia, often influenced by OSS alumnae, were initiating area-studies programs for Russia and Asia. But in New England only BU had taken the plunge into Latin America, and Halperin was made for the job. He was already known on both sides of the language divide for his prewar publications, and his experience with the OSS was exactly what the university wanted.

HALPERIN: So I was invited to take that job. Certainly I was the indicated person with my OSS background. And I was very happy to get back. Now, in a much smaller way than I had anticipated when I wanted to "sell my machine" to the United Fruit Company, I was able again to do something with my experience. There was a geographer and there was a historian, and I also appointed some new faculty. The whole approach was interdisciplinary. I set up a core program in the department. And then there were the adjunct studies that the students were to take as well.

The first full-time appointment that Halperin made was an Argentine named Walter Beveraggi Allende. To that point in his life, Beveraggi's claim to fame was that he had tried to assassinate Juan Perón in Argentina and had escaped to tell about it. He was just finishing his Ph.D. in economics at Harvard, and Halperin found him to be a welcome addition to the department. He was excellent in his field, perfectly fluent in English, and a very personable young man. He was also, as it happened, an excellent polo player, because as a youth he had been sponsored at a local club by a wealthy Jewish manufacturer.

At the time Harvard had a kind of continuing education program in which they gave lectures, held roundtables, and produced radio programs. At one point Halperin, Beveraggi, and a young Latin American historian at Harvard were invited to give a series of round-table discussions for this program on the situation in Argentina, and these were then broadcast over the local CBS station.

HALPERIN: Beveraggi was there and none of us was pulling any punches about what we believed about Latin America. All of a sudden Beveraggi got word of a big scandal that this program had created in Argentina. Very shortly the newspapers came from Argentina to Beveraggi. And splashed on the front page is, "Traitor Beveraggi" had been deprived of his Argentine citizenship. Then there was a story, and in addition to Beveraggi, it turned out that Maurice Halperin had also lost his Argentine citizenship. The other guy somehow got off. He didn't lose his citizenship.

It was ridiculous because Maurice did not have Argentine citizenship. Apparently some officials in Argentina had confused him with an Argentine historian whose name was also Halperin, and who, as it happened, was rather vocally anti-Perón. And so the poor Argentine Halperin nearly lost his citizenship because the American Halperin had attacked Juan Perón. Fortunately the situation was cleared up with no further damage to the man.

But that was not quite the end of it. The Argentine counsel in Boston picked up on the matter and informed his superiors in Argentina that CBS was tied in with the Morgan banking interests. Of course, in a corporation the size of CBS, one would not have to dig too deep to find a connection with one large banking house or another. It was just that in certain quarters the House of Morgan carried a particularly negative image of ruthless, exploitative American capitalism. For the Communist party it had served for years as a symbolic shorthand for the enemy in America. It had also been a convenient target for embattled American farmers over the decades. Now the Argentine press was using it as a symbol of Yankee imperialism. In some sinister way, the House of Morgan was attempting to subvert Argentina. Maurice had almost grown accustomed by then to being an agent of the Communists. Now he had to adjust to being a tool of Wall Street as well. It was a new experience for him.

Years later, after Perón went into exile, Beveraggi returned to Argentina as a professor and became active in national politics. According to Halperin, he was associated with the most reactionary elements in the Argentine Navy, a group that expressed the most virulent brand of anti-Semitism. One of Beveraggi's books, says Halperin, came right out of Goebbels. "Amazing! Came from Goebbels. That same stuff. Interesting evolution." It was certainly an ironic evolution for a man whose first opportunity in life came from a Jewish millionaire and whose entry into academia was made possible by a Jewish radical.

Another of Halperin's appointments was a wealthy young man from Colombia, Virgilio Barco Vargas, an engineer who was doing graduate work at MIT. His American wife had finished three years in the Latin American program at Stanford University before coming east, and Halperin was able to arrange for her to finish her degree at BU. At the same time Barco decided that while he knew a great deal about Colombia, he knew very little about the rest of Latin America. So he enrolled in the graduate program with Halperin, wrote a thesis on Colombian politics, and was appointed as a lecturer in the department the following year.

The appointment of Barco precipitated a minor bureaucratic crisis at BU. His visa was not accompanied by a work permit, so technically he was unemployable in the United States. Now, as it happens, Colombia is one of the Latin American countries that is—or was, before the rise of the "drug barons"—virtually owned by a handful of very rich, aristocratic families, and Barco's was one of those families. Moreover, his wife was the daughter of an American oil company executive, so there was money on both sides of the marriage. They lived in a luxurious flat in Boston, although neither of them was employed. So Barco was not worried about the visa because he was quite willing to work for nothing. The problem was with the university, which was simply not programmed to handle such a thing. Regulations mandated that employees, whether secretaries, professors, or janitors, be paid. It is precisely the sort of crisis that occurs when common sense collides with bureaucratic regulations. Halperin had to go to the president of the university and plead his case. Eventually sanity prevailed, and Barco joined the faculty. He was never paid.

After that the Halperins and the Barcos became good friends and stayed in touch over many years. When Maurice was in Moscow in the early 1960s, he read that Barco, recently the mayor of Bogotá, had been appointed to a cabinet position. Halperin needed a particular Colombian publication for his own research at the time, so he wrote to congratulate Barco on the appointment and asked if, by the way, Barco could send him a copy of the book. The book arrived, along with a very pleasant letter. Many years later, Vancouver played host to an international conference on housing and the environment— "Habitat"—and Barco came as head of the Colombian delegation. Again the families were united, and they spent a pleasant time together. Some years after that, Barco served as president of Colombia and is perhaps best known in the United States as the man who declared war on the drug lords of his country.

Halperin's third appointment came about in a circuitous fashion. During the war he had assigned a few minor OSS tasks as a favor to a New York public-relations man named Win Nathanson. When Halperin was about to leave New York for BU, Nathanson returned the favor. Among his other accounts at the time, he handled public relations for the Brazilian coffee industry in the United States, and he was on good terms with important people in Brazil. He arranged for the governor of the state of São Paolo to receive Halperin for six weeks in the summer of 1949. The trip was a bit nerve-racking. When Halperin arrived in Rio de Janeiro, he discovered that there was no connecting flight that would get him to São Paolo within hours of the appointed time. Eventually he impressed upon the authorities in Rio that this was an important journey and that there would be a reception committee awaiting his arrival. They finally put him on an unscheduled cargo plane, which completed the last leg of the journey and arrived in São Paolo at precisely the appointed hour. To his surprise, local dignitaries were indeed on hand to welcome him, although no flight was due from Rio anywhere near that time. They were there, as they told him, because they knew that Americans were always on time.

São Paolo was the heart of Brazil's burgeoning industrial area and was already undergoing the population explosion that would make it a nightmare metropolis in the next several decades. Halperin worked with university people there on local economic problems, in this way more or less earning his keep at a posh hotel in the city. The trip put him in the good graces of important people there and would serve him well on trips to Brazil in the future.

When he returned to Boston, he organized a two-day conference on Latin American affairs to launch his new department, and he packed it with local luminaries, academic and otherwise. Nathanson helped him with the publicity, and the conference was a resounding success. One of the surprises there was his announcement that he was going to establish a special program in the department for the study of economic problems in the region of São Paolo, something that was made possible by his new connections in Brazil and made promising because there was nothing like it anywhere in North America. To seed the program he hired Paulo de Maura, Brazil's consul-general in Boston. As it happened, de Maura's strengths were in Brazilian literature and anthropology, not in economic affairs, which was supposed to be the focus of the new program. But he lent a certain glamour to the department and worked out quite well. He was Halperin's final appointment.

In Moscow, years later, Halperin encountered Paulo, who had come as the head of a Brazilian trade delegation. He was trying to persuade the Russians to buy cheap Brazilian coffee, instead of the more expensive Colombian or Costa Rican beans. There was a certain charming forthrightness in his approach that must have been rare in the world of trade delegations. Good Brazilian that he was, he took his coffee seriously and was appalled by the way Russians prepared it. He found it undrinkable. Unfortunately he told them so. His sales pitch was that since they didn't know how to brew coffee anyway, they might as well save money by ruining it with less-expensive beans. He even offered to set up a coffee stand in Moscow and teach the Muscovites how to brew it. Apparently there was something lacking in his sales technique, for the Russians continued to brew their coffee in the same old way with the same old beans. It remained undrinkable.

The Brazilian connection proved fruitful, and the program flourished in the next few years. By 1952 the wheels were turning for an exchange that would prove fruitful in a different way. Halperin arranged for the governor of São Paolo, a man named Adhemar de Barros, to receive an honorary degree at BU. Officially, of course, the invitation would come from the president of the university, and Nathanson would make all the necessary logistical arrangements. When de Barros came for the June convocation, he brought along five hundred books on Braziliana as a gift to the department. It was an unexpected and very welcome windfall. The affair proved to be quite a coup for the university, since the prevailing political wisdom was that de Barros would be the next president of Brazil. This meant that everybody who was anybody in Boston society wanted a piece of the action. Harvard's Latin American historian attended, and the Harvards did not ordinarily pay much attention to the BU's. Heads of local banking institutions were glad to assist, and officials of the United Fruit Company surfaced. There was even a Cabot in attendance. Luncheons, dinner parties, and banquets were given by the cream of Boston society, and Halperin went along to all of these affairs, though whether as a chaperon, shield, or gourmand is not clear. Everybody wanted to rub shoulders with the next president of Brazil. The Latin American Regional Studies department had made it. On the other hand, de Barros never did. When he ran for the presidency a few years later, he lost.

The other part of the deal was that Maurice and Edith, along with the children, went to São Paolo as guests of the government after the festivities in Boston were over. Just as de Barros had been a celebrity in Boston, Halperin was now a celebrity in São Paolo. Professors are generally more prestigious in Latin America than in the United States, and since he was coming from Boston he was doubly honored, because a Boston university meant Harvard to the locals, and Halperin saw no reason to disabuse them of the notion. After all, he was a Harvard man. So he was wined and dined by local businessmen, government officials, and the social elite, just as de Barros had been in Boston.

Halperin gave a few lectures while he was there, but mostly he just traveled all over Brazil with the family; they even took a spectacular trip to the Amazon basin. The grand finale came when they returned to São Paolo, and Halperin was awarded the Order of the Southern Cross, an honorific medal of great prestige in Brazil. True, Maurice was only awarded the Southern Cross, second class, but first class was reserved for Brazilians, and he did at least beat out the unfortunates who had to settle for the medal, third class. The actual medal was presented to him at a formal dinner and ceremony at the Brazilian Embassy in Washington at the end of the year.

Halperin had joined the OSS quite naive in some ways. Now, after ten years of high-powered work in Washington, New York, and Boston, he had become an exemplary academic operator. How many professors, after all, are awarded the Order of the Southern Cross, any class? He had reason to be satisfied with his life. Indeed, if things had gone on that well much longer, he might have become positively smug. But fate had other things in store for him. For once the intervention of the supernatural was cruel.

It involved his politics and his past, and it could not have come at a worse time. There had been warning tremors before—the allegation by Drew Pearson and some of Elizabeth Bentley's testimony before HUAC in 1948—but nothing had come of them, and in the glow of the Brazilian triumph, danger must have seemed quite remote. When it came in March of 1953, the earthquake that destroyed Halperin's life was part of that larger seismic pattern in American society at the time known too narrowly as "McCarthyism."

McCarthyism did not occur in a historical vacuum, but against a backdrop of national and international events that saw dreams of postwar amity dissolve into uncertainty, anxiety, and eventually, fear of nuclear catastrophe in a third world war. It started for many Americans when Winston Churchill told them that an "Iron Curtain" had descended to divide Europe, and after that it was an almost rhythmic litany of bad news: civil war in Greece; the Berlin blockade and air lift, which had the Americans and the Soviets at the edge of war for almost a year; the triumph of Communism in China; the news that Russia had exploded its own atom bomb; and finally the outbreak of the Korean War in the summer of 1950.

How did it all happen? The easy answer to this complex question was that it was the result of Communist aggression abroad and Communist subversion at home. Evidence of this domestic subversion was soon forthcoming, beginning with the revelations of a defecting Russian embassy clerk in Canada that there was a Soviet spy ring in North America, then progressing to the allegations by HUAC that the "Hollywood Ten" had insinuated Communist propaganda into the movies, then ballooning in 1948 with the spectacular charges before HUAC that important government officials had committed espionage for the Russians, and culminating in the arrest of the Rosenbergs for their role in transmitting information about the atom bomb to the Russians.

The solution to all of this seemed abundantly clear. Where domestic Communism existed it must be exposed and cauterized. No mercy must be shown this ruthless and cunning enemy. He might be anywhere, and he would use any foul means available in his quest for world domination. Today this might sound like caricature, but that is precisely the sort of reasoning that one encountered in the political dialogue of the era. Stripped of the melodramatic language, this was still very serious business, and there were plenty of people prepared to investigate it for reasons ranging from patriotism to political exploitation. Senator McCarthy neither started nor monopolized it, but he came to symbolize it because he had a flair for publicity and a talent for manipulating the compliant media that set him apart from his less-talented competitors. It seemed that every day brought new revelations about the sinister mischief of Communism.

The effect was cumulative and the consequences devastating. Nothing was sacred, and no one was above suspicion. Many times accusation was taken as evidence of guilt, and the accuser was often permitted to remain anonymous. In some cases the allegations were valid, in other cases, not. In some cases they were provocative, in others, preposterous; it made no difference. Jobs were lost, careers terminated, reputations destroyed; revered statesmen were reviled; the media were attacked; the Voice of America was investigated for subversion; American overseas libraries were purged.

Critics of all this have referred to the decade as a time of scoundrels, or they have drawn analogies with the Salem witchcraft trials, and still further analogies with the "Great Fear" of the French Revolution. To be sure, fear *was* on the land, and after a while, fear takes on its own reality and generates its own responses. In a very different context, Franklin Roosevelt had made that point when he was first inaugurated in 1933. It is quite possible that most people took the charges with a grain of salt, but if so they kept silent before the onslaught of a passionate minority who took innuendo for accusation and accusation for proof.

The responses to this great fear ranged from silence to moral cowardice to hysteria. Reasonable people who were above suspicion panicked. I was a slightly overage university undergraduate at just that time, and I recall rumors flying around the University of Iowa that FBI agents were enrolling in courses anonymously to monitor the thinking of the faculty. One morning I was furiously taking notes during a lecture on nineteenth-century French utopian socialism, when I got a short breather because the professor paused for perhaps two or three seconds before going ahead to finish the lecture. At the end of the hour I approached him to ask a question about the lecture, but he seemed distraught. He ignored my question and asked, "Did you notice that I hesitated once in my lecture?" "As a matter of fact, I did," I answered, "because you never do." He said that he had been about to make a comment on Fourier, the early utopian socialist, when it occurred to him that his point could be misunderstood as endorsing Fourier, and therefore socialism, and therefore, in the minds of some, perhaps, Communism. "I changed my wording to make sure that couldn't happen," he said dismally. "When they make you do that, the bastards have won." He turned from me and wandered away down the hall. The professor was a devout Christian and a Burkean conservative. If the whole situation smacks of paranoia, then I have made my point.

At first McCarthyism appeared to be a partisan political attack by Republicans against past Democratic administrations, but when it continued after Eisenhower's election, it could no longer be explained simply as a means by which the political outs were trying to get back in. At that point it took on an even more ominous tone. Thus, the Senate Internal Security Subcommittee (SISS) began its investigations under Democratic Senator McCarran in 1952, but it continued them under Republican Senator Jenner early in 1953 without missing a beat. And several universities had already fired professors for taking the Fifth Amendment before various government committees.[4] That was the climate in which Maurice Halperin was subpoenaed to testify before SISS in March 1953.

This climate of fear might help explain Halperin's hasty departure for Mexico the following autumn, but it does not dismiss the allegations made before the committee. Those allegations had first come to public attention several years earlier, but Halperin had not been called to testify before a congressional committee until the subpoena from the Jenner Committee arrived.[5] Overnight, Halperin had a major crisis on his hands. He realized that he was not in control of the situation but could only react to the initiatives of others in what would surely be a hostile ambience.

---

4. Ellen Schrecker discusses SISS and the universities at length (although without mentioning Halperin) in *No Ivory Tower: McCarthyism and the Universities* (New York: Oxford University Press, 1986).

5. Halperin's name came before HUAC a few times in those years, but in no threatening way. One witness took the Fifth Amendment when asked if he knew Halperin and gave the same response when asked about more than three dozen other people; two other witnesses said they did not know Halperin; and Bentley appeared before the committee again early in 1952 to warm over her charges against Halperin and others. These fleeting references were generally ignored by the public and the press and were scarcely noticed by Halperin.

HALPERIN: Let me see if I can reconstruct this thing. Well, I was called to meet this [Jenner] Committee in Executive Session and I had, of course, decided I had to make up my mind what I was going to do beforehand. I consulted a friend of mine who was a lawyer, and with whom I used to play duets and trios. He gave me an idea as to what the options were. And also he gave me some idea as to where to look in some of the legal books, so I did a little personal research on what's involved with the Fifth Amendment and the First Amendment, etc. And by the time I was in the Committee it was very clear in my mind I was going to plead the Fifth Amendment. What were the alternatives to it? My word against Bentley's in this climate. My word against Bentley's.

If he had never met Bentley, it would have been easier. In that case, his word against hers might have led to a stand-off and a return to the status quo. The trouble was that if he started to testify, he would have to admit that he had indeed known Bentley, had known that she was a Communist, and had hosted her in his home a few times for the sole purpose of discussing Latin American affairs with her, in the belief that the information was destined for Earl Browder and not the Soviet Union. It was all part of what he called the "climate of indiscretion" in Washington at the time. But times had changed. With all of that out on the table in 1953, his word—his credibility—would be seriously compromised. The political breezes being what they were that spring, he says that the Fifth Amendment was the only realistic option for him.

The way the hearings generally worked, the witness appeared first before the committee meeting in executive session to respond to such questions as it might ask, and then he or she might be asked to appear before a public session of the committee.

HALPERIN: So it didn't take a minute or two in the Executive Committee—very businesslike—nobody there, no press or anything. And I took the Fifth Amendment to one or two questions—two questions, I think—and I was then put down to be interviewed or examined in the open meeting. That's how they worked it. First the closed meeting and then into the open meeting. I went to see the President of the University,

*whom I knew very well, a very decent person in every respect. And I
said, "Well, I think maybe I had better warn you that in another day or
two I am going to be in the newspapers." Well, we discussed the thing
and he pled with me, "Don't take the Fifth Amendment—take the First
Amendment." And I pointed out that the First Amendment people had
gone to jail. . . . I didn't have the feeling that I wanted to be a martyr;
this isn't my business at all.*

Unfortunately for Halperin, the committee and its counsel, Robert
Morris, had more than two questions on their mind in the open session
that afternoon. In addition to asking about Communist party membership and espionage activities in connection with Bentley, Morris
dug back into Halperin's life, asking about his politics at Oklahoma
University, the politics of his contacts in Mexico, his voyage to Cuba,
his purchase of a Soviet bond, his politics at the time he attended
the UN conference in San Francisco, and his possible acquaintance
with a raft of people—generally those named at various times by
Whittaker Chambers and Elizabeth Bentley. The committee had done
its homework on Maurice. In almost all cases he pled the Fifth Amendment. There was one notable exception, and even that was to clarify
a point rather than to answer a question. Referring back to a possible
misunderstanding of one of his answers at the executive session that
morning, he said,

My intention was to deny any crime of espionage, but it was not my
intention to answer any specific details relating to that particular crime.
For the record on all specific questions, my position is one of not
answering.

Morris: Miss Bentley has testified you did give her information. Did
you?

Halperin: I refuse to answer on the basis of the fifth amendment. *But
I did not commit espionage* [my emphasis].[6]

6. This excerpt from the committee hearings is quoted from the *Boston Herald* of
March 27, 1953, the day after Halperin testified.

Halperin says he thought it necessary to go on record on this matter, and of course he did it under oath. At the end of his testimony, Halperin issued a statement pointing out that the First and Fifth Amendments were the bedrock of democracy and attacking congressional hearings for chipping away at both. His statement was entered into the record of the hearing and published by at least some of the press.

That isn't all the press published. The next morning Halperin was going to work on a crowded streetcar. He glanced over the shoulder of someone standing near him who was reading the morning newspaper, and he almost jumped out of his skin. A blaring headline told of a BU professor refusing to testify about alleged Communist activities, and below it there was a prominent picture of him. Given the constraints of space allotted to the story in different papers, the accounts of the hearing were reasonably accurate and generally not too inflammatory. The headlines were another matter. The *Boston Post*, rather gentler than most, notified its readers that "FOUR BALK AT RED QUERIES"; "4 TEACHERS DEFY RED PROBERS," proclaimed the *Boston Herald*; the *Boston Globe* said gruffly, "PROF AT BU WON'T TALK"; but the prize went to the tabloid *Daily Record:* "REFUSES TO DENY TREASON." One might note that Halperin also refused to deny armed robbery, income tax evasion, and child molestation, because he was not asked about them. He was not asked about treason either. Treason was not an issue; espionage was, and espionage on behalf of an ally does not define treason. But "treason" has a keener edge to it than "espionage" in much the same way that "defy" has more bite than "balk." These headlines did no honor to the Boston press.

Halperin appeared before the committee on a Thursday in late March. Back in Washington the following Monday, the committee heard another witness, this time one who gave testimony about Halperin's prewar political affiliations. The man was Nathaniel Weyl, an admitted former Communist. Weyl had been a Communist in New York City before coming to Washington in 1933 to work for the New Deal's agricultural program in the AAA. While working for the government he joined a secret Communist party cell, most of whose members were later identified by Whittaker Chambers. He left the New Deal in 1934 to work full time for the Communist party by organizing farm workers in the Midwest.

Weyl told the committee that he first heard about Halperin from Homer Brooks, the district organizer for the party in the Southwest, who told him that Halperin had been "accredited" as the Texas-Oklahoma representative of the Communist party to the Mexican Communist party. At the time Weyl was living in Houston. A short while after his meeting with Brooks he went to Mexico, where he learned from a highly placed Mexican party functionary—he thought it was Valentín Campa, the number-two man in the party, but he could not remember with certainty—that Halperin had presented his credentials in Mexico and had attended various meetings of the Mexican party.[7]

Weyl had long since left the party but had remained silent until after the outbreak of the Korean War. Although his testimony was hearsay and had nothing to do with Halperin's alleged wartime espionage, it was nevertheless damaging. Weyl was a credible witness, and his testimony supported other allegations that Halperin had been a Communist while he was at Oklahoma University. It certainly did nothing to ease Halperin's situation.

The day after Halperin appeared before the committee—the day that the *Daily Record* warned darkly of Halperin's treason—*Bostonia*, the BU alumni magazine, came out with its April edition. The cover featured a huge globe of the world with Brazil facing the reader. Above it was a picture of a Brazilian notable pinning the Order of the Southern Cross on Halperin's lapel; below it was a replica of the medal itself. Most of the issue was a hymn of praise to Halperin and his program at the university. Halperin learned later that Senator Jenner's sister or sister-in-law (he does not recall which) was associated with the alumni magazine and that when she found out that Halperin was to appear before the committee she asked the senator if he couldn't

---

7. *Hearings Regarding Subversive Influence in the Educational Process*, before the Subcommittee to Investigate the Administration of the Internal Security Act and Other Internal Security Laws of the Committee on the Judiciary of the United States Senate, Eighty-Third Congress, first session (March 30, 1953), 714–15.

somehow shuffle the professor out of the deck. Jenner told her that if only she had asked him a week earlier he could have done something about it, but that it was too late. It is not so much the intervention of the supernatural that sits at the center of Halperin's life; it is irony—sometimes funny, sometimes poignant, sometimes bitter, but always irony.

After the hearing, President Case of Boston University set up a faculty committee of what Halperin calls "elders of the establishment" to conduct their own investigation into the situation. Halperin appeared before this committee on a few occasions, but he was at an impasse with them. They wanted him to answer questions that he would not answer before the Jenner Committee, and he explained that he could not do that. The committee was unhappy with Halperin's silence but reluctant to take stern measures, if only because it might make BU look bad in the academic community alongside Harvard, a university in the same city that had chosen to ignore unsupported charges against some of its own faculty at the time.

The matter appeared to be settled in June when the committee and Halperin arrived at a compromise. He would make a statement to them that he had never been a Communist while he was at BU, but he would continue to plead the Fifth Amendment if he came before any government investigating committee again. For its part, the committee would reprimand and censure him for his uncooperative attitude but would then drop the matter. Halperin, who had continued to teach during this investigation, would remain on the faculty as before, the head of the Latin American Regional Studies Department. The matter settled, Halperin went off to Mexico for a summer of research.

When he returned in September he was uneasy about the future. The clouds were dark, he says, and he sensed a storm coming. So he offered President Case a kind of deal.

HALPERIN: I said, "Look here, I think we have to assume it's not over. Now I have an idea about what we can do about it. I will take a sabbatical year of absence beginning in the fall. I will leave you a post-dated resignation which you can use or not as the situation would warrant at the end of my sabbatical. This way I am out of the way, and if there is still an interest in me you can say that he has actually resigned. In other words, use this resignation if and when and how you think you need to use it. And we will go to Mexico, and I am pretty sure I will be able to make a living there, and this way possibly you won't be embarrassed any more."

Certain that the worst was over, and not persuaded of the morality of such a deal, Case rejected the suggestion, and Halperin resumed his teaching duties with the university.

The storm broke some time later in the narrow confines of Halperin's living room. He was watching the evening news on television and suddenly he *was* the evening news on television. There was a film clip of Attorney General Brownell testifying that afternoon before the Jenner Committee. Brownell read into the committee's record a letter that FBI Director J. Edgar Hoover had written to President Truman in November 1945, briefly identifying a spy ring that had been functioning in Washington during the war, and sketching in a few of its activities. The letter was a summary of the deposition that Bentley had just made to the FBI. Halperin was cited as one of the spies.

The issue this time was different from what had emerged at the Jenner Committee hearing in March. At that time Halperin was asked about Bentley's allegations and asked specifically if he was a member of her "espionage ring" during the war. The point is that he was asked, not accused, although an accusation was certainly implied. In the fall, Brownell was not just fishing in the testimony of such a controversial witness as Bentley; he was revealing the blunt accusation of the director of the FBI. To be sure, Hoover's letter was based on Bentley's allegations, but his endorsement, especially since it originated in 1945, gave those allegations a power they had previously lacked. The letter had not appeared at the springtime hearing because it had still been classified "Top Secret." Now it was declassified, and its impact was profound.

The next day was a disaster for Maurice. It started, as it had some months earlier, on the streetcar; Halperin again saw his name and face on the front page of the local newspapers. And it got worse.

HALPERIN: Well, I had a class—I forget at what time—-11 o'clock or so—and just as I finished, a messenger came in with a very urgent message and my recollection is, "Go to the Dean's office immediately." And I went to the Dean's office, and I don't remember whether the Dean himself or somebody else gave me the word. "You are suspended with pay pending an investigation." Well, very clearly this Brownell business shook them up. In a way, you can't blame them. What are they going to do?

What they were going to do was have a faculty committee dig into the whole situation and see what this was all about. Was Halperin an innocent victim of the growing hysteria of the era? Or was he actually complicit in the dark machinations of the spy world? There was so much irresponsible red-baiting at the time that many honest people believed it was all irresponsible red-baiting.[8] The faculty committee was supposed to see if there were grounds for taking further action against him, or whether he was indeed innocent because not proven guilty. But Halperin did not see it that way.

HALPERIN: Naturally I discussed this with Edith and my brother, Teddy. And my mother and father were still there too. It seemed as if this was going to go on indefinitely and I couldn't see a positive outcome. There were many pressures, you know, on the University. I remember specifically there were some newspaper items in which members of the Regents were calling for my dismissal. It didn't look good. And so we decided there was no point in hanging around. We would simply leave and, as I had anticipated could easily happen, we'd make our way to

8. Not long ago I made the acquaintance of a conservative federal employee who had an interesting perspective on this matter. He feels that irresponsible red-baiting was the worst thing that happened to anti-Communism in the era. The only issue, he says, should have been Soviet espionage, not party membership or Communist beliefs. When McCarthy and others blurred that distinction and then ran amok, charging the Democrats with "twenty years of treason" and impugning the loyalty of such moderates as George Marshall, Dean Acheson, and Adlai Stevenson, they alienated liberals and divided the nation. It is not surprising, he says, that many liberals responded by refusing to believe that anyone did anything at all out of line.

*Mexico where we had contacts and where as a Latin Americanist I
should have been able to make a living. And if I didn't make a living,
it would be proof that I was a very poor Latin Americanist.*

His recollection was that Brownell appeared before the Senate committee in early or mid-October, and that he "waited and waited and
waited" for the faculty committee to get around to him. After five
or six weeks, further delay seemed futile, so he and Edith packed up
and drove to Mexico City. They stayed the first night in Washington
with Luis Quintanilla, an old friend from Mexico, who was at that
time ambassador to the Organization of American States, and then
spent four more days on the road before arriving at their destination.
They spent the second night in Chattanooga. Maurice remembers it
quite well because it was Thanksgiving. He emphasizes that there
was nothing precipitous in their departure. They gave the faculty
committee plenty of time, as he recalled it, and then left because they
did not know what the future held at home and because they were sure
they could get by in Mexico. And both Halperins did get jobs almost
immediately. They were settling in when they heard from Boston.

*HALPERIN: I get a letter from Case in a sense summoning me to come
and have a meeting. The Committee finally was going to have a meeting
and offered to pay my fare. Well, I talked it over with Edith. What's
the use, I'm established here now. I have this thing here. Suppose they
even say I can come back to teach. It is still on the record. How can
I go back to teach in this terrible mess there. . . . If they sent back a
letter saying that I was reinstated or something, then I would have to
consider whether I wanted to go back or not on that basis. But to go
back on some unknown basis?*

Moreover, he asks, "What assurance did I have that once in . . .
U.S. jurisdiction I could get back to Mexico? A subpoena, another
subpoena. . . . New trumped up 'evidence.' " This was not paranoia,
he says, but a sober assessment of possibilities in the political climate
of the time. In addition, Edith was under considerable stress, and he
was reluctant to leave her alone in Mexico. All in all, he says, there

were more reasons to remain in Mexico than to return to BU for his hearing.

Back in Boston, however, they saw things quite differently. Remembering back over decades, friends and colleagues say that they were ready to go to the wall for Halperin, and felt disappointed, even betrayed, by his behavior. One of them said recently,

> Yes—a group of us did rally to Maury's support. We were ready to go to bat—gung ho—when we heard he had skipped town. President Harold Case was very decent . . . asking him to return to B. U. from Mexico and meet with the Committee to explain his position (and offering to pay travel costs for the round trip). But Maury—for reasons of his own—preferred to stay put.[9]

Rather more brusquely, another erstwhile colleague recalled that "Halperin was invited to meet with a faculty committee and the president, and refused. The faculty was quite disturbed by this response."[10] Still another, a member of the Political Science Department at the time who says he rallied behind Halperin, remembers sharing the belief with many of the faculty that Halperin was a "victim of the red-baiting" of the era. He agrees with the others that President Case, a conservative man in a delicate situation, acted with honor throughout and was fully supportive of Halperin; and he agrees with the others also that most of the faculty were firmly behind Halperin. All Maurice had to do, he says, was deny the charges before the faculty committee, and he would probably have come through the ordeal with flying colors.[11] (What might have happened, however, if Halperin had gone before the committee and refused to answer the charges is anybody's guess.) As for Halperin's departure, Newman says it was a "shocker." One moment he was in Boston; the next, he was gone forever. Nobody seems to have had any forewarning—the faculty, the committee, and the president were all taken by surprise. Those who had "gone to bat" for him came away with egg on their faces and a bad taste in their

9. Solomon Lipp, letter to author, January 18, 1990.
10. Ernest Blaustein, letter to author, May 21, 1990.
11. William Newman, telephone conversation with author, December 3, 1990.

mouths. They were angry and many of them were now quite ready to believe that Halperin was guilty after all.

There is certainly a wide discrepancy in the way different people recalled and evaluated the situation. Halperin's former colleagues feel that he had a good chance of surviving the affair with his job and reputation intact. Instead, they point out, he bolted without giving the committee or the president a chance even to hear his testimony. He, on the other hand, feels that these erstwhile colleagues were "naive" and that "the chances of reinstatement looked slim." Moreover, he does not remember any support at all coming from the faculty. On the contrary, he felt totally abandoned. Nevertheless, he says, he gave the committee ample time to launch its inquiry, which, for some reason, it never did. Eventually he and Edith tired of marking time, so they left.

It turns out that Halperin's memory did not serve him well in this instance. He did not wait and wait and wait; he did not wait at all. The 1945 letter in which Hoover accused Halperin and others of espionage was declassified on Monday, November 16; Brownell entered it into the Jenner Committee's proceedings the following day; Boston University suspended Halperin on Wednesday, November 18, not in early or mid-October. The next day the university bureau of publicity released a brief statement by Halperin:

> Five months ago Boston University, with great courage and singular devotion to duty, stood firm in the face of a radical assault on academic freedom. The conservative position adopted by Boston University did honor to its long tradition of integrity and fundamental Americanism.
>
> Today the same issue has been raised as an incident in a larger struggle for political power of unequaled partisan ferocity. There is every reason to believe that Boston University will again refuse to yield to hysteria, and that after calm appraisal of the situation, will reaffirm its decision of last June.[12]

12. *News about Boston University*, University Bureau of Publicity, press release no. S-3835, November 19, 1953: "Text of Statement from Boston University Professor Maurice Halperin." Note that Halperin was still describing the issue as an "assault on academic freedom." That might or might not have been the issue in March, but it was certainly not the case in November. The only issue at that time was espionage.

The same evening the *Boston Globe* reported, "Spokesmen predicted it would be impossible for the preliminary board to sit as a body until the first of next week because of faculty schedules."

Thus, one week before Thanksgiving, Halperin claimed to be serene and confident that the university would exonerate him,[13] and he had to be aware of the fact that the faculty committee would not meet until Monday of the next week at the earliest. When the committee did not meet on Monday, the Halperins apparently decided to leave immediately. They made all arrangements on Tuesday and were gone early the following morning. Maurice had not appeared before the committee, had not heard from it, and, most important, had made no effort to contact it to find out when it would meet.

This alters the timetable drastically. Maurice did not give the committee five or six weeks to call him to a hearing; he gave it one day, from the Monday the committee did not meet until the Tuesday the Halperins decided to leave.[14] Moreover, the committee had not set a firm Monday date for the meeting; it had only said that faculty schedules would prevent it from meeting *before* then. And as one of my colleagues observed recently, anyone who has been around academia for a while knows that faculty committees are notoriously sluggish about doing anything that does not involve their own salaries.

Considering what was at stake, and considering the fact that Halperin made no effort at all to contact either the faculty committee or the president, it is clear that he gave the university no chance at all, which is exactly the way his former colleagues remember it. However Halperin recalls the affair, the conclusion seems inescapable: he bolted.

All right, but why didn't he return from Mexico to Boston at university expense to appear before what, from all accounts, would have been a friendly committee and a president who insisted on

13. He says now that he was neither "serene" nor "confident" at the time but that he was "whistling in the dark, hoping to rally support."

14. Halperin says he is concerned about this memory lapse. Reflecting back upon the situation, he claims that the week he waited after the hearing must have *seemed* like an eternity, and in the decades since he began to remember it that way—he internalized it as an eternity. That, he says, could explain his recollection that it was five or six weeks from suspension to departure.

evidence of wrong-doing before he would act against Maurice? Here the situation is less clear, and Halperin has a plausible response. He is not persuasive when he says that even if the university returned him to the classroom, the whole affair would still be on the record. How could he teach under those conditions, he asks? Well, why not? The only thing on the record that mattered would presumably be the university's conclusion that there was no evidence to support the charges against him.

He is on more solid ground when he points out that he had no guarantee that he would be permitted to return to Mexico once he had returned to the United States. In that case, if he were fired from his position at BU, he would be left without a means of earning a livelihood anywhere. It was all well and good for his colleagues to have projected a favorable verdict for him. They were assessing the situation from the perspective of people who had nothing to lose. By the time he was in Mexico, Halperin was viewing the matter from the angle of someone who had everything to lose. So he rejected the idea of returning "on some unknown basis." He had built a life in Mexico and felt that he risked losing it by returning to Boston for his hearing.

However he wants to explain it, Halperin rejected the framework of due process that the university offered him both before and after his departure. Before he left he had absolutely nothing to lose by waiting for the hearing. The Jenner Committee might or might not have recalled him. If it did, he would surely have pled the Fifth Amendment again, leaving the committee with no more evidence than it had had in March, which was none at all. The faculty committee would have heard him out and made its recommendations to the president, who would also, no doubt, have been under a variety of pressures from civil libertarian groups, from the AAUP, and from conservative regents. How would Case have acted? Nobody knows—not Halperin's former colleagues and certainly not Halperin himself. That is what makes his hasty departure so difficult to fathom. Halperin was a fighter, and it was out of character for him to duck a situation like this one. He says he had no wish to become a martyr, but there is no strong reason to believe that martyrdom would have been his fate. At worst, he would have lost his job and then gotten on with his life—whether in Mexico or in the States—at a later date; at best, he would have salvaged his career and life in America. By refusing from the outset to appear before the committee, he left the university with no alternative but to fire him. The choice was always his, and it was a curious one. We shall have to reexamine Halperin's departure from Boston University again in the final chapter. Having made his choice, Maurice Halperin was settled more or less permanently in Mexico when the university fired him in January of 1954.

5

South of the Border

The departure from Boston was hurried, but it was not reckless because the Halperins were old hands in Mexico. They had made their first trek south of the border in 1932, and in the years since then they had visited often and at length. A warm, approachable, congenial couple, they had also accumulated a storehouse of friends by the time of their troubles in the 1950s. Some of these friends were just neighbors and acquaintances of no particular significance; some were quite important in the national life; and some were unknowns who later became quite prominent in their own domains.

In 1934, for instance, the Halperins befriended an unknown young Frenchman named Henri Cartier-Bresson, who was to become one of the renowned photographers of the postwar world. Maurice remembers accompanying Cartier-Bresson on a trip to Tlascala, where he learned something about European anti-clericalism. Every so often, when they passed a church, Cartier-Bresson would angrily pull out a chalk and express his sentiments by scrawling "MERDE" on the wall. Halperin also learned something about photography on the trip. He learned not to stint on film. Cartier-Bresson would take hundreds of shots, often of the same subject. He explained that there was always the possibility that something might go wrong with any one photo, and also that the next shot you took might be the perfect one, just a shade better than all the others. Maurice never forgot the lesson. Following Cartier-Bresson's advice, he amassed loads of spectacular slides from his various travels in years to come.

When Judith's third birthday approached in September 1934, Maurice asked Cartier-Bresson to take a photo of her. Cartier-Bresson proposed instead that Maurice give the commission to another talented young unknown, a Mexican photographer who desperately needed the money. His name was Manuel Alvarez Bravo, and he became almost as famous as Cartier-Bresson in later years. On the way to Bravo's house, Judith banged her finger in a car door and had it all bandaged by the time they arrived. Bravo removed the bandage from the pained toddler, stood her against a white wall, and caught a wonderfully complicated expression on her face. At a retrospective of his work decades later at Chicago's Art Institute, Judith brought this photo, and the man in charge of the exhibit was, she says, "panting after it." He immediately identified it as a Bravo because of the particular use of light in the photo. It was Bravo's trademark.

Maurice met another man in those years from whom he was to learn much about Mexico and the curious ways of its males. His name was Palomo Valencia, and he was governor of the state of Yucatán. Initially Palomo had come to power forcibly through a coup d'état, and then had had his authority legitimized when the Mexican government recognized the fait accompli and made him governor of the state. He invited Maurice to be a guest of the government one Christmas, and Maurice traveled all the way to Merida in the south of Mexico for the holiday. After coming to power, Palomo had instituted an agrarian reform in the state, and he took Halperin on a tour of his domain to show him some of the results. The professor was impressed with the reform, but he was also appalled to see that there were still many plantation owners who provided better quarters for their horses than they did for their workers. Palomo's reform was only a beginning. The tour had a profound influence on Halperin's understanding of Mexico.

One night, during the brief holiday, Palomo took Halperin on one of his regular trips to the local zoo, where he petted the lions and tigers, who apparently recognized him and rubbed up against him in a display of devotion that had Maurice terrified. Another time they went to the beach, where Halperin witnessed a strange ritual. In the Yucatán (though apparently not in Mexico City) Palomo always wore a pistol. When they got to the beach there was not a person in sight, except for Palomo's bodyguard, so the two men stripped completely for their plunge into the ocean. And then, with no one even remotely in the vicinity, Palomo buckled on his holster and pistol for the twenty-yard walk to the water. He was stark naked. At the water's edge he unbuckled his paraphernalia, laid it down, and plunged in for his swim. After the dip, still dripping wet, he buckled it back on for the walk to their clothes, took it off, dressed, then put it back on again. Halperin was beginning to learn that the violence of American life was small potatoes alongside the gunplay of Mexico, and that the display of a pistol had a symbolic charge of inestimable value in macho Mexico.

Now Halperin was back in Mexico again, but this time he was faced with the prospect of building a life there. The first order of business was to earn a living. He had made some preliminary inquiries along those lines during the summer before his departure from Boston, and he was assured that there would be enough work at least to feed his family. On those terms he set about to put together a patchwork career. Characteristically he did it through personal contacts.

One of these contacts was Enrique González Aparicio, a friend from before the war. It was Aparicio, in fact, who had introduced him to Palomo Valencia. Aparicio came from a prominent old colonial family in Veracruz, and, when Halperin met him, he was a wealthy banker and close adviser to President Cárdenas. In later years their friendship had consequences that Halperin could never have foreseen. Aparicio, for instance, was married to the sister of Luis Quintanilla, who was the Mexican ambassador to the Organization of American States when Halperin left Boston in the 1950s. It was Quintanilla who had helped him launch what was to be a series of pamphlets on contemporary Latin American topics. The series was published by Boston University, and Quintanilla wrote the first monograph for it. As it happened, it was also the last monograph for the series, because Halperin was soon dismissed by the university, and the venture collapsed with the departure of its founder/editor.

Although Aparicio died shortly before the war, he still managed to help out Halperin in his time of trouble years later. The aid actually came from a close friend and disciple of Aparicio, who was a top official in the Bank of Mexico in the 1950s. Through Aparicio he had known about Halperin for years and was aware that he was now in Mexico because of political troubles in the States. He was pleased to get an appointment for the American as research consultant with the government's economic development bank, the *Financiera Nacional*. Halperin directed studies on the feasibility of developing the chemical and coal industries in Mexico. The job required only two or three half-days per week, it paid well, and Halperin learned things from it about the Mexican economy that proved to be quite helpful during his stay in Moscow some time later.

Halperin likes to say that Aparicio helped him "from the grave." The assistance might have been more direct if the man had not met an untimely death before the war. He broke his leg playing baseball, and while he was having it set in the hospital, the doctors decided to take care of a few other things that needed fixing. His appendix, for instance, was still around. Why not remove it before it caused trouble? And his teeth were in need of repair. They decided to do those too. They were going to really fix the man up completely while he was there. They did, and he died, a victim of over-repair.

Another of the prewar contacts who helped Halperin in Mexico was Vicente Lombardo Toledano, a left-wing labor leader since the 1930s. Although he was a reliable fellow traveler, Lombardo headed his own political party, which gave him freedom of action he would not have had in the Communist party. Moreover, since his party usually supported the government when the chips were down, the government reciprocated by subsidizing his party's newspaper. He was also on the executive committee of the World Federation of Labor, which was the East Bloc's answer to the Western-oriented International Labor Organization. Lombardo was a complex man, who knew how to play both sides against the middle effectively.

Halperin had referred rather unflatteringly to Lombardo in his article for *Current History* in 1934. When he first met the Mexican labor leader two years later, he was astonished not only that Lombardo had read and remembered the article, but also that he now agreed with Maurice's 1934 comments about him.

HALPERIN: What impressed me was that he took no offense at being criticized. This was in '36. So that started a long friendship. I don't mean I saw him every day, but I would see him from time to time at his

*home. Once or twice I had dinner there. He lived well. And the reason
was, I guess, that his wife owned two or three textile factories. She,
incidentally, was an enormous woman. Obese, super obese. Fantastic.*

Halperin's friendship with Lombardo now paid off in a very practical way, when the Marxist labor leader introduced Maurice to Jesús
Reyes Heroles, the editor of a journal that represented a group of
small industrialists, most of whom were in chemicals and textiles.
Being Mexicans, they were almost by definition anti-American, and
being small industrialists, they were very anti-multinational. They
were related to Lombardo's party and, at the same time, supporters of
the government.

Halperin and Reyes Heroles impressed each other favorably. Later
in life the Mexican held various cabinet posts, and, according to
Halperin, would probably have become president if his father had
not been a Spaniard, which, in Mexico, disqualified him by law from
the presidency. Reyes Heroles gave Maurice a job editing a section
on international economic developments for the journal. The job came
with all the important trimmings, including a desk, an office, and a
salary. It wasn't much of a salary, but it wasn't much of a job either.
It absorbed only a small part of Halperin's time.

Not long after that, Lombardo introduced Halperin to the minister
of the economy. This man hired Maurice to prepare a summary of the
main trends in the American economy every month. The job did not
call for any analytical skills, but it did assume a certain knowledge of
the subject. In this sense, Maurice was fortunate, because both jobs
required a combination of skills and knowledge that he had long since
mastered, and workers with them were not otherwise readily available
in Mexico City.

Then Halperin received an appointment as an adjunct professor
at the National University in Mexico City. Full-time appointments
were reserved almost exclusively for Mexicans and a few Spaniards.
Halperin's was a kind of semipermanent, temporary appointment. It
not only helped to fill out his income, but, far more important, it was
the basis for his continuing status as a legal immigrant.

The final piece in this patchwork of jobs fell into place when Edith got a job at the American School in Mexico City. The school was funded, at least in part, by the American government and was attended primarily by the children of American diplomats and by children whose parents wanted them to get an English-language education. Edith was quite a catch for them. She had all the credentials and years of experience, culminating recently in the Brookline (Massachusetts) schools.

The Halperins had arrived in Mexico City around the beginning of December 1953, and in less than two months they had enough work to keep them in the middle-class style they had grown accustomed to over the years.

It was at this time that Maurice got the call from President Case to return to Boston. By then, the Halperins had confirmed that they could survive in modest comfort in Mexico, which played a major role in their ultimate decision not to return. He had burned his last bridge and made the necessary preparations for a life in Mexico. Maurice did what he had to do, and Case did what *he* had to do. Case's reply only formalized the situation. It also created a brief stir in the Mexican press and made Maurice a minor celebrity, more notorious, unfortunately, than noteworthy. The Halperins were soon able to get on with their lives fairly quietly.

Judith was married now and no longer with them, but David joined his parents when his school year ended in Boston. With Lombardo's help they were able to enroll him in one of the best high schools in the city. David's facility with languages was such that he became editor of the school paper in his final year, and his mastery of Spanish continues to play a major role in his life today.[1]

Maurice and Edith were able to establish themselves at a reasonable level of material comfort in Mexico City, but at a more subtle level, there was something missing. For all their visits to Mexico over the past twenty years, home had always been the United States. Now they

1. David currently resides in southern Mexico, where he is director of a medical research project.

were suddenly rootless. Home was no longer the United States, yet neither was Mexico. What Mexico gave them was a haven, rather like the sanctuary provided by the Medieval Church. The problem with sanctuary is that it provides physical safety without psychological security. Even though the Halperins had not been driven out of the States, their mentality was more that of exiles than emigrants. What they lacked was a feeling of permanence in and a sense of commitment to life in Mexico. In their minds, there was always the possibility of returning home, so they never really integrated themselves psychologically into Mexican culture. On the contrary, their emotional moorings were primarily in Mexico City's highly visible community of American expatriate radicals, and their involvement in that community only further insulated them from Mexican society.

This psychological distance between the Halperins and their hosts was not helped any by the Mexican press, which periodically attacked the American expatriate radicals as the vanguard of a Communist plot to take over the country. After a brief period of grace, Maurice took his share of these barbs and grew perhaps a bit cynical toward those Mexicans who wanted to have it both ways—to attack the American Establishment as Yankee imperialists and the American leftists as Communist subversives.

Among the expatriates, there were some who had achieved a measure of renown as political dissidents in the States before coming to Mexico. Dalton Trumbo, one of the more colorful of the Hollywood Ten, had spent some time there in the early 1950s, before returning at just about the time that Halperin was arriving.

A more durable member of the community was Albert Maltz, another graduate of the Hollywood Ten. Maltz, a longtime member of the Communist party, and a talented screenwriter and novelist, was one of Halperin's closest friends in Mexico. He and his Hollywood colleagues were the first significant group brought before HUAC after the war, when no one knew what the rules were and few people took HUAC very seriously. That is probably why they decided to rely upon the First Amendment, which turned out to be a serious mistake. As they saw it, it was the First Amendment that gave them the opportunity to transform the hearings into an arena for ideological confrontation with the Congressmen, and it was not yet clear that the First Amendment was an unacceptable defense in their situation. They wanted confrontation, but they were not out to martyr themselves. They certainly never dreamed that they would pay for their decision in federal prisons. Jail cells were for criminals, not writers.

Their second mistake was that they misjudged their foe. The game was played on HUAC's turf under its rules, and only HUAC knew what those rules were from moment to moment. The Ten didn't have a chance. They were slaughtered. Having chosen confrontation, they proceeded to alienate public sympathy by climbing down into the gutter for a slanging match with the committee. The cameras caught it all—flashbulbs popping, the gavel pounding, middle-aged men demeaning themselves by screaming at each other. The writers could not have scripted a better scene of pandemonium. In retrospect, it is difficult to know whether to feel more contempt for the patriotic treacle and political opportunism of the committee (espionage and subversion, after all, were not issues at these hearings) or for the effrontery of a few Stalinists trying to lecture America on the meaning of freedom.[2] Maltz, mercifully, was not one of the aggressive spokesmen of the Ten, but that did not spare him from doing time, along with the others, for contempt of Congress.

After his release from prison, Maltz, bitter at what he felt to be mistreatment for honestly held political convictions, had abandoned the United States and chosen to live in Mexico. At the same time, he had quit the Communist party and had become ambivalent toward the Soviet Union itself. He was increasingly critical of its rigidities, yet still often inclined to praise a silver lining where others saw only a cloud. He was groping his way toward the land of the ideologically homeless, a terrain that restless former Communists by then had been pioneering for almost two decades.

Maltz and others like him, of course, were blacklisted in Hollywood. The studios were already in trouble from the emerging challenge of

---

2. In later years all, or almost all, of the Hollywood Ten admitted to having been members of the Communist party either at the time of the hearings or within a few years of them.

television. The last thing they needed was for militant anti-Communist organizations to impose a boycott on them for employing political outcasts. Courage was at a discount in the media those days. As it is, Maltz was one of the lucky ones. The blacklist did not work a severe hardship on him, because he had enough money left from his Hollywood years to live reasonably well in inexpensive Mexico.

Still, he was a writer, a good one, and he wanted to continue writing. The trouble was the blacklist. No one would touch a script by Albert Maltz. But what about a script by John Doe or Joe Smith? The answer to that question gave birth to a new profession in the 1950s: the "front." The front was a conduit between the blacklisted writer and his market. The writer would give a script to the front, who would then submit it to a studio (or, in the case of television, to a station or network) under his own name. The producers, delighted to discover fresh talent just when they needed it, would cheerfully buy the script, and the front would then pass the money on to the real author, usually keeping some agreed-upon amount for his troubles. The only talent the front brought to the whole affair was his name, but that was a priceless asset to a blacklisted writer. It was a lovely example of entrepreneurial ingenuity, and everyone benefited. The whole process was described some years ago in *The Front*, a witty and angry movie that was made when it was safe once again to make such a movie. The writer, director, and some of the actors had all been blacklisted. Woody Allen played the front. It was in this way, by using a front from time to time, that Maltz was able to supplement his income and, more important, to stay creatively alive.

Another member of the group in Mexico was Hugo Butler, who was, like Maltz, a radical and a former Hollywood screenwriter, although he had not had the privilege of appearing before HUAC with the Hollywood Ten. Also like Maltz, Butler availed himself of a front whenever he felt that he had a worthy script to sell. In one case he was even able to double his pleasure. He sold a script to one of the studios through a front, pocketed the money, and then put the affair out of his mind. Some weeks later he received a thick package in the mail, which, to his amazement, turned out to be the script he had just sold. Amazement turned into amusement when he read the accompanying letter from the producer who had bought the script. In effect, it said, "Dear Hugo. We bought this script recently and it is just the sort of thing you used to do so beautifully. There are a few problems with it, as you will see, and we would be pleased to pay you a healthy fee to solve them. Of course you will understand that this must all be done on the Q. T." Butler understood and was delighted to help out his old friend—on the Q. T., for a healthy fee.

Another member of the expatriate community was Frederick Vanderbilt Field, who might have spent his life in relative obscurity were it not for his middle name. For Fred was a Vanderbilt, the great grandson of Commodore Cornelius, who founded the family fortune, and the grandson of William, who doubled it. In addition to being a Vanderbilt, Fred was a Communist. It was an odd pairing of traits, since the Vanderbilts and the Communists did not ordinarily hobnob with each other. The old Commodore was one of the more colorful of the freebooting buccaneers who helped build industrial America in the nineteenth century. His son, William, a Scrooge-like character, worked assiduously to rationalize the old man's empire and multiply his fortune. Because they were one of the richest families in America, and because fraud, labor-baiting, and corruption were frequently found in the vicinity of their achievements, the Vanderbilts were a perfect symbol for the Left to attack, and the Left rarely missed an opportunity to do it. But Fred was different. He was an errant piece of fruit that fell off the family tree into the lap of the Communist party. He says that he never actually paid dues to the party or held a membership card, but that he was a "member at large."[3]

Like Maltz, Field had spent time in jail for his beliefs. Called before various congressional and judicial tribunals in the early 1950s, he had tried to use the Fifth Amendment selectively, answering some of the questions put to him, and standing on his Fifth Amendment right

3. Frederick Vanderbilt Field, *From Right to Left: An Autobiography* (Westport, Conn.: Lawrence Hill & Company, 1983.) The party probably did not miss Field's dues. He estimates that he has given away about one-third of his fortune since the 1930s (276), and it is a safe bet that the party got its share. Born in 1905, Field was still a member of the party living in Mexico when he wrote his autobiography in 1983.

in refusing to answer others. It did not work that way, however. If you answered any substantive question, you were then compelled to answer other questions relating to it. Your initial answer disqualified you from claiming your Fifth Amendment right for related questions. That explains what otherwise appears to be the absurd extremes to which some people carried the Fifth Amendment during those years. It is one thing, after all, to refuse to say whether you were ever a member of the Communist party. But isn't it just a bit ridiculous not to acknowledge that you spoke at some political rally, when the newsreels plainly show that you did? And isn't it silly not to admit that you wrote a particular book, when you are shown the book with your name on it as author? No, it isn't ridiculous or silly, because once you answer either of those questions you might be compelled to answer others relating to it, or risk being cited for contempt. You have forfeited your right to silence.

The right not to testify is one of England's great contributions to the concept of civil liberties in the Western world. It emerged from bitter experience with confessions extorted by the state or the church under various types of duress, including torture. One need only think of the way confessions have been extorted in various parts of the world, including the Soviet Union, during the twentieth century to grasp the significance of this right. The Fifth Amendment may permit some people to hide their guilt, but the Bill of Rights implicitly assumes that this is a small price to pay for the protection it affords the innocent from coercion by the state. Field's mistake was not in using the amendment, but in not using it consistently. For that mistake he spent nine months in prison. Those months in a cell, plus the political harassment his wife endured, persuaded him that Mexico would be a pleasant place to live when he got out.

As it happened, Mexico City was not the first territory that Halperin and Field had occupied at the same time. Thirty years earlier they had been classmates at Harvard. That was while Field was still very much a Vanderbilt and Halperin was still very much an upward-striving Jewish scholar. Halperin was aware that Field was a classmate, but he had not known him at Harvard because they hardly traveled in the same social circles in those days. The long and sometimes painful political journey that each had taken in the decades since Harvard now brought them together in a situation where last names and family backgrounds were inconsequential. Even in Mexico City, they were not close friends as much as they were amicable acquaintances, but they were nevertheless members of the same general community of expatriates. Now, finally, they did travel in the same circles.

Somewhat more important than Field in Halperin's life in Mexico were Alfred and Martha Stern, another rather anomalous couple. Martha was the daughter of William Dodd, a University of Chicago history professor who had been Roosevelt's ambassador to Berlin in the 1930s. Later she wrote a book about her experiences in Berlin.

HALPERIN: Stern was a big philanthropist, among other things. He was a millionaire. His father was a banker in Fargo, North Dakota, of all places. He was of German ancestry and spoke German very fluently. They lived in a palatial apartment. Mainly we were invited to their luxurious place for luxurious meals. He was a sort of patron of the arts and of the intellectuals. And he had connections, political connections. For example, when O'Dwyer became ambassador to Mexico—O'Dwyer was an old friend of his—he got O'Dwyer to hire me to write a series of reports and articles about Mexico. Here he was the new ambassador to Mexico and apparently he didn't know where it was on the map.

The common denominator of this community was a pro-Soviet orientation in political matters, although the degree of commitment varied widely among them. Some were rigid party-liners for whom the Soviet Union could do no wrong and the United States no right. Others, including Halperin, took the party line with a few grains of salt and had reservations about certain aspects of the Soviet Union. Still, Halperin did agree with the analysis of world affairs that held the United States primarily responsible for the Cold War.[4] Although these

---

4. He changed his mind on this issue during his sojourn in Moscow, especially after talking with some of the "Progressives" during the "Khrushchev Thaw," who told him he was crazy to believe that the Americans were responsible for the Cold War.

people shared certain ideals, and talked politics often enough, there was an unwritten rule among them that no one would ever ask anything about the political background of another. The political discussions never got personal, Halperin says.

More than politics, music united Halperin's closer friends. Maurice had put away his violin before he entered Harvard, and he had not picked it up again until the 1940s. During the war he began to play chamber music with other amateurs in Washington, including his boss, William Langer, who was a fair violist. Halperin continued to play chamber music more or less irregularly after the war, and in Mexico City he found a community of amateur musicians of varying ability. Home base for the group was the home of Kurt Odenheim, an American businessman of German descent who had been involved in radical politics and might have been a member of the Communist party at some time. Odenheim, like the others, had found Mexico more congenial to him than the United States in the postwar years and had established himself quite successfully there as a luggage manufacturer. Each Sunday, he held an open house that featured music, potato pancakes, and on occasion, politics. Some people came to play and eat, others to listen and eat, and perhaps a few just to eat, since the potato pancakes had a great reputation in the expatriate community. The sessions lasted for hours, and generally served as an anchor for the dozen or so families that were regulars.

In addition to Halperin's various jobs in Mexico City, he took a flier at business that proved the wisdom of his previous choice of academia for a career. It was a disaster at the time but is quite funny in retrospect, as disasters often are. Not long after he arrived in Mexico, Halperin ran across a man named Bob Strand, whom he had met some time earlier in New York at the home of an erstwhile Oklahoma colleague, Ben Botkin. Botkin, a noted folklorist, was genuinely enthusiastic about Strand. His imprimatur was most important to Maurice, who held Botkin in the highest esteem.[5] Halperin was almost overwhelmed by

5. Botkin was a cousin of George Gershwin's. Halperin says that Botkin was Gershwin's first choice to write the lyrics for *Porgy and Bess*. When Botkin rejected

Strand, who was a salesman-promoter and therefore, almost by definition, an extrovert with a flamboyant personality. He had recently been
making a living selling fire engines in Peru, and was now organizing an
ice cream company in Mexico. As it happened, Maurice had around ten
thousand dollars—his life's savings—he was just itching to invest. So
he put five thousand dollars into Strand's ice cream venture. Halperin
and Strand—it was a match made in heaven—Strand's heaven.

*HALPERIN: Yes, that's right. He's organizing a company that was to
sell soft ice cream from trucks that would be circulating around the
city. Small little trucks with a freezer and the cones and so forth. It
looked like a good proposition. Well, the corporation would consist of
owners of these trucks. A person who wanted to invest bought a truck
and Bob managed the business and he got a fee for managing the
business. He had already signed up Albert Maltz and other reputable
people, including Frederick Vanderbilt Field. And so I had this money
in my hand. He was a man sent by the Lord, you know. You could trust
him. I had to do something with the money, so I bought a truck. I never
saw my actual truck, I just knew I had one because I had bought it. . . .*

*Incidentally, this corporation had to be set up a little bit illegally,
according to Mexican law. I recall that 51% of the ownership has
to be in Mexican hands, or something like that. Now, people had
specialized in setting up these corporations. The difficulty is that if
the corporation got into trouble and there was some kind of a conflict,
you are out of luck. The thing's illegal, you see. I hadn't thought about
that beforehand, but I knew about the system of making it apparently
legal so that at least the inspectors are satisfied. In other words, dummy
shareholders who did this for a fee, you understand.*

*Well, this business was a wonderful thing. It paid some enormous
dividends monthly. I forget the details now, but I think on an annual
basis maybe you were getting 30% profit on your investment. Which
wasn't unusual in Mexico and other underdeveloped countries. Capital
was very scarce and interest was very high; in this particular business,*

---

the offer, Gershwin asked his brother, Ira, who turned out to be not a bad second
choice.

interest was among the highest. One of the best businesses in Mexico.
Well, I think I saw a truck once or twice. I tasted the ice cream and it
was very nice. The ice cream machines came from Seattle, a company
by the name of Sweden. My friend, Bob, pointed out how clever that
was because people would think that the machine was made in Sweden
and not in the States, so you would get away from the anti-Yankee
prejudice. I don't know how many machines he finally sold—fifteen,
twenty, God knows. He, himself—blowhard is the word I am thinking
of. He was a blowhard.

So Halperin and the other budding entrepreneurs marched cheerfully
to the beat of this blowhard with a heart of gold. Strand was selling
the trucks and getting commissions for them, as well as taking a slice
of the profits for himself. He entertained a lot, and he generally lived
better than the investors, but no one thought much about that for a long
time. Gradually, however, Maurice grew suspicious. The investors
were asking for annual or semiannual accounts, which is standard
business practice, but Bob delayed and then delayed some more, until
the delays began to look like stalling to Maurice.

HALPERIN: So I blew the whistle. The first reaction on the part of
Maltz and some of the others was that I was unjust and paranoid. Talk
about Maltz being a little naive, you know. The others also. Actually
I think they said I was paranoid about this thing. But the data never
came up and finally what happened—what he was running was really
what we used to call a "Ponzi scheme."

A Ponzi scheme, named after a financier–con artist from an earlier
era in Boston, is a variation on the pyramid scheme. Using *Cremrica*
(for that was the name of the ice cream company—"Rich Cream")
as an example, let us say that Strand got two or three people to buy
trucks at ten thousand dollars each. They were his first investors. Then
let us say that he found two more investors at the same price. From
their twenty thousand dollars he paid interest to the initial investors at
the end of the year. This came not from profits, but from capital. The
following year he might attract three more investors and would now

pay interest from their investment to all the earlier investors. The man behind the scheme could keep this up as long as he continued to draw new investment capital, and as long as no one asked for an accounting. In the case of *Cremrica*, no one knew how much ice cream, if any, was being sold; no one knew if Strand had even bought all the trucks he was supposed to have bought.

The affair lasted perhaps three years for several reasons. First of all, he had a bunch of suckers who did not know the first thing about business. Second, his suckers were leftist suckers, which meant that they not only didn't know anything about business but that they didn't care anything about business; basically they held it in contempt and didn't care to learn anything about it, although they did not object to earning 30 percent on their investments. Third, when innocent lambs are making a huge return on modest investments, they are not likely to ask probing questions, even as they are being led to the slaughter. If they had looked into the matter, they might have learned that the money Strand was putting into their hands was coming out of the money he had lifted from their pockets. And finally, the fraud lasted as long as it did because Strand was so good at what he did. He was charming and sincere and therefore completely credible, as any good con artist must be.

HALPERIN: I have never been able to decide whether he started out with this in mind as a Ponzi scheme, or whether he was fundamentally —well, he was a salesman, of course, so he couldn't be completely honest—whether he had really expected this business would make a go. And when he saw it wasn't working he converted it into a Ponzi scheme with the hope that eventually some miracle would save him. I don't know. He was either a fraud to start with or a fraud who developed out of these difficult circumstances. He left Mexico in a hurry, and we were able to rescue something from it. We were able to sell some of the trucks. I got something like $2,000 back from my original $5,000 investment.

The final act of this tragicomedy was directed by the Mexican press, and they had a field day with it. According to their version, the great ice cream caper had actually been a successful business venture organized by foreign Communists to replenish the party's treasury. So these aspiring businessmen first got taken in by a snake-oil salesman, and then got raked over by the press for filling party coffers with tainted profits they never made. Privately fleeced and publicly vilified! It had cost the investors quite a bit of money, of which most of them had precious little to begin with, to learn that they were really not cut out for business.

When Maurice first entered the ice cream business, he had been feeling rather washed out. Before long he was very ill with a low-grade infection that nobody could locate in his body. It would respond to antibiotics and then flare up again a week after the treatment stopped. So the doctors put him in the hospital and gave him massive doses of antibiotics with the same results as before. He seemed to get better; they released him, and soon he was as sick as ever with his chronic low fever, general debilitation, and jaundice. The latter symptom suggested that something was wrong with the liver, but what?

Halperin's physician through all this was another radical American expatriate, a veteran of the Spanish Civil War named Jake, who was known fondly to his patients as Jake the Fake. After the illness had dragged on for too long, Jake decided that an exploratory operation was necessary. The symptoms were too vague. There was no pain and therefore no way to pinpoint the problem. But the indications of liver trouble had Jake worried. "I can't get any information from you at all," he said to Maurice. "It's like trying to do veterinary medicine. I'll find out what's wrong with you after the autopsy." It is a physician's joke. The patient has the option of not laughing.

HALPERIN: So I had this operation. They opened me up top to bottom. They found a liver problem which wasn't very advanced, but they also found a pelvic appendix. A misplaced appendix, which happens maybe once every hundred thousand times. The appendix is supposed to be in a certain place. Mine had slipped down into the pelvis. Therefore, no pain, no normal symptoms. Interesting. . . . It was appendicitis with a liver complication, so they took out the appendix and I healed.

By then Halperin was extremely weak from months of illness and medication, and finally from the heavy surgery he had undergone. The prescription was complete rest—away from work, away from the city, away from everything. So they sent him to a Jewish sanitarium and old-folks home in Cuernavaca. The place was not so bad, considering his earlier self-diagnosis. He had heard the whispers behind his back, and he was inclined to agree with them—cancer! "What surprises me," he says, "is that I didn't panic. I figured it's the end, so it's the end and I'm going." Fortunately it wasn't and he didn't.

The sanitarium wasn't an exciting place to spend several weeks, but it wasn't supposed to be. What it offered instead of excitement were peace, quiet, and an extraordinary individual, a man considerably older than Maurice who was also recuperating there. His name was I. N. Steinberg, and as it turns out, he was Lenin's very first minister of justice in the new Bolshevik regime of Russia. Maurice found the man fascinating. He would talk for hours about his experiences, and Maurice, too weak to talk much, listened and lapped it up.

It happens that Lenin's first government was a coalition that included some members from other parties. Steinberg was not a Bolshevik, but a Social Revolutionary, and he was appalled at Lenin's increasingly draconian approach to opposition. He told Halperin, "So I would say to him, 'Vladimir Ilyitch, look, I'm Minister of Justice. Where is the justice?' " And Lenin would reply, "Before you have justice you have to have injustice." Steinberg was concerned with justice; Lenin was concerned with revolution. Given Steinberg's perception of Lenin's personality, he felt that there was no likelihood of compromise. He was bound to lose this argument, and before long he began to feel that he might lose much more. So Steinberg left the Soviet Union not too many months after the revolution. His decision was prudent and timely, because the Social Revolutionaries fell victim to Lenin's zealous pursuit of prejustice injustice not long after that.

By the 1950s, Steinberg was busy trying to promote Jewish colonization somewhere in Africa. This was a quixotic endeavor because the state of Israel already existed. But Steinberg had grave reservations about Israel and was an outspoken anti-Zionist. "Statehood necessarily means involvement in some kind of force," he said, "some kind of crime. This is not what Jewish destiny is supposed to be. This is not our contribution to world civilization. Our contribution is ethical—to give an example." Nearly forty years after he left Lenin's Russia he was still agonizing over ethical questions. Where was the justice? One wonders what his position on Israel would be today.

Apart from occasional harassment from the more sensational exemplars of the Mexican press, the expatriate community was left pretty much to its own devices and generally cruised on a reasonably calm surface. Then, in February 1956, Nikita Khrushchev dropped his bomb at the Communist party's Twentieth Congress in Moscow, when he told the assembly that, yes, Stalin had indeed committed unspeakable atrocities for twenty years behind the facade of the cult of personality he had erected.

No single event since the German attack on the Soviet Union in 1941 so thoroughly rocked the Communist world. But there was an enormous psychological difference between the two events. The Nazi attack led to the reversal of what was only a two-year-old policy that most Communists had never really been comfortable with anyhow. Now they could once again direct their wrath toward the fascist menace that had drawn many of them into the party orbit in the first place. It would be too much to say that they welcomed the Nazi attack, but it did release them from the stress of having to swallow their hatred for fascism.

Khrushchev's speech was of another order altogether, for it told them that they had been living a lie for years, ignoring extensive testimony to the contrary that had been available to them all along. It is necessary to emphasize here that Communism, for many of the deeply committed, was not simply what they believed or how they voted. It was a way of understanding the world and a way of life. Nowhere have I ever seen this more poignantly described than in the recollections of a former party member years after her bitter break with the party:

> All my life . . . from the time I was fifteen years old, the Party was an enormous support system which came through in every crisis, political and personal, with love and comradeship. . . . And even beyond

that, beyond crisis, it was a total world, from the schools to which I sent my children to family mores to social life to the quality of our friendships to the doctor, the dentist, and the cleaner. . . . People now long for community, they're dying for lack of it. Community can't be legislated. It's an organic sense of things that comes up out of the social earth. It's a commonly shared ideal. . . . And we had it. We had it in every conscious as well as unconscious response to ourselves, to each other, to the world we were living in, and the world we were making. Right, wrong, errors, blind pro-Sovietism, democratic centralism, the lot notwithstanding. In our lives, as Communists, we had community. . . . We had that civilizing sense of connectedness, it's the heart and soul of all civilized life.[6]

For the deeply faithful, the homeland of this profound feeling was the Soviet Union; the visible symbol, while he lived, was Joseph Stalin; and the source of authority was the party, above all, the party. To understand the power of this vision, one need only look at the experience of Halperin's close friend in Mexico, Albert Maltz.[7] Maltz had joined the party in 1935, and was always more of a liberal humanist than many of the hack writers whose edicts set the party's guidelines for art. He was also more talented. The strictures of "socialist realism" had never sat comfortably with him, and finally in February 1946 he published an article in *New Masses* that called this dogma into question. Citing such authors as Galsworthy and Steinbeck, he argued that great fiction could be written by people who had no affinity for the party. Moreover, he continued, fiction that conformed to party ideology was often characterized by wooden characters mouthing puerile platitudes. The result was propaganda, not art. At bottom the article was an argument for artistic freedom, which one would think is a modest request for the artist to make.

The party did not see it that way. First the literary editor of the *Daily Worker* wrote a series of articles attacking both Maltz and

6. Norma Raymond, quoted in Gornick, *Romance of American Communism*, 115–16. Raymond's feelings toward the party were hostile, but her memories of life in it were sweet: "It was ambrosia," she said.

7. This account is taken from Victor Navasky, *Naming Names* (New York: Viking Press, 1980), 288–302.

the essay. Then Maltz was called to defend his position before a party meeting. Rational discourse was not the purpose of the meeting, however; humiliation was. It was like the feeding frenzy of a school of sharks, and Maltz was the bait. The party attached enough importance to his heresy to ship in (to Los Angeles) what Leonard Atlas, who attended the meeting, calls an "intellectual goon squad" from the East to preside over the ritual. Maltz uttered a few sentences in defense of his essay, and then he was subjected to brutal invective shouted from every corner of the room. The one or two people who tried to speak up for Maltz (including Atlas) were shouted down. The meeting ended with the admonition to Maltz that he reconsider his position before the group reconvened the following week.

The following week, the meeting, according to Atlas, was like a "hyena attack." The assault on Maltz was relentless and merciless until finally it "made him crawl and recant." He stood before the assemblage and confessed his sins, like a heretic broken by the Inquisition. He completed his self-abasement in April with a second article in which he retracted his February thoughts, admitting, among other things, that they had given ammunition to social democrats who used them to support "slanders" against the party.

This pathetic performance has become a legend over the entire spectrum of the American Left. To the non-Communist Left it was an example in microcosm of the totalitarian brutality of Soviet Communism. To Communists it was a reminder that criticism of any aspect of party ideology was intolerable because it put the entire structure of world socialism in jeopardy.

One scarcely knows whether to feel anger or sympathy for Maltz in this affair. But to say that Maltz "was humiliated" or that the party humiliated him is off the mark. The explanation does not belong in the passive voice, and the blame does not rest with the party. Maltz could have faced the tribunal and said, as Martin Luther had told *his* tribunal four hundred years earlier, "Here I stand. I can do no other." Nor was it simply a failure of courage on the part of Maltz. He humiliated himself not out of cowardice, but in the end because he agreed with the party's analysis of his behavior. His commitment to art paled before his commitment to the party.

The degree to which one accepted that kind of slavish adherence to party dogma explains the various reactions to the Khrushchev speech. To most observers at the time, the only surprise was that Khrushchev made such a speech at all. When party members confronted it, however, they were dumbfounded. I attended a debate between a Trotskyist and a Communist in 1962 at which the Communist, Herbert Aptheker, dismissed the "revelation" about the Stalin years as an "aberration." Two-thirds of Soviet history an aberration! The deeds of Stalin had been common currency outside of the party, including the non-Communist Left, for decades. To the party faithful in 1956, however, they came as a revelation.

Eventually it proved to be too much for many party members to swallow, and they left by the thousands. Within a year, party membership in the States had faded to insignificance. In Mexico the speech was debated endlessly. A hard core of true believers simply refused to accept it. There had never been such a speech, they insisted. It was all a plot, an act of CIA disinformation.

The will to disbelieve was not monopolized by the Americans, nor was it limited to the feeble-minded. Narciso Bassols, a leading Mexican intellectual and former cabinet minister and diplomat, was convinced that it was a CIA fabrication. Halperin could not budge him from that position, but Bassols was in some ways an innocent in such matters. More surprising to Halperin was Lombardo's resistance to the news. Even after he finally accepted it, he couldn't understand it. Apparently it haunted him. When he was in Moscow a few years later, he came to Halperin's apartment and admitted his confusion. How did it happen? How *could* it happen?

HALPERIN: Well, I was taken aback by this and I had to think fast and I gave him the following story. Suppose Pancho Villa took over the Mexican Revolution in 1915. What kind of a government would Pancho Villa have set up? He would talk about democracy and justice for the peasants and working class, while he established a "people's" dictatorship and murdered thousands. I said, "That's it. It turns out that Stalin was a Pancho Villa, that's all." To explain it to this Mexican all you had to do was imagine that Pancho Villa took over. A very true-

blooded revolutionary who meant the very best for Mexico. But what kind of government would you have with Pancho Villa? How many crimes would he commit for the benefit of the Mexican people?

Most of the community accepted the news and tried to fathom its meaning. To Halperin it came as a shock. He says he had never been a party member, had never been able, for one thing, to submit himself to party discipline of the sort that humbled Maltz, and he had had his doubts for years about some of the developments in the Soviet Union, such as the purge trials in the 1930s. But he had long since put these doubts "on the back burner" and had left them there, almost forgotten. He continued to believe that the Soviet Union offered a path to the future, if only to a very remote future, and he continued to accept the party line on the Cold War.

Now he was forced to address the purge trials and worse. If it had all been a lie, then what could he believe in now? What was left? What was left was not so much a belief anymore, but a hope that the speech at least proved that there was a correcting mechanism in the Soviet Union after all. It was the same hope that allowed Aptheker to see the Stalin era as an aberration. Halperin conceded that he had been wrong about Stalin's Russia, but perhaps there was still the hope that Soviet socialism would transcend the errant ways of the dictator. That hope too would dissolve in time, but for the moment it sustained him and some of the others.

Life might have gone on this way indefinitely, half in the cocoon of leftist American expatriates and half in the larger Mexican community around it, but in 1958 something disturbed this irenic situation, and to this day Halperin does not know exactly what caused it. Maurice's son, David, had just finished his first year of medical school, and was back in Mexico visiting his parents.

DAVID: It was August. We had just gone for the weekend to a resort called Valle del Bravo outside Mexico City. We came back on Sunday afternoon. We had literally just walked in the house, when the phone rang, and it was a friend of my folks who said, "Get out of the house.

Everybody is getting picked up and deported to the States." By "every-body" she meant this circle of friends in the dissident community, these political exiles. And she mentioned that Schlafrock had been dumped in Laredo [Texas] *. . . There was clearly a danger. So we walked right out of the house. We did not even unpack our suitcases. We went back to the car and drove to the house of Domingo Lavín, who was a Mexican industrialist friend of my father. So we went to this house, a very fancy house in the Lomas de Chapultepec, and they were having dinner when we got there. There was some hurried conversation between Dad and Domingo, and we were put into one of his cars, and his chauffeur drove us to Cuernavaca, about an hour-and-a-half's drive away—to his house in Cuernavaca, which was a very palatial establishment surrounded by a high wall. We were introduced to the housekeeper as the Smiths. And basically he said, "You'll be safe there. So just go there and let's see what's going on."*

Frederick Field recalls the same situation in his autobiography. He was informed by a lawyer in the Mexican bureaucracy that orders had been issued for his arrest and deportation. The message advised Field to disappear for the time being, which he did without further urging. He had already spent time in a federal prison, and he had no desire to do a second stretch. So he hastened to Cuernavaca (Halperin did not know that he was there at the same time), spent two days there at a renowned and expensive inn, and then proceeded to Acapulco, where he stayed, with a second (unnamed) American fugitive, at the house of another Mexican bureaucrat for ten days. "Ten of us in all had been targeted for this round-up," Field says. Three were caught and immediately flown out of the country, never to return. "The others, including myself, were luckier. They were warned of what was about to happen and managed one way or another to keep out of the way of the authorities."[8]

Like Halperin, Field did not know exactly what triggered the act. He thinks that the American embassy, unhappy at the hospitality shown

8. Field, *From Right to Left*, 289.

these leftists by Mexico, brought some sort of pressure to bear on the Mexican government. David, on the other hand, links it to some general unrest in Mexico at the time. He recalls that the electrical, telephone, and railroad unions were having big demonstrations and that some elements of the press blamed Maurice and the other "American revolutionaries" for arousing domestic discontent. In any event, after ten days in Acapulco, Field was given the all-clear signal, and he resumed his normal life in Mexico City.

Halperin received no such signal. The Mexicans were still looking for him, and he had no wish to return to the States. He did not know what awaited him there, but federal "correction" seemed a possibility, and he had no desire to be corrected. This put him in something of a quandary, because he, a Yankee in Mexico, could not expect to remain incognito indefinitely. The only realistic alternative open to him was to move to Europe. But how realistic was that? He still had to eat, and America's NATO allies were not enthusiastic about sheltering her political exiles at the time.

Actually, Maurice had been facing the likelihood of a bleak future in Mexico for some time already. There was a possibility that some of his sources of income would dry up, and he seemed to be at a dead end for others. He was able to get by, but how long could he continue to do so? He had been discussing this situation with a few influential Mexican friends for some time already, and two of them in particular, Lombardo Toledano and Narciso Bassols, had been trying to persuade him that there was a way out.

Lombardo was the preeminent labor leader in Mexico and a long-time fellow traveler. Bassols had been, at various times in his career, secretary of the treasury, secretary of education, and ambassador to the Soviet Union. Like Lombardo, he was a fellow traveler insistent upon maintaining his independence from the party. Yet, he was even more admiring of the Soviet Union than Lombardo. Both men were Marxists, both were fellow travelers, yet they had been carrying on a bitter public polemic and had developed a deep personal animosity toward each other. Of the two, Maurice preferred Bassols, who lived modestly and was a man of immovable integrity, while Lombardo lived almost lavishly on his wife's money and operated comfortably in Mexico's political Establishment.

Both of these men told Maurice that they could help him get situated in the Soviet Union. At first the idea seemed far-fetched. The Soviet Union had always existed as an abstraction for Halperin. Other people lived there, but the thought of setting up housekeeping there with Edith had never entered his mind. At the urging of his friends, he now began to consider the proposal more seriously. The Mexican police were looking for him, and some sort of move was imperative.

But first he had to get out of Mexico. The key person in the deal that was eventually worked out was Domingo Lavín, who was a personal friend of former president Lázaro Cárdenas.

DAVID: In those days the tradition in Mexican politics was that ex-presidents had their political fiefdoms. Cárdenas had a state—Michoacán—that he owned. And a huge following. And although his faction wasn't in power, he was extremely powerful. What got communicated to me was that through the connection with Domingo Lavín— the lesson was that Cárdenas was very powerful and that you could get a favor from Cárdenas. But Dad said, "You must understand,"—he was telling me; I was 21—"You must understand that sometimes you're in a position to get a favor from somebody who's very powerful, but you only get one chance. So you don't use that lightly." He said, "The fact that I have connections to Cárdenas is very important. I've never used it. Now is when I will use it, because this is the only chance. He won't do me another favor."

It was a bit like the genie in the bottle, except that you only got one wish. And it was not the intervention of the supernatural this time at all. Cárdenas was very much alive, and what he had to offer was power, which happened to be in very short supply in the Halperin household just then.

David, young as he was, was chosen as the intermediary because he was not in jeopardy. He went to Mexico City and called the minister of the interior to confirm the deal that had been made through the intervention of Cárdenas. If Halperin was allowed to return to Mexico City, he and Edith would leave within three months.

DAVID: It was an important lesson to me about connections to powerful people. You may have a friendly acquaintance with someone who is powerful, and in fact they may do you a favor—once. So you want to guard that relationship very, very carefully. And you may never use it, which is probably best of all. But if you need to, you must know that you're only going to get one chance.... So I went back to Chicago and within a few months they left. They were expelled from Mexico.

Once Maurice and Edith left Mexico they were out of peril and off to the unknown. For David it was just the opposite. He returned to the familiar, and he was about to learn that being the son of Maurice Halperin was, in itself, perilous.

Actually, David thinks that his admission as an undergraduate to the University of Chicago a couple of years earlier was facilitated by the Dean of Students "to kind of make up for the sins of academicians who kept their mouths shut while everybody else was suffering." And it helped that David had a bag full of strong recommendations, including one from the head of President Eisenhower's Committee for the Arts and Sciences. It was written by Robert Rogers, who had been Halperin's administrative assistant at R&A during the war. A man of impeccably moderate political credentials, Rogers praised the "fine and loyal family" that David came from. A letter like that makes it easy for a dean to do a good deed.

The trouble did not begin until after David was in medical school and his parents were in Russia. He drove with some friends to Mexico over the Christmas vacation of 1959, and after a spell in Acapulco, they went on to Mexico City, where David saw several old family friends. The University of Chicago Medical School had a system at the time that allowed its students to spend part of their clinical year studying elsewhere, and it seemed to David a perfect opportunity for a reunion with his parents. So while he was still in Mexico, his father arranged for him to spend an academic quarter working with a prominent cardiac surgeon in Moscow, a man who later became minister of health. By no means did David have to lower his standards for that appointment either, since cardiac surgery was very advanced in the Soviet Union at the time. David received the school's permission to go ahead with the plan, and he was elated.

DAVID: Well, I got back to Chicago and it so happened that my next rotation was the obstetrics rotation and I was working in the Night Birth Room. So I had no reason to be anywhere except the hospital at night. In the daytime I was mostly asleep. And that was my rotation for the next two or three weeks. So it was probably a month after I had gotten back—at the end of January—that I wandered into the Dean's office. His secretary looked at me and she just turned green. And she said, "My God, you're here!" I said, "Sure. What's the problem?" She said, "Just a minute." And she went and got the Dean and he came out, and he turned pale. He said, "Come into my office." And he said, "We were told that you had defected to the Soviet Union from Mexico, carrying documents." The FBI—this information came from the U.S. FBI. They got the information from the Mexican FBI.[9] I said, "Did it occur to you to call my apartment to see if I was there? Or maybe to call one of my roommates? Did you check to see if maybe I was in the Night Birth Room where I was scheduled to be?" You know, they just took it on faith. . . . The practical result was that the Dean said, "I don't think it would be a good idea for you to go to Moscow." I said, "Gee, you know, it's all set up and everything." He said, "Well, not only do I not think it would be a good idea, but I don't even know if the Admissions Committee would readmit you to school next year." So I said, "Well, actually I didn't want to go anyway."

That was the beginning. When David was called before his draft board in 1961 he was given a list of mostly left-wing organizations of the past and present and asked if he had ever belonged to any of them. Ordinarily this was a routine matter for all draftees, but given

---

9. David was elated when he received the appointment, and he told some of Maurice's old Mexico City friends about the forthcoming trip to Moscow. It is quite possible that there was an FBI informer among them.

David's background, he did not see it as routine. David was not a Communist, but he was a socialist of a newer breed, and he had attended a Communist party meeting or two out of curiosity at the University of Chicago. He feared what might happen if he said that he was not a member of the party, and then someone came forward to say that he had seen David at a party meeting on such and such a date. Feeling that he did not need that kind of trouble, and that no one had the right to ask him such a question anyhow, he refused to answer.

DAVID: So I got called up for a special interview by the Selective Service people. There were some uniformed people there and they asked me the questions all over again, and I refused to answer them. This time I had a lawyer with me. So they said, "Would you submit to a lie detector test?" My lawyer, who was very smart, said, "Wait a minute, you don't believe that he's refusing to answer this question? You think that's a lie? You think he really wants to answer that question? What do you use a lie detector for if he refuses to answer the question?"

But the army had the last word. Since David was a physician, he could only be called up as an officer. He was not called up. Instead, he was given a 1-y classification, which meant that he was mentally or morally unfit. In the upper right-hand corner of his draft card was a "p," which meant political.

Even that was not the worst of it by a long shot. Politics returned to haunt him while he was doing his residency in general surgery at the Hines Veterans Administration Hospital outside of Chicago. With two thousand beds, Hines was the largest VA hospital in the country. To receive an appointment to a residency there was an honor, and David was more than pleased with it.

DAVID: Three or four months after I started, I got called in. Actually I was on call in the evenings in the Emergency Room, and before my shift I got called in by the administrator of the hospital, who was a very elevated figure, a big shot in the VA system. He said, "I've been instructed to inform you that you are hereby separated from the Veterans Administration." I said, "Why?" He said, "I'm not at liberty

*to tell you." Then he said, "Have you talked with your father recently?"
I said, "Well, no, we write letters." He said, "Oh. Okay, if you'd like
to, you can work tonight's shift in the Emergency Room." Tonight! So I
said—by this time I was a grown-up—"Well, first of all, I don't accept
being fired. I can't imagine that you can fire me for no reason. And
second of all, while I deal with this, I'm not going to work tonight in
the Emergency Room."*

This was far more serious than anything he had faced before, so
he went to his lawyer, who agreed to take the case without a fee
since David had no money. This meant that David had to do the basic
research for the case himself, laboriously copying all the relevant VA
documents on employment for the lawyer. What the documents told
them was that it was almost impossible to fire someone from the
VA, except for total incompetence. Furthermore, there was an appeals
process that ended with the president. Armed with that information,
they challenged the decision; they appealed, and David was ready to
take it up to the president if necessary.

He took other steps as well. First he called Walter Palmer, an old
professor of his who was head of gastroenterology at the University of
Chicago. Palmer was, in David's words, "very wealthy, very WASP,
and very Gold Coast of Chicago." David had been his intern for a
while and had a very close relationship with the man. Palmer was
appalled by David's story and immediately called the medical director
of the VA, who happened to be a good friend of his. He was off the
phone in five minutes and told David that the order to fire him had
not come from the VA at all, but from "another government agency,"
and that his friend, the medical director, could not do a thing about it.
Interestingly enough, the medical director had not even had to ask his
secretary for a file on the case. He already knew all about it. Palmer
was not able to do more than that, but he did at least confirm David's
suspicion that someone from outside had put pressure on the VA. To
David this could only mean the FBI.

He was right. Years later he applied for his file under the Freedom
of Information Act. References in the dossier that arrived indicate that
some documents were withheld, and much of what he did receive

was inked out. But the censor was curiously lax with the VA affair. Enough remains to draw a fairly clear picture of what happened. David was hired by the VA on July 1, 1962.[10] In a memorandum of August 15, 1962 ("Subject: David Carlos Halperin") to a Mr. Mohr (whose identity is unclear) from Cartha DeLoach, one of J. Edgar Hoover's top assistants, DeLoach says, "It is recommended that I confidentially brief Jack Gleason, Administrator for the Veteran's Administration, who is personally known to me, concerning the background of Maurice Halperin." Remember that this was years after Maurice had left the country and that this memo about him was in David's file. In a communiqué of August 24, Hoover directed the Chicago Bureau to "submit a letterhead memorandum concerning the employee [David] suitable for dissemination, succinctly characterizing his parents to reach the Bureau by 8-31-62." The memo went on to note that "arrangements were made through Mr. DeLoach's Office to confidentally [*sic*] clue VA Administrator re Halperin's background. This was done on 8-21-62." On August 30, the Chicago Bureau replied that it had very little relevant information on Maurice and Edith and that Hoover should try the Boston Bureau.

Evidently sufficient information was found somewhere, because in a September 25 memorandum to William Sullivan, Hoover's assistant director of the Bureau, W. A. Branigan says that they "confidentially furnished this information verbally to John S. Gleason, Jr., Administrator of VA, and subsequently forwarded to that agency a letterhead memorandum prepared by Chicago setting forth some background data concerning subject's father." The memo goes on to note that David was fired by the VA on September 10 and that on September 21 the hospital was notified by his attorneys that he was appealing his dismissal. Two days later Hoover referred to a Bureau "airtel 7-18-62 concerning captioned individual [David]," and notified the Chicago Bureau to "check your files for any pertinent information available concerning (David) Halperin and alert your sources for any

---

10. The following account is taken from relevant documents in David Halperin's FBI file. Instead of standard footnote citations, I have alluded to the relevant documents in the text.

data relating to his action." This airtel from Hoover included a cover memo of uncertain date from Branigan to Sullivan, stating that "previous investigation conducted by us regarding David Halperin developed no information indicating that he was a member of the Communist Party (CP) or of communist front groups." The memo went on to note that the VA had "dismissed Halperin on the basis of information furnished concerning his father's background and Mr. Turner, VA, advised he would greatly appreciate any additional information we could furnish him concerning David Halperin himself." Branigan said that the VA should be advised "that we have no further information regarding David Carlos Halperin."

Pieced together, these fragments reveal a most disturbing picture. David Halperin started to work for the VA on July 1, 1962. By July 18, the Bureau knew about his job and had circulated some sort of memo about him. By August 15, somebody "recommended" that Cartha DeLoach brief the VA administrator, John Gleason, about Maurice—not David, but Maurice—Halperin. Since there were few people in the FBI senior to DeLoach, and since Hoover himself was active in this affair, it is obvious that it was Hoover who "recommended" DeLoach's action. On August 21, DeLoach spoke to his friend, Jack Gleason, about the unsavory history of David's father and subsequently had the Chicago Bureau confirm that informal discussion with "background data" about Maurice in a "letterhead memorandum." There can be little doubt that he asked Gleason to have the younger Halperin fired and that Gleason passed the word on to the director of Hines Hospital. David's dismissal was justified in terms of his "failure to meet VA standards," which was demonstrably absurd. In fact, David was fired solely because of derogatory information about his father, as the FBI itself admitted.

This whole grim tale is a case study in anti-Communism gone berserk and an object lesson in the abuse of power. For what is painfully clear is that Maurice was the real target in the affair, not David. The problem was that Maurice was out of Hoover's reach. David wasn't, however, and David's name undoubtedly came before the FBI in the routine security check that accompanied his appointment to Hines Hospital. Hoover was evidently apprised of this and directed his agents in Chicago to see what political dirt they could dig up on David. They found nothing, but that did not stop Hoover. He then had a little package of information prepared on Maurice and Edith and presented it to the VA administrator, who used it to justify David's dismissal, although there were no security issues involved in David's job at all. When David fought the dismissal, Hoover once again directed the Chicago office to find something on him, and the Chicago office once again drew a blank. The inescapable conclusion is that the FBI—Hoover, really—made a willful effort to destroy the life of an innocent man because it was the only way to punish the man's father.

A rancid aroma surrounds this whole affair. For some reason Hoover was carrying on a vendetta against Maurice. Angry because there was no way to get at him in Havana, where he was living at that time, Hoover saw a way of getting at him through his son. But why was Hoover doing this? Maurice had been out of the country for nine years and presented not the slimmest threat to American security. Anyhow, in the larger scheme of things he was small fry, so why spend all that effort on him?

Well, we know that Halperin had unwittingly embarrassed Hoover early in 1942 with his report to Donovan about the situation in Mexico. And Hoover was known not to forgive and forget easily.[11] Perhaps he was upset that Halperin had slipped away when things were heating up in 1953. Perhaps he was even more upset when Halperin escaped deportation from Mexico back to the United States in 1958. Perhaps he

11. Melvin Purvis was a case in point. Purvis had been in charge of the FBI "G-Men" who tracked down and killed both John Dillinger and Charles "Pretty Boy" Floyd, two of the legendary gangsters of the 1930s. After the completion of each case in 1934 he received a lavish letter of commendation from Hoover. By mid-decade he was a national hero, better known than his chief. At that point, Hoover apparently began to perceive him as a rival, or perhaps as a publicity hound who was a threat to the Bureau's integrity. For the remainder of Purvis's life, Hoover seized every opportunity to downplay his role in the Dillinger case and to send out damaging reports to prospective employers. Hoover was almost obsessed with the need to destroy Purvis. Purvis, terminally ill, committed suicide in 1960. See Richard Gid Powers, *Secrecy and Power: The Life of J. Edgar Hoover* (New York: Free Press, 1987).

was furious at his failure to even the score with this man after fifteen years. And perhaps he finally saw a way of getting back at Halperin by destroying his son. Absurd? Of course it is, but it is consistent with the Bureau's outrageous effort to destroy a man (David) against whom, by its own admission, it had nothing and could find nothing even when virtually ordered to do so. It is pure conjecture, but it will have to do until a more convincing explanation comes along.

David had no way of knowing any of this in 1962, although he suspected FBI involvement from the outset. So he proceeded along such paths as were available to him. He took his tale to Rabbi Weinstein, a prominent Jewish clergyman in Chicago, who was on President Kennedy's Commission against Discrimination. Weinstein balked at first, saying that he was only supposed to deal with matters of discrimination. David pointed out that he was Jewish and that there just might be some discrimination involved here. Weinstein agreed and said that he would have his Washington office look into the matter.

Next, David contacted the two senators from his state with interesting results.

DAVID: This is very instructive. Let me start with Senator Douglas. We had Mr. Liberal and Mr. Conservative.[12] *I called Douglas and I talked to his legislative assistant in Chicago, who said to me, "You know, the Senator just can't afford to be associated with this kind of problem. Your father lives in Cuba, and the Senator does so much good work that he can't afford to be tainted with this. It would destroy his effectiveness, which none of us would want to happen." Then I called Senator Dirksen's office, and it was absolutely routine for them. "The Senator's constituents come first. His job is to deal with federal agencies. I'll have this on his desk on Monday morning." Absolutely straight. No Communist stuff. You got a problem with the VA? That's what the Senator does. I don't know what he did about it, but the attitude was very businesslike. The constituent is king! I was amazed.*

---

12. In terms of their popular images, this is not an inaccurate characterization. Douglas was thought to be one of the two or three most militant liberals in the Senate. Dirksen, who had a talent for self-parody, was commonly (and inaccurately) paired with Barry Goldwater in the far Right of the Republican party.

Time passed and they had gotten only silence from the VA. David was beginning to get very worried. Then a friend and former classmate from medical school called with another possibility. He was from a small town in Montana, and his sister had once gone out with Mike Mansfield, another of the Senate's staunch liberal Democrats. "If you don't mind," he said, "I'll call Mike Mansfield and see if he can do anything about your situation." No, David said, he didn't mind at all. A week later he got a call from Hines Hospital and was told that he had been reinstated without prejudice and with full back pay.

There is an epilogue to this story. Years later David returned to Chicago for a dinner honoring the long-time chief of surgery at Hines Hospital, who was retiring. All of the man's residents from years past attended.

DAVID: Puestow was his name, and he was a very prominent, and also a very conservative, society surgeon. Dr. Puestow called me aside and he said, "So glad you came all the way from Maine. You know, I was asked to fire you for professional incompetence. And I felt really pressured because this was the FBI. They said it was a matter of very important national security. But I just couldn't do it, because you weren't incompetent and I told them so. I asked them if they couldn't find some reason that had to do with the problem of national security, and that ended the interview." Again it was an example of somebody without politics, or with politics I would have been opposed to, who was so principled. . . . It would have been so easy for him to accede. I mean, the FBI is a powerful organization. He had integrity and he felt safe because he was getting old, had money, was WASP, and so forth. But for me it had been a matter of life and death, because if I had been fired for professional incompetence, I would have had no recourse. It would have ruined my career for the rest of my life. So I feel incredibly indebted to Dr. Puestow.

So the FBI first tried to get David dismissed on a charge of professional incompetence. Such a charge would probably not have withstood a legal challenge from David. But the charge was never made because the Bureau was unable to budge an honest doctor. The FBI then apparently turned to officials somewhere well up in the VA bureaucracy and persuaded them to do the job. The trouble was that they had no justification for their action.

The only mystery remaining from this sordid affair is who or what persuaded the VA to take David back. To this day he doesn't know. Was it his letter working its way slowly through the bureaucratic process? Was it the rabbi? Or was it perhaps one of the senators, and, if so, which one? There is another possibility that shows up in one of the FBI documents. In an October 10 memorandum, D. J. Brennan notified William Sullivan that Halperin had been reinstated five days earlier and that "his previous termination was wiped out administratively from the records of VA as if it had never happened." The reason? The VA's general counsel "advised that the manner in which Halperin had been dismissed was technically wrong and the deficiency in the way it was handled could not possibly stand up in any court proceedings brought against VA by Halperin." In other words, faced with a lawsuit, perhaps the VA simply caved in because it didn't have a legal leg to stand on.

Of course, with the Halperin family, there is always the possibility that the supernatural was at work again.

6

Eastward Ho!

For the second time in five years the Halperins prepared to move. They had taken their earlier moves more or less in stride. The youthful venture in Texas had been eased by the fact that they shared a language and some cultural symbols with the Rangerites, and also by the knowledge that it was not going to be permanent. In Paris, the language, the history, and the culture were Halperin's intellectual equipment as well as his bread and butter. Maurice had prepared for the move to Oklahoma with two years of graduate work and teaching there; and Washington, New York, and Boston were no problem at all. Mexico had been more difficult, because it meant leaving families, friends, and cultural roots for an indefinite period, perhaps forever. It was a foreign nation, but at least he and Edith were familiar with the land and its language because they had been going there with some regularity for twenty years. They could adapt easily enough to Mexico.

The move to Russia was unlike all the others. For years the Soviet Union had been an ambiguous symbol for Halperin. He had had reservations about its political excesses since the 1930s, but he was always able to see the glowing ideals through the dark realities. He differed from the true believer by conceding those dark realities instead of denying that they existed. But he could not fully resist the promise of ideals that had been dear to him since he was a young man who had not even given any thought yet to the Soviet Union. These were the ideals of the French Enlightenment that had enchanted him since his days at Harvard. If reality fell short of the ideal, there was reassurance in the knowledge that a revolution is not made in a day or a year or even a generation. It was that hope that led him to interpret the Khrushchev speech as a sign that there might be a correcting mechanism in the system, even as it confirmed some of his worst fears about what had been going on in Russia for years.

But Russia had always been remote from his personal world. Now it was to become his home and he had no idea what to expect. He knew little about day-to-day life in the Soviet Union, he couldn't speak a word of the language, he didn't even know the alphabet. He did have one thing going for him, however: he had a job waiting for him in Moscow. Lombardo Toledano had arranged for him to receive an appointment to the Institute of World Economics and International Affairs of the Soviet Union's Academy of Sciences. Maurice was taken on as an expert in the Latin American section.

At that he was fortunate. When he arrived in Mexico he did not have a passport, but that was no problem because he didn't need one in Mexico. To travel elsewhere at the time would have been a problem, because the passport office of the State Department was making it extremely difficult for some people to get them. In 1952 the State Department announced "that members of the Communist Party, those who supported its goals, or those whose activities abroad would advance the Communist movement could be denied passports."[1] And the sole apparent arbiters of what activities might advance the Communist cause were Ruth Shipley of the passport office and her successor in 1955, Frances Knight. In the hands of these two militant anti-Communists, and especially in the climate of the early 1950s, Halperin would never have been issued a passport.

This placed enormous discretionary powers in the passport office, and it raised serious questions about the constitutionality of the State Department's edict. Various lower court decisions had overturned specific passport denials during the decade, and finally, in 1958, the Supreme Court severely trimmed these discretionary powers in the case of the artist Rockwell Kent, when it said that the passport office could not, as a rule, deny a passport on political grounds.[2]

---

1. Stanley Kutler, *The American Inquisition* (New York: Farrar, Straus & Giroux, 1982), 97.
2. Ibid., 89–117. Stanley Kutler discusses the political and constitutional issues involved.

Halperin applied for his passport soon after this decision, but he was told that it could take an exceedingly long time for his application to be processed, and that there was still no guarantee he would get a passport at all. In other words, he was being stalled. At this point he was put in touch with Leonard Boudin, who was Rockwell Kent's lawyer, and who was having passport problems of his own. Boudin was specializing in such cases at the time, and he agreed to press Halperin's suit against the State Department. Since the generic decision had already been made in the Kent case, the passport office was really defenseless, and Halperin got his passport at the eleventh hour. The case of Halperin v. John Foster Dulles never came to court.

The Halperins left Mexico in the fall of 1958 and decided to make their journey a sightseeing vacation. They traveled at a leisurely pace down through Central America to the northern coast of South America and then on to Europe. They spent some time in Lisbon and then went on to Switzerland, visiting Zurich, Geneva, and beautiful Lugano. From Switzerland they flew to Prague, which they gave a mixed review. The city had survived the war intact and had a great deal of charm. They were especially impressed with the well-preserved old Jewish ghetto, and with the cemeteries, which, for lack of ground area, had had to expand vertically underground, with headstones on the surface pointing in every direction, like an expressionistic fantasy. They were less impressed with the way the Czechs were treating the city. This was Halperin's first actual contact with Eastern Europe and it was, he says, "an eye opener." After Switzerland, the city seemed dismal and polluted with the smoke of brown coal.

From Prague, the couple headed for Moscow in a train crowded with Russians who were returning from vacations at Czech resorts. Some of them could speak English, which eased the journey somewhat, and all of them were strikingly open and friendly. It reminded Maurice of a similar experience in Spain almost thirty years earlier, when everyone had wanted to help the Americans, telling them what to do, where to eat, and how much to pay for this and that. He found the same sense of hospitality in the Russians. "It is what you wouldn't find," he says, "if you walked into a railroad car full of Frenchmen." The other thing he noticed about the Russians was their tremendous curiosity about the outside world. They wanted details about everything. Introduced to the Soviet Union in this way, through its people, Halperin was relieved and encouraged about the future.

The trip to Moscow took two days through terrain that was blanketed with snow and as flat as Illinois. Along the way they came within twenty-five miles of Gritsev, the town that Halperin's family had left at the turn of the century. They arrived in December and were met by the Intourist people who put them up at the old Metropole Hotel, pending the completion of a security investigation of Maurice. By this time Maurice was an accomplished hand at being investigated. He had undergone an extensive security investigation in the OSS. By the time he was cleared, he reckoned he was the most secure person in the agency. Having proven during the war that he was no Communist threat to capitalism, he was now forced to wait until the Soviets could prove to their satisfaction that he was no capitalist threat to Communism. It took about three weeks before he was cleared to receive an apartment and go to work at the institute.

Throughout Halperin's discussions of Russia there is a sense of otherness. He never seems to be at all integrated into what he is describing, not even to the extent that he had been in Paris and Mexico City. Whether he is describing the topography, the architecture, the people, or the job, he always speaks as an outsider, an observer looking in on something he is no part of. He speaks, as always, in the first person, but reading the transcripts of our interviews on Russia is more like reading a novel or a travelogue written in the third person. There is that much separation between the observer and the observed. That was never the case when he talked about his experiences anywhere in the States, or in Paris and Mexico City.

Perhaps it is this sense of estrangement that explains what seems to be Halperin's heightened awareness of his Jewishness in Russia. In a land where everything else is strange, there is security in anything that is familiar. Generations of immigrants from Europe, Africa, and Asia have impressed that reality onto American life, and now Maurice was reversing the pattern of his own parents. He was the stranger in a strange land. He did not actually seek out the company of other Jews in Russia, but he was intensely aware of it, and he welcomed it because he felt comfortable with it.

In one way his Jewishness came up just as a matter of day-to-day life. His family had come from Russia where the name—Halperin is pronounced Galperin there—is quintessentially Jewish. Thus just introducing himself was a way of identifying himself. "Hello, my name is Galperin." That sentence included the unspoken tag line, "I'm Jewish." And from time to time the introduction was met with the rejoinder, "Oh, you're Jewish. So am I." On occasion, that identification was uttered almost furtively by people who did not particularly want to be known in public as Jews. Why were they reluctant?

The question of anti-Semitism in the Soviet Union has been a matter of public debate in America for years. Officially, of course, there was no anti-Semitism there because it is against the law. In fact, one of the things that made the Soviet Union attractive to many Jews was their awareness that the Bolsheviks had made anti-Semitism a crime shortly after the Revolution. That the Bolsheviks felt compelled to do this is a comment on the ferocity of anti-Semitism in tsarist Russia, both among the people and in the regime itself. After that, anti-Semitism was never a matter of official policy as it had been under the tsars, although the sentiment survived the Revolution, and the government was not above playing on it when it suited its purposes to do so.

But what about the fact that Jews had to have their Jewish identity stamped on their passports? Actually this is not as insidious as it sounds. Jews were considered a nationality group in the Soviet Union, and all of the many nationality groups had to have their national identities stamped on their passports. The intent was not consciously anti-Semitic, although the consequences might have been, because anti-Semitism was imbibed by many Russians with mother's milk. On the whole, though, it remained possible for Jews to do reasonably well in Soviet society, especially if they were not too visibly Jewish, and above all, not Zionist in their sympathies.

Halperin illustrates the existence and the effects of a subtle anti-Semitism in an interesting way. One day he met one of the researchers at the institute who worked in a geographic, rather than an area, section. "My name is Galperin," said Maurice. "Oh, are you Jewish?" was the response. "Yes I am," said Galperin. "So am I," said the Russian, although he had a Russian, rather than a Jewish, name. As they got to know each other better, and as it became clear that the man was anxious to talk about things in general, Maurice invited him several times to come to dinner with his wife, but the answer was always the same—his wife was too ill and they couldn't make it. Maurice got the message: I'll see you at work but not socially, and that was that.

The following summer the Halperins took a holiday in Karlovy Vary (the famous Carlsbad spa) in western Czechoslovakia near the East German border. It was a long way from Moscow, but through the institute they were able to arrange for a room at one of the hotels reserved for Russian tourists. To his surprise, Halperin ran into the Jewish geographer from the institute there, and he was like a different man. He peppered Halperin with questions and wanted to talk and talk, though always away from the hotel, where, he feared, the walls had ears. "Let's take a walk," he would say, and they would talk, but always outdoors. He was starved for knowledge about the outside world, and, as it turned out, often totally misinformed about it.

It was in his observations on Jews in America that he completely amazed Maurice. He was convinced, for instance, that the Rockefellers were Jewish, and Halperin took pains to disabuse him of the notion. On another occasion he informed Halperin that wartime ambassador Harriman was Jewish. Maurice did not know whether to laugh or cry. He described Harriman's family background and brought the man grudgingly around to the realization that Harriman was not Jewish. "But Harriman visited a synagogue while he was here," the geographer said. Maurice explained that Harriman did this not because he was a Jew, but because he was a politician. That explanation entailed in turn a brief discussion on the nature of ethnic politics in the States. It was difficult for the man to grasp, because in Russia the only people who visited synagogues were Jews. Here, then, was a highly educated Jewish professional who had taken as gospel the anti-Semitic stereotyping the government had found it convenient to use in its anti-American propaganda. In order to discredit capitalists, you make them out to be Jews. Hence the Rockefellers and the Harrimans were Jews.

In the Halperins' years together, it was Edith more than Maurice who had provided a Jewish environment in the household. Maurice did not have a religious bone in his body, and had it been left to him, the household would not have had a strong Jewish framework. He had no problem with his Jewish identity, but it was tied to cultural factors in which religion played no role, and about which he did not have intense feelings. It was just there, a significant part of family life, but nothing he ever really worked on. In his discussions of Oklahoma and Boston, for instance, he makes occasional references to things Jewish—a friend, a situation, a job. But these were things usually mentioned only in passing. At the same time, he almost never mentioned in passing that such close friends as Woodrow Borah and Albert Maltz were Jewish. It was just taken for granted. Only after he came to Russia did the subject play a larger role in his mind, and that seemed to have more to do with the circumstances of his isolation than with the circumstances of his Jewishness.

It was not so much a general sense of Jewishness as a specific quest for his own roots that led Maurice to search for any of his family who might have survived the war. The opportunity came unexpectedly when he was hospitalized for minor surgery in 1959. The doctor assigned to his case spoke English, and when he saw the name Galperin he identified himself as a Jew also, although he had a purely Russian name. The doctor, whose name was Viktor Krylov, agreed to help Maurice try to get in touch with his relatives in Gritsev, and he wrote a letter in Halperin's name to the governing council of that town. The quest for lost relatives was still common in the late 1950s, and Halperin's request was turned over to the leader of the Jewish community in Gritsev. Most of the Jews had been evacuated from this area of the Ukraine before the Nazi advance, and many had returned after the war.

The leader of the community wrote back, saying that the family survivors were actually living in the Moscow area right at that moment, one family in the city and another in a nearby village. When Maurice contacted the Moscow family through an interpreter-friend, it became clear immediately that these people wanted nothing to do with an American relative. Instead, they put Halperin in touch with a first cousin, a woman who agreed to bring her husband along to see Maurice at his apartment, but not at hers. They discussed relatives and made small talk and agreed to meet again in Halperin's apartment. She had two brothers who were members of the party. They would have loved to see him, but they hoped he would understand why they could not afford to. She returned to see Maurice some months later and stayed only briefly before leaving. Maurice walked her to the subway.

HALPERIN: And she said, "You know, we live in this thing. In a sense we already have Communism in my apartment. We have a communal apartment with four families sharing a kitchen and toilet." She talked about the difficulties and also the question of the neighbors and of being a Jew. And she said, "You know, if you came to see me—an American—it could endanger us. I mean, they would hold this for blackmail against me. They could squeal that we had an American come to visit us." And I don't think that was paranoia on her part. Of course, this wasn't supposed to happen any more with Mr. Khrushchev. But nobody was taking a chance. Everybody knew the machinery was still there. So it was a memorable walk in which she unburdened herself about how things were absolutely horrible in every respect. And I never saw her again.

Maurice was learning that meeting people outside of work would be no easy task for him. It did not make any difference whether they were relatives, chamber musicians, or those met at chance encounters. Either they would have him at their house but would not come to his, or they would go to his but could not have him at theirs; and in a few cases they would simply not see him anywhere. The reason was the same in all cases: they were afraid to be seen with an American.

Maurice had still not seen the relative in the village outside of Moscow, so one day he went out with Dr. Krylov to see the man. When they arrived, they were warmly welcomed into what Halperin calls a comfortable "shack," where the parents and their grown daughter lived together. In some ways the visit was a replica of the visit with the Moscow relative. This one did not mind speaking more or less openly in his shack—Who would bother to wire a shack, after all?—but he asked Maurice not to visit him at the Moscow supermarket that he supervised, where the likelihood of surveillance was much greater. The daughter worked as a stenographer in Moscow, and the Halperins offered to put her up in their apartment when the weather was particularly bad, but they met with the same rejection. It was impossible. She could not afford to be seen consorting with Americans. The fact that they were first cousins meant nothing. The sense of frustration that Maurice felt at this behavior was overwhelming. "How these people survived this fantastic thing. . . . I still think of it now," he says. "And I still think of what Gorbachev has to face."

Other complexities of being a Jew in Russia were illustrated by the doctor. After their professional encounter in the hospital, Maurice and Viktor became good friends, and they remain in touch with each other to this day. One day Krylov opened up to Halperin and told him the story of his own background. His grandfather had been kidnapped from the ghetto at the age of eight and "drafted" into the tsarist army. The machinery for military conscription was not very efficient in those days, and kidnapping was a fairly common way to fill the ranks. The term of service for these child recruits often ran as long as forty years.[3] At the end of their time, they were released, given a modest pension, and permitted to settle anywhere in Russia. For Jews caught up in this process there was one definite advantage; it meant that after their discharge they did not have to return to the Pale—the areas where Jews were compelled to live. Of course, those who were impressed as young boys were inevitably baptized during their military service, and often they had little or no recollection of being Jews when they got out anyhow.

Krylov's grandfather did remember when he was released forty years later, and he resumed his life as a Jew when he settled in the city of Sverdlov, where he married a Jewish woman and started a family. One of their children was the parent—Halperin does not know

---

3. Histories of immigration often mention escape from military service only in passing as a reason why some Europeans came to America, especially after the Civil War. In fact, it was a powerful incentive for many immigrants. Conditions and length of service were particularly onerous in the Russian and Austro-Hungarian armies. The prospect of twenty to forty years of service motivated many to search for an alternative.

whether it was the father or mother—of Viktor Krylov. Krylov thought of himself as a Jew, and was so identified on his passport, but there was little of Jewish culture about this completely Russified man with a Russian wife. Because of their mixed parentage, his children were permitted to choose their nationality for their passports, and chose Russian nationality. This neither surprised nor bothered the doctor.

Krylov was not simply a physician in the North American sense; he had a Ph.D. in medicine and was a highly skilled specialist. He was also the protégé of a very powerful man in the medical bureaucracy, so he was reasonably well protected in the system. With a career in an elite profession, an apartment of his own, and a car, he lived quite a comfortable life. There seemed to be no barriers to his advancement. Yet, while the system permitted him to move upward, it did not permit him to move outward. He was not happy that men who were junior to him in years and competence were allowed to leave Russia for professional meetings elsewhere in Europe, while his own applications for permission to attend these meetings always got lost in a bureaucratic fog.

The fact is that the government was afraid to let highly trained Jews out for fear that they would never return. So Krylov was aware that being Jewish imposed occasional minor disabilities upon him and that anti-Semitism had a way of flaring up after periods of dormancy, but he was quite content with his life in the Soviet Union and had no wish to flee. That is what made his near-confinement inside Russia so galling. It was not until years later that he was finally allowed to attend professional meetings out of the country.

The Jews that Halperin knew in Russia fell into the same category. They were not tradespeople, or artisans, or blue-collar workers; they were professionals whom he usually met one way or another through his work at the institute. They were part of an elite, and on those grounds they had some claim to middle-class creature comforts. They were highly assimilated and not overly troubled by the discrimination they occasionally encountered. The Khrushchev thaw was treating them well. The rising clamor for emigration in the 1970s reflected different realities and perceptions, but Halperin saw little of this in the early 1960s.

The Halperins moved into their apartment in January. It was in a new building, and by Soviet standards, it was quite comfortable. They were twice blessed because they didn't have to share it or its bathroom with anyone else. Many middle-class Soviet couples were not so fortunate. It was located directly across the street from the Ukraine Hotel, which Halperin describes acidly as "one of Stalin's architectural wonders." It might have been ugly, but it was convenient since Maurice had only to cross the street to buy a newspaper. Even that was not easy, since at first the only papers available there that he could read were the *London Worker* and the *Paris Humanité*, both of which were Communist party organs. Before long, however, he pestered the hotel into bringing in the *New York Times*, a lifelong addiction of his. Now, with his regular *Times* fix, he felt in touch with the world again.

The apartment itself was the smallest space he had ever lived in. The living room and bedroom were each about eight by twelve feet, the kitchen even smaller. There was a toilet in a small cubby hole, and a bath (no shower) and sink in the kitchen. And there were problems.

HALPERIN: I couldn't imagine a new building like this, the workmanship so shoddy. Even the outside—some of the bricks were crumbling already and it had just been put up. There was an elevator there that used to creak, and a dingy staircase. It was a building that had no youth. It was born old. I didn't know how they could do it.

The building was enormous. It was built around an inner courtyard and housed hundreds of families. It fronted on Kutovsky Prospekt, a major boulevard that was dominated by the Ukraine Hotel. To the rear it looked out on another world, an old Moscow village of small shacks, a bit of tsarist Russia surviving intact. Occasionally the Halperins would gaze down on this village and see people bundled up to their ears against the searing cold, scurrying from their shack to and from an outhouse, because there was no indoor plumbing in the entire village. At thirty-five below zero, one does not make a leisurely visit to the outhouse.

When Halperin's daughter, Judith, visited with her husband in the spring, Maurice took them for a tour of this village. It was like going back four centuries in time, he says. But the people, as always, were warm and friendly—and curious and astonished. Amerikanits! Here were Americans in their obscure little village. The Halperins might as well have been Martians. They were as unreal to the villagers as the village was to the Halperins.

When the government tore down this village and moved its inhabitants to a new area, the old people wept. They didn't want to leave. The young people were delighted, of course, because to them it meant progress, which included indoor plumbing on wintry mornings. The old people had no objection to indoor plumbing, but they did not want it at the expense of their community. It was an ancestral home with family roots curling back through centuries. If they were moved to new quarters, they would lose that sense of organic relationship with an area and with each other that defines community. But they had no choice. The bulldozers came, the village disappeared, and they moved.

There were parallel experiences with "urban renewal" in some American cities at the time, and Halperin encountered the same phenomenon a few years later in Cuba—people being moved to new apartments and weeping as they watched their old shacks being demolished. The sense of community is a powerful force that taps deep into our feelings and does not always fit comfortably with modern techniques of rational planning. Halperin, always the rational man, had a kind of epiphany in this experience with an ancient village and its people in Moscow.

When Halperin started his job at the institute, he spoke only the few words of Russian he had picked up in his first weeks there, which is to say that for all practical purposes he spoke no Russian at all. Fortunately this was not an obstacle in his work, because all his colleagues in the Latin American division spoke Spanish and understood English as well. But it was an impediment to social discourse, and it certainly did not make things easier at work, Spanish or no Spanish. So the government assigned him a tutor. With the lunatic logic that often characterizes bureaucratic decisions, the government chose a tutor whose specialty was teaching Russian to Arabs. He was marvelously fluent in Arabic, but he did not speak a word of English. At that, the problem was an advantage in some ways, because it prevented Halperin from using English as a crutch. He was forced to learn Russian (or Arabic) in order to communicate with his tutor at all.

That did not bother Halperin as much as the antiquated techniques of language instruction this fellow had been taught. After all, Maurice had taught language himself for many years and had the expertise to make such a judgment. But bit by bit he learned. He also grew quite fond of his instructor in the months they worked together. The lessons were held in Halperin's apartment, and in time a friendship grew out of their professional relationship. The tutor had a great curiosity about the outside world and a healthy skepticism toward the official explanations available to him. Halperin calls him a "closet dissident."

Like most teachers, and especially teachers of language, Maurice wanted to speak the language correctly—to get the right gender and the right number and the right case, and to get the accent to the point where it was at least comprehensible. As a result, he usually spent so much time trying to put a sentence together correctly that he had a devil of a time communicating at all for some months. Then one day he read about a Turkish poet who had come to Moscow suffering from that same beginner's disease: make it perfect. The Turk learned quickly to pay no attention to the grammar; he just spoke the language. His Russian was atrocious, but he communicated.

HALPERIN: And that gave me an idea, and I started in and it was wonderful. Just paid no attention. Made all kinds of errors, but I could be understood by educated people. With less educated people I had trouble. I remember once I went shopping and I made a slight mispronunciation and the girl behind the counter didn't understand me. But somebody beside me—and I could tell by the clothes that she was a cultured person—explained to the girl what I was saying. So we made it. Of course, I couldn't do a deep philosophical discussion, but once I got onto the idea of just speaking without paying attention to the grammar, I got by.

The institute where Halperin worked was part of the Academy of Sciences, which is the most prestigious academic institution in the Soviet Union. It dealt with the non-Communist world (another institute dealt with the Communist world), which it divided into geographic sections. There was a North American section, for instance, and a European section. Halperin worked in the Latin American section. His impression was that the best people were assigned to the North American section, the worst, to his own section on Latin America. In fact, he was shocked at the level of ignorance that prevailed among a group of people who were supposed to be specialists in Latin America.

The institute was housed in a pre-Revolutionary building, where the facilities were predictably antiquated. By the time he started to work there, he was beginning to feel that anything old was shabby and anything new, shoddy. The administrators and section heads had private offices. The rest of the personnel sat at assigned places in large reading rooms. There was indoor plumbing, but the toilets fell below Halperin's standards. By now the toilets of Moscow were becoming a concern of his. At best they were unpredictable. Among Westerners, he figured, only the French would be oblivious to such deviant toilet behavior. When they worked they seemed to groan in protest. And they didn't always work. The toilet paper was usually *Pravda*, which he judged to be superior to sandpaper, but not really up to the standards of the *New York Times*. Because of the stench, the windows were always kept open, which made going to the toilet in winter an adventure.

The cafeteria stood in about the same relationship to Western cafeterias as the toilet did to Western toilets. This *stolovaya*, as the cafeteria was known, was a kind of lunch counter where the average meal would consist of meatballs, perhaps, along with cabbage and potatoes. Halperin found the food there uniformly unpalatable and indigestible. Consequently, for dessert he usually popped a couple of antacid pills, a huge supply of which Albert Maltz had brought along on his visit in 1960. Halperin called them "stolovaya pills" in honor of the cafeteria. He never went to work without them. He notes, by the way—without further comment—that this restaurant was for the elite.

It was not just the convenience facilities that were deficient at the institute. There were also serious problems with the way work was carried on, and these problems were built into the system. Library facilities were a case in point. There were two libraries at the institute, one closed and the other open. Both of them were closed to common citizens. No one could just walk in off the street and use them. Within the institute the open library was available to all researchers, but the closed library was open only to senior members. Halperin was considered a senior member. The idea was to keep "dangerous" material from inexperienced hands.

It was all quite alien to Maurice, since most of the material in the closed library would be on open shelves for undergraduate use in any university library in North America. The *New York Times* was in the closed library. Stranger still, sets of encyclopedias were broken up, with some volumes of a particular set found in the open library and others from the same set found in the closed. If the authorities, in their wisdom, decided that a particular encyclopedia handled a particular subject in an unacceptable way, the entire volume containing that subject would be wrenched from its set and placed in the closed library. If you wanted to look up "Texas," you might have to go to the closed library because someone did not like the way that volume handled "Trotsky." The safe volumes in the set remained in the open library. If you happened to be a junior member doing research on Texas, that was too bad. You would have to look it up in an encyclopedia that had a more satisfactory treatment of Trotsky.

The institute itself had no control over this situation. Instructions came down from the Censorship Office, and the directors had to obey them. Like any bureaucratic agency, the Censorship Office had to justify its existence by producing. Since its product was censorship, the more it censored, the more it proved its worthiness. It followed from the logic of bureaucratic procedure. On those terms it proved its worthiness to a fare-thee-well. Halperin had to go along with this, but he never got used to it. On one occasion he got fed up with the system and rebelled.

HALPERIN: I remember one time I was in the closed library and there was a book that had just come in, some book of geography, and I couldn't imagine for the life of me why it was in the closed library. There was a girl sitting there at the desk, and I asked her, and she said she had no idea. So then I said, "You know, this is extraordinary. If an airplane dropped a million copies of this book in Russian over

Moscow, it wouldn't possibly be subversive in any sense you can think of." I was indignant and I looked around—there were people there— and everybody had his head way down. Nobody had heard anything like this ever, you understand. Once in a while I would engage in a little indiscretion like this. It was a habit of many years.

It was such indiscretions that had gotten him fired from Oklahoma University, and performances like this one did not win him any bonus points in Moscow.

Still, it is necessary to look past these deficiencies in order to understand what the institute represented, and, in a larger sense, to grasp what was going on in Russia at the time. For one thing, this was the period of de-Stalinization known as "the Khrushchev thaw." How this thaw was perceived was largely a matter of perspective. Halperin, who had not known Moscow before the thaw, was annoyed by the censorship and bureaucratic nonsense that made his work difficult, but Russians were exhilarated by the air of liberation wafting from the Kremlin. This air definitely settled on the institute. Its director was the brother-in-law of Anastas Mikoyan, the number-two man in the Soviet hierarchy at the time and a reformer. Consequently, the institute was the academic center of "progressive," essentially anti-Stalinist, sentiment. This meant that many of the people there spoke quite openly and frankly with Halperin. They voiced grievances and expressed hopes for change. The same statement, the same sentiments, would have been unthinkable ten years earlier. This sense of change, of hope, was exciting to Maurice and a necessary antidote to the censorship and other depressing realities he encountered all around him.

Although the scales had tilted toward the "progressives" at this time, their counterpoise existed in the "reactionaries," as the progressives called those who opposed the Khrushchev reforms. That the progressives also sometimes referred to their opponents as the "Black Hundreds" is revealing. The Black Hundreds had been essentially private armies employed especially by provincial elites to overturn the liberal Revolution of 1905. They were little more than hired bands of thugs who represented the most retrograde elements of the old regime in Russia. In this way the progressives used one of the most hated memories of tsarist Russia to characterize those who stood fast for the hard-line policies of Stalin. The term clearly evoked images of reaction, repression, and thuggish violence. No greater insult was possible.

The institute sponsored several kinds of work. At one level it served as a kind of think tank where researchers carried on projects and wrote reports at the request of the government. Another kind of work was done according to the plan that was laid out for the institute at the beginning of each year. The various geographic sections would be given specific projects and would then divide up the work among the personnel for completion by the end of the year. This was probably the least successful aspect of the institute. There was something almost ritualistic about it. Since there was supposed to be a plan for everything in the Soviet Union, the institute had a plan each year. And each year it would be unfinished by the time the plan for the following year came down. Meanwhile, individual researchers were permitted to work on their own projects if they had the time to do them. Finally, the institute served as an academic training center where young researchers could work on their doctorates. For the few people admitted to this program the demands were high and the work difficult. They were expected to produce a very substantial dissertation—in effect, a book on a significant subject.

In time, Maurice was able to do most of his assigned work at home. That presented him with a problem, however. He worked with a small portable typewriter that he had brought with him, but he had no furniture of the proper height to type on. And one did not simply go out and buy a typewriter stand in Moscow. The solution was easy enough. He stole. He went out at night and pilfered bricks and boards from construction sites until he had enough to hold his typewriter at the proper height. After all, he thought, it was just moving materials from one government project to another. This has been a standard solution to similar problems among American servicemen for years. To describe the process they invented the term "scrounging," a pleasant euphemism that disguises the fact that necessity is often the mother of felony.

Halperin's job at the institute was what he wanted to make of it. He was considered a political guest who had come highly recommended by Mexicans, which carried some weight in his section. If he wished, he could have put in his time by just sitting there, or at home, doing nothing, which was a privilege that was not extended to Russians who worked at the institute. Thus he was treated with considerable deference, at least for a while. He worked because he wanted to work, and he managed to publish a few things while he was there.

But he was appalled at the low level of competence of most of the personnel working with him. He couldn't help comparing them with the team that had been assembled in the Latin America Division of the OSS. The difference was awesome. Moreover, the ignorance of the Russians was compounded by the hidebound dogma that many of them imposed upon their work. He remembers one occasion when he was invited to participate in the discussion of a paper by one of the women working there. Halperin took the invitation seriously and prepared for it accordingly. He even had a colleague help him with the Russian.

HALPERIN: Well, I read this miserable piece and I decided that I had to do something about it. After all, I was living there high off the hog in Soviet terms, and I felt a sense of obligation. Or maybe it was indignation. I don't know what moves me on these occasions when I become imprudent. So there was this discussion, and then it came my turn and I just laced into this thing fiercely, no holds barred. I said at the beginning, "You know, I have a lot of things to say and I want to say them as clearly as I can, so I am going to use English instead of Spanish." They all knew English. OK. So I laced into the thing, ripped into it and just tore it to pieces—interpretations, data, and everything—and I talked about dogma and about I forget what all. I may have talked for an hour or more. I just went on, page by page, line by line. Well, these people were listening and when I finished, not a word. Dead silence. It was very interesting. Dead silence. I looked around and nobody wanted to look me in the eye. The lady who wrote the stuff was right there. She was a regular member of this outfit. She had some kind of academic degree or she wouldn't have been there.

They all had some kind of academic degrees. Well, the session ended then. Not a word. We all got up, left the room and started for the stolovaya, *and people were talking to me as if we had been somewhere else. It was as if the whole thing had never happened. But I am sure that one of the reactions was that some people were glad I did what I did. There were among those people those who were fed up with the dogma.*

The abysmal quality of this paper and the silence that greeted Halperin's critique only hardened his already low opinion of the Latin Americanists at the institute.

On other occasions it was not so much dogma as politics that interfered with Halperin's work. Not long after the Bay of Pigs disaster he wrote an article for a Soviet publication in which he angrily attacked President Kennedy's Latin American policies. But somewhat surprisingly so soon after the aborted invasion, official policy in Russia was to go easy on Kennedy. The editor of the journal called Halperin in and suggested a few softenings and a few deletions that would have altered the tone of the article and brought it into line with official policy. He was very nice about it, suggesting rather than insisting, but Halperin was adamant: he would not change a word. To his credit, and perhaps to his peril as well, the editor printed the article as submitted.

Halperin could understand the editor's problem. He operated under well-defined if changeable political restraints; Maurice was challenging these and putting him in jeopardy. It was a different matter with the personnel at the institute. Perhaps there wasn't much they could do about the dogma that hobbled their thinking, but he felt that they could at least inform this dogma with accurate information. There was nothing to prevent them from informally upgrading their credentials by doing a little extracurricular reading in the closed library, which was well stocked with a wide variety of uncensored material, except for the occasional excised "slander" emanating from the West—an unflattering cartoon of Khrushchev in the *New York Times* perhaps or some highly critical analysis of Soviet economic problems.

Halperin even found a copy of Djilas's *The New Class* there. Djilas was the Yugoslavian Communist who had incurred Tito's wrath with his argument that the great ideal of a classless society had produced instead a self-appointed and self-perpetuating ruling class that was responsible for the bureaucratic inertia of Soviet-type societies, and for the economic and political problems that followed from this situation. The presence of a book so critical of the Communist social system indicates that nearly everything was available there. Indeed the book was a revelation for Maurice himself. He says it was "like a searchlight" for him. He was aware of all the details it spoke of, but Djilas was the first person in a Communist nation to put those details together and explain them to his satisfaction.

Halperin did find highly competent people at the institute, especially in the American and Italian sections. The younger people in particular impressed him as being bright, informed, and inquisitive, if somewhat cautious in the range of their inquiries and the boldness of their observations. Many of them would seek him out for conversation in the *stolovaya*, when they might have been prudent to steer a wide path around the American. They tended to be skeptical about the ideological implications of Soviet scholarship and enjoyed questioning this outsider in a way that revealed their reservations. It occurred to Halperin that these relatively open-minded and critical youngsters were part of a cadre who would one day challenge their elders for control of the nation. He told Edith that he would not be surprised to see the emergence of a leader from this corps who would move the Soviet Union in new directions. At the time, however, the prospect seemed quite remote.

The Halperins took advantage of their tenure in the Soviet Union by traveling extensively, often to places that seemed quite exotic to their American eyes. One of these journeys took them into the southern Ukraine to make a movie down near the Black Sea. Mosfilm, the large state movie production company, was doing a movie that called for someone to play an American professor. Maurice was born for the role. He tested for it, and it was his. He was given the title of "artiste," an overblown term for a walk-on who had about thirty words to speak.

HALPERIN: It was a film that extolled the life of a very famous academician whom Lenin had persuaded to work for the Revolution. He was an expert in animal husbandry and was associated with an institute that was actually very close to where we were filming. . . . The picture was really a pot boiler, basically speaking, but the whole experience was extraordinarily interesting. I didn't see it until much later, and I didn't know the whole story, but the part that I was involved in was where the academic goes to the United States to buy sheep for breeding stock. And I think this was in Kansas. My job was to stand beside the academic when the sheep were sent down the runway and try to persuade him that these were good sheep when they weren't. In other words, I was supposed to try to swindle the academic. I was doing my patriotic duty as an American—trying to swindle him. When I saw the picture I was watching for my part and it came and went like that. Zing! About twenty-one seconds. Edith and I sat and looked at each other. And to get those twenty-one seconds we spent a week there.

Halperin does not recall what the sheep were doing in Kansas. Perhaps the meeting took place at a railhead. Or perhaps it was a case of sacrificing geography to art. In any event, the call for American professors in Soviet films being somewhat limited, this was the end of Halperin's career as a matinee idol.

More of an eye-opener than the movie was the town in which the film was shot. Maurice does not recall the name.

HALPERIN: Well, this town—let's say approximately 5,000 people— was incredibly run down. The shops, empty. This was 1961. The streets were full of mud, half paved, half unpaved. There was no hotel in town, no movie house, no pool parlor, no bowling, no tennis. I don't know what they did. It was a depressing place. We were billeted in the City Hall. They put up beds there, sort of a collective. But there were no indoor toilets there or anywhere else in town. There was a large public outhouse with no indoor plumbing. They had to come and shovel it out. I don't know how often they cleaned it, but certainly not often enough. They should have cleaned it three times a day and they maybe cleaned it once a week. So you find the shit all piled up and the odor absolutely deadly. This was for the entire town, a brick building in the center of town.[4] *It's the worst thing I've ever seen. Much better to go out in the fields somewhere. Actually, I couldn't use the place. If I went in there I would want to puke. I suppose one can get accustomed to anything, but coming from the States we had been used to indoor toilets and good plumbing. I had been in outhouses where it was possible, but this was just terrible. People coming in and out. And the irony was that on the outside there were big signs that said "Long Live Our Glorious Communist Party" or "Forward to the 22nd Party Congress" or whatever they said. All the slogans were there on the outside of the outhouse.*

To Halperin it seemed inane. You don't decorate an outhouse with sacred slogans. It was like putting frosting on a pile of garbage. Still, as with everything else he experienced, judgment was relative. Halperin's point of reference was American middle-class plumbing, and his judgment was merciless. For all he knew, however, this was a nice new brick outhouse that had replaced a rickety and dangerous old wooden one. From that perspective the judgment would probably be quite benign.

Unfortunately that perspective was clouded by the town's proximity to the Institute of Animal Acclimatization, where scientific research was done on the relation of animals to their environment. This was the same institute that had been featured in the movie, and it was a different world from the town; it was clean, neat, hygienic, and thoroughly modern, as far as Halperin could see. And it was immediately adjacent to the town. He says it was like crossing the street from one century to another. "The research center apparently had no influence on the town which was right next to it," he says. "You would think there would be some part of the culture seeping into the town. No. The two could have been separated by a thousand miles."

When Halperin thought about it, he couldn't help but compare this town with Ranger, Texas, where he had begun his adult life more than

4. The image of a brick outhouse brings to mind a slightly different American expression of purely metaphoric dimensions and rather different intent. There was nothing metaphoric about this brick outhouse; it was memorably real.

thirty years earlier. It was about the same size as Ranger, and about as far from Moscow as Ranger was from New York. But there the similarities ended.

HALPERIN: Ranger in 1926 had paved streets, indoor plumbing, movie houses, restaurants, pool parlors, bowling alleys, a hotel. The railroad went through. That's right. In 1926, 5,000 population, several thousand miles from New York, and it had practically all of the creature comforts. I mean, you couldn't get caviar in Ranger, and you couldn't get gourmet foods, but you had all of the contemporary creature comforts in a town of that size and that distance from the center. And here is this town in 1961 still extraordinarily primitive. And I could see what the problems are of development in a place like that. I mean, with all of the mistakes they made and all of the crimes they committed they really had a formidable task in modernizing this barbarian people. I would bet this place that I visited in '61 hasn't changed. From what I read it would be one of the last places that Perestroika *would reach. . . .*

The Soviet Union was an experience that one couldn't possibly anticipate in any way. You could be an intellectual giant and have read everything and you wouldn't have anticipated the details, and the details are so important. You live the details.

While Halperin was in the Ukraine he got to know several of the scientists from this nearby institute because they were artistes in the same movie. He sat with them on the grassy plain outside of town, and they talked for hours. The scientists, most of whom spoke English, were anxious to "unburden," which they felt safer doing out under the stars than on the set. They spoke of their harrowing experiences under the Stalin regime. Surprisingly, many of them were not much more sanguine about a future under Khrushchev than they were about the past under Stalin. Perhaps there would no longer be the midnight knock on the door, but as one of them said to Maurice, "Listen, you have to remember that our people until very recently have been semi-barbarians." The implication was that it would take a long time to educate semi-barbarians to function effectively in a modern society.

Later that year, in the summer of 1961, the Halperins pressed their travels in a different direction when they went touring through Uzbekistan in Western Asia. In those days the Soviet Union meant Eastern Europe to most Westerners. It meant Moscow and Leningrad and perhaps the Ukraine. Only recently, first with the internal strains revealed by *glasnost* and then by the disintegration of the Soviet Union, have we become aware of Soviet Asia. Uzbekistan lies well to the east of the Caspian Sea. The ancient city of Samarkand is less than two hundred miles from Afghanistan and not much further from Pakistan; it is more than two thousand miles southeast of Moscow. It is a different world, and the Halperins were dazzled by it.

When they set out eastward they expected the worst. They had only recently come from the disheartening trip to Ukrainia, and they carried with them stereotyped images of the squalor of Afghanistan and Pakistan and India, images of open sewers, beggars in the streets, and filth everywhere. They were therefore relieved and delighted when they found cleanliness, a sense of order, and even a modest degree of prosperity compared to what they had expected. It occurred to them that anyone entering the Soviet Union for the first time from the East would be quite favorably impressed after leaving the grinding poverty of Pakistan, for instance. Entering from the West, however—even from Czechoslovakia—created exactly the opposite impression; one sensed a steep drop in all expectations about standards and styles of living. Again, it was a matter of one's point of reference.

Their first impression of Uzbekistan was confirmed as time passed. They found food to be better than it was in Russia itself. There were pleasant teahouses scattered about the cities that lent an air of leisure that was absent from Moscow. Halperin had the impression that this Asian republic adapted the best features of its indigenous culture to the Russification that the Soviets were imposing on the region. In that sense, it was somewhat similar, he says, to what American imperialism did for Cuba in eliminating some tropical diseases and bringing pure water and modern techniques of sanitation. Of course, it also brought a certain amount of economic and cultural exploitation, and created a huge reservoir of resentment. That, too, was replicated in Uzbekistan, where Soviet efforts to Russify the population were met with fierce resentment and resistance.

By this time the Halperins were seasoned tourists. Their travels had carried them all over the Western Hemisphere as far south as Brazil and through much of Europe as well. Ordinarily they satisfied their hunger to learn about the places they visited by chatting with the local population, as well as with people in more exalted positions. Now, for the first time, they ran into a stone wall with a local population. With varying degrees of proficiency they could get by in French, Spanish, and Russian. But they didn't speak a word of Uzbek, and the Uzbekis, it seemed, did not speak any of the Halperins' languages, including Russian.

They breached this communications barrier by accident one day in Tashkent, the capital of the republic. They were walking in the main park when they overheard two women speaking Yiddish as they sold soft drinks from a pushcart. Halperin was startled at first, because in Moscow Jews would not speak Yiddish in a public situation like that. He approached them and spoke to them in Yiddish, and they were more shocked than he. Strangers rarely stopped them to speak in Yiddish; Americans never did. It turned out that the women were European Jews who had come to Uzbekistan during the war. Maurice recalled then that Stalin had sent perhaps as many as a half-million European Jews to Soviet Asia as the German armies advanced in the summer of 1941.

To this day no one is sure why he did it. Did the anti-Semitic Stalin seize upon the German invasion as a pretext to rid Soviet Europe of hordes of Jews? Or was this an act of charity aimed at saving Jewish lives? Whatever his motives, the deed did save a few hundred thousand lives, and most of these refugees simply remained in the East after the war.

From Tashkent the Halperins traveled to Samarkand, one of the fabled cities of the world. Samarkand had been on the path of trade routes and warring armies since antiquity. Alexander the Great had stopped there on his way to India; the Moslems had overrun it and brought to it their religion in the seventh century; Tamarlane had conquered it and used it as a base of operations at the end of the fourteenth century; and the tsars had brought it into the Russian Empire in the nineteenth century. Halperin was amazed by the presence of all this before his eyes. He found that he could go out into the fields and actually pick up artifacts that lay there loose, including coins that dated back almost to the time of Alexander. Of course, these had long since been picked over for the most valuable finds, which were now safely housed in the town's museum. There were also buildings standing from the time of Tamarlane, including a magnificent mosque and Tamarlane's mausoleum. The Soviet government was taking good care of these buildings, restoring those that were in disrepair.

One thing that struck Halperin was the widespread use of tiles on the buildings, tiles of a light blue color and specific designs that he immediately recognized from his travels years earlier in Spain and Mexico. He realized that the source of these colors and designs was Arabic culture. The Arabs had brought them along in their conquest of Spain, where they were an integral part of southern Spanish culture by the time the Moors were driven out. From Spain they were brought to the New World, where they were integrated into Mexican and other Latin American cultures. Just as the Arabs had brought them westward across the Mediterranean, they had also brought them eastward and northward in their conquest of Central Asia. It was a fascinating lesson in the spread of culture. Here, however, unlike Spain and Mexico, the religion as well as the cultural artifacts had survived.

From Samarkand the couple proceeded to Bukhara, another ancient city that had fallen to the Moslems. What particularly interested Maurice here was the existence of a sizable Jewish community of quite a different kind from those he had encountered elsewhere. European (and therefore North American) Jews had originated, of course, in the Middle East, then spread westward over the Mediterranean basin, and then northward and finally eastward through Europe. One strain had lived in peace under the Moors in Spain for centuries until both Moors and Jews were driven out at the end of the fifteenth century. Most of these "Sephardic" Jews resettled elsewhere in the Mediterranean basin, especially in North Africa. The rest of the European Jews, far more numerous, had settled north of the Pyrenees and as far east as the Urals over many centuries, and by the nineteenth century were themselves extremely diverse in cultural and religious traditions. These were the "Ashkenasim," and were the source of most of the immigrants who came to North America.

The Uzbeki Jews, who were so plentiful in Bukhara, were not part of the westward diaspora. They had come directly northward from Palestine, following much the same route that the Arabs had pursued in the seventh century. And now both groups lived, apparently amicably, in Uzbekistan. Halperin did not even know about these Uzbeki Jews until he noticed that most of the locals wore one kind of skullcap, while the remainder wore quite a different kind. He was told that the prevailing style identified the Muslims; the rest were worn by the Jews.

In European Russia, Halperin had found some comfort in sharing a common heritage with the Jews he encountered. What struck him in Uzbekistan was that he seemed to have nothing in common with these Asian Jews. To whatever extent such generalizations are valid, their appearance, like that of the Muslims in the region, was characteristically Middle Eastern. They were, on the whole, smaller and darker than the European Jews. Unlike the women with the soft drinks in the Tashkent park, these Jews spoke no Yiddish, which is, of course, a European language, and Maurice spoke neither Hebrew nor Uzbek, so there was really no way for them to communicate. Since Halperin is not religious, he began to wonder just what he did have in common with these people. Perhaps there was some vague awareness of a shared heritage of old traditions, but if it existed it formed no significant bond. Even the North African Jews he had met had struck a familiar chord. They spoke French together, their clothes were similar, and they looked at least somewhat alike. But he shared none of these things with the Uzbeks. "I guess I had nothing in common with them," he says, "except maybe one thing. Uzbek Jews and Jews like myself were always candidates for the gas ovens. Maybe that's the common denominator." Whether Uzbeki Jews are aware of this remains unknown, but it is a rather grim comment on a crucial factor that shapes the mentality of Halperin and others who share this feeling.

In some ways life in the Soviet Union for Halperin consisted of occasional bright events punctuating the otherwise humdrum day-to-day life at the institute. The movie in Ukrainia was one such event, the trip to Uzbekistan, another. Many of these events taught him things about Russia that he had not known when he arrived. He did not need his time at the institute to teach him about the perils of dissent, although it certainly verified what he had been hearing for years. But he had not really known much about the remarkable cultural variety of this huge nation. That lesson was brought home to him when he experienced it in Central Asia. He learned other, less pleasant things during his stay in a Soviet hospital.

Halperin was already suffering from a hernia when he came to the Soviet Union, but he had tried to avoid surgery by wearing a truss. It was not enough, so eventually he agreed to have surgery. Through the Academy of Sciences, he was assigned to an eminent surgeon by the name of Petrovsky, who later won the Lenin Prize for surgery and became the minister of health. This was the same man who was Krylov's teacher and sponsor.

Now, most Soviet citizens cannot ask the Academy of Sciences to find a surgeon for them, and the surgeon they do find is not usually someone of Petrovsky's stature. Halperin, however, received preferential treatment. It wasn't supposed to be that way in a classless society, but there it was. And Halperin did not protest at all. He went to Petrovsky's office in the Surgical Institute, another pre-Revolutionary structure, for an examination, and Petrovsky agreed to do the surgery.

HALPERIN: He said, "Now, I can do the operation in the Kremlin hospital or in my own hospital here, whichever you prefer." Well, having the spirit of adventure, I knew I would learn nothing in the Kremlin hospital; I would just get my hernia repaired. I would be comfortable and enjoy life, but I just couldn't resist the idea of seeing what went on in Petrovsky's hospital. So I said, "No, might as well do it in your hospital." Well, I went at the appropriate time and they had an English-speaking doctor to admit me—take my history and the usual thing, you know. In our conversation he said, "You are Jewish, of course, aren't you?" I said, "Yes." And he said, "So am I," although he had a Russian name, and didn't look at all Jewish. [This was Krylov.]

As always, Maurice felt vaguely comforted by this as he was being led to his room. He felt rather less comfortable when he arrived. The tiny room had six beds in it—three on each side of a very narrow aisle—and they were close enough together so that one could reach out and touch the next bed without stretching. Although it was late winter, the window was kept open—he later found out why—and the room was freezing cold. Fresh air was one thing, but this was ridiculous. There was a refrigerator in the corridor, and wives, mothers, and other assorted helpmates were encouraged to bring in food for the patients to supplement the institutional salami and porridge that was otherwise the daily fare.

The next day Maurice came down with a cold, and the operation had to be postponed. That was all right with him, since he could return home and at least escape the porridge and salami until he had to go under the knife. But his scheme ran afoul of the authorities, who told him it was against regulations for him to leave until after the surgery. Halperin had stood up to the Jenner Committee, and he was not about to back down now before a bunch of hospital bureaucrats. He raised such a racket that they sent Krylov in to explain things to him. He explained that if Maurice left, it would create a big scandal. It just wasn't done. Maurice replied, "Okay, there will be a scandal." He left. Later he found out why the patients thought he was mad. For most of them the hospital was a step up in living standards. Although many of the facilities in the hospital were antiquated, they were better than those that the patients had at home. And so was the food. Salami and porridge do not qualify as haute cuisine, but there was plenty of both, and one did not have to stand in endless lines to buy them.

When he returned to the hospital after nursing his cold, he was placed in another six-bed room, and this one was filled with men who had all sustained major injuries during the war and were still in bad shape almost twenty years later. It brought home to him just what these people had gone through to survive the German invasion. It was on this second trip that Maurice learned more about the facilities of the hospital. He learned that the tap water was not potable, because the pipes were from the turn of the century and managed, on occasion, to transform water from a modern purification plant into something on a level with toxic waste. In the one huge communal toilet on the floor, he learned why the windows were kept open. The toilets were as old as the water pipes and about as reliable.

HALPERIN: They also had big benches in this toilet where the enemas were given. They were given, you might say, in a communal spirit. Certainly a communal atmosphere. And who gave the enemas? Elderly women who were specialists in enema giving. They weren't nurses or anything, but they wore a frock and that was something, you know—a line of women giving enemas. People stretched out on these benches, and then they rushed to the toilet, and again, everything was primitive.

His "adventure" was turning into a nightmare, and Maurice was beginning to wonder if it would ever end. Finally the day for surgery arrived. This was a teaching hospital, so he was wheeled into an amphitheater and given a local anesthetic, which the doctors explained was safer and better than a general. They finished their preliminaries, and, with the eager students gathered around, they applied the knife. What the eager students learned was that a local anesthetic improperly administered might as well not be administered at all. Whoever had injected the anesthetic had botched the job somehow, and the anesthetized area was as live as a hot wire. Halperin says that never before or since has he felt pain like that. His howl of anguish got the message across. The team stopped immediately, of course, and gave him another local, and they were then able to proceed without further incident. Sometime later Halperin discussed the matter with his son, who is an experienced surgeon. David explained to his father that a local anesthetic was definitely not called for in this situation. He concluded that the only explanation was that the hospital either had too little anesthesia or too few anesthetists, and the doctors reserved what they had for the most serious surgical procedures.

Well, Halperin had proceeded with the whole affair in "the spirit of adventure." He wanted to find out what went on in the common citizen's hospital. He found out that, no matter the eminence of the surgeon, what went on was erratic and in some ways anomalous. Surgery was available to anyone at no cost and might even be done by a famous surgeon. At the same time, procedures were slipshod, even perilous. American medicine, by contrast, had probably achieved a more consistent level of efficiency, and certainly better facilities, for those who could afford to pay for it. Certainly the health delivery system in the Soviet Union was a quantum leap better than it had been under the tsars, but knowledge of that fact was no consolation for Maurice when the knife plunged into his live flesh.

Maurice later compared notes about his hospital experience with Albert Maltz. Maltz came over in 1961 for a month or so to oversee the publication of one of his books and to receive royalties from some of his earlier works that had been published in the Soviet Union. Halperin describes Maltz as a "well-behaved Jewish bourgeois," a thoroughly decent and gentle person who was sometimes a bit out of touch with practical realities. Like any good writer he had a shrewd understanding of human nature, yet paradoxically he was an erratic judge of specific human beings. For instance, he was a prime investor in the great Mexican ice cream caper, but he ignored growing evidence that there was something very fishy about it and tried to silence the alarms that Maurice was setting off with assurances that Bob Strand was too nice a guy to cheat his friends and partners. Only after Strand and the money were gone did he admit that he had been wrong. Maltz was also generous to a fault. When Maurice heard that he was coming to Moscow, he wrote to Albert and mentioned that he could not get either antacid tablets or dental floss in Moscow, and would Albert please bring some over with him. Maltz apparently brought over a bit less than a carload. Thirty years later Halperin is still using the dental floss that Maltz had brought to Moscow. In all the annals of floss, surely no batch ever served so well as this one.

While he was in Moscow, Maltz had some work done in the Kremlin hospital, and he described his experience there to Maurice. After Halperin's experience in the Petrovsky hospital, it sounded like heaven—superb facilities, ample and excellent staff, edible food. It was as if they had imported the Massachusetts General Hospital intact. When Halperin complained about his own miserable experience to Maltz, Albert agreed that perhaps the local hospital had a few technical deficiencies, but he reminded his friend that the health care system in

Russia was more humane, just as the factory system was more humane than its American counterpart.

HALPERIN: He had once been to an American automobile assembly plant and compared it unfavorably to a Russian plant he had visited recently. He said, "Well, you know the Russian plant was very inefficient—people walking around, kind of dirty. But it's more human. Nobody is being rushed. People take their leisure. They are treated more like human beings." And I said to him, "Well, that's very nice, of course, but Albert, have you noticed that you can't buy a car here? They don't produce cars with this fine, humane attitude towards the workers; there are no cars coming out." He hadn't thought of that.

Some time later Edith came down with pneumonia. The doctor insisted upon hospitalization, but her own spirit of adventure had been dampened by Maurice's experience in Petrovsky's institution. She knew all she cared to know about it and elected to enter a brand new hospital built for Academy of Science personnel. Its staff and facilities were more or less on a par with the Kremlin hospital. It existed in a different world from the Petrovsky hospital, and it brought home to the Halperins once again the inequities of life in this nation that was supposed to have abolished inequities.

One of the spin-offs of Maurice Halperin's life on the Left was his acquaintance with many near-famous and famous (some would say *infamous*) people. In some ways this was a function of the era. After all, in the 1930s and 1940s most artists and intellectuals who were at all political were on the Left for at least a while, and most of those on the Left were in or near the orbit of the Communist party. Halperin's rather unpleasant encounter with Clifford Odets in 1935 was a consequence of the era's politics.

Not all of these acquaintances were as distasteful as Odets. On one occasion he and Edith were invited to the Moscow apartment of Ilya Ehrenburg. Ehrenburg had been a controversial character in the West for years. At his best, he was a novelist of impressive proportions; at his worst, he was a hack journalist and apologist for all the tortured twists in the party line for years. Ehrenburg had a vast apartment on Gorky Street. The first thing Maurice noticed when he stepped inside the door was that there was art everywhere. But not just art; these were paintings by Degas and Picasso and others, many of them dedicated to Ehrenburg personally, and most of them hung in slapdash fashion all over the walls. The collection's value must have run to millions of dollars. Halperin remembers in particular a conversation they had about Suslov, the official party ideologist then and for many years afterward.

HALPERIN: I had read the day before a statement by Suslov which seemed to me extraordinarily stupid. Remember this was during the Khrushchev thaw, and some people were beginning to talk openly. Maybe I never would have gotten there if it weren't for that particular period. So I told Ehrenburg I thought the statement was extraordinarily stupid, and I said, "How do you account for that, a man of such importance?" He didn't deny that what Suslov had said was stupid. He said, "Well, you see there is something you don't understand about revolution. To get rid of the capitalists is very easy, but to get rid of the idiots? Very difficult."

Whatever else Ehrenburg was, he was a survivor. He had been around for a few decades and had come through the worst repressions unscathed and unfettered. No doubt part of that was due to his timely shifts of position. But there were others who shifted position, who tried to remain loyal to Stalin, and still got caught up in the machinery of repression. Ehrenburg's only explanation was a shrug. "I had a winning lottery ticket," he said. He survived by chance. It was probably as good an explanation as any.

Halperin also met the renowned Chilean poet Pablo Neruda while he was in Moscow. They were, in fact, renewing an old friendship. Halperin had first met the future Nobel Prize winner in 1940, when he was spending the summer in Mexico City with Edith and the children, and Neruda was there as Consul General for Chile. His was already one of the great names in Hispanic literature, so Maurice made an appointment to interview him for an article in *Books Abroad*. Neruda failed to show up for their first appointment, and when they finally did meet, Halperin chided him for this. Neruda took it well, and the two men hit it off from the start.

They met several times after that, ate together in restaurants with their families, and talked interminably. It helped that they were both men of the Left, although this was the period of the Nazi-Soviet Pact, when Halperin's attitude toward the Soviet Union had chilled completely. In fact, he thought Neruda's politics were as naive as his poetry was profound. The man was blind to any criticism of Soviet politics and foreign policy. But when Halperin asked him what he thought of socialist realism, which was the prescribed mode of literature for party members everywhere, Neruda replied, "I don't understand what that means at all." He was all for the liberation of the world proletariat by the Russians, Halperin observes, but he wasn't about to let anyone mess with his poetry.

The next time they met, Maurice was with the OSS during the war, and Neruda had come to Washington with some sort of Chilean political delegation. They talked over old times and when they parted, Neruda wrote a special inscription on one of his long poems and gave it to Maurice. So when Maurice heard that the famed Chilean poet was in Moscow, he called him, and the old friends spent a pleasant afternoon together. The Nobel Prize was still far in the future, but the thought occurs that without having to worry about surviving in Soviet society, Neruda was already the literary figure that Ehrenburg might have been under similar circumstances.

One of the acquaintances that Halperin remembers with special fondness was a man introduced to him as Mark Frazer shortly after he arrived in Moscow. Frazer was an Englishman, and his style immediately identified him as an Englishman of some substance— public school, Cambridge University, proper accent, and all. He held a very important post in a different division of Maurice's institute, had an American wife, and was most congenial. The Halperins and the Frazers had so many things in common, not the least of which was language, that they soon became very good friends, visiting back and forth with some regularity. This was a pleasure for the Halperins, because there were so many people who were reluctant to be seen at their apartment.

On one occasion the Halperins were invited over to meet Frazer's American mother-in-law, who was visiting at the time. Speaking to Frazer at one point in the evening she called him Donald. "Don't you think this, Donald?" and "Don't you think that, Donald?" Halperin was puzzled. "Donald? I thought your name was Mark." "Well, Mark is how I'm known here, but you see, my name really is Donald. Donald MacLean, actually." Halperin's jaw dropped. Donald MacLean! Burgess and MacLean! Everybody in the Western world who could read a newspaper knew that they were the British spies who had defected to Moscow one jump ahead of arrest in 1951.[5]

MacLean did not surface until he and Guy Burgess were "presented" at a press conference in Moscow in 1956. Of the two, Burgess had always been the more flamboyant. At a time when homosexuality was still very much a hush-hush matter, he was outrageously gay, which is to say that his highly visible behavior was intended to outrage. He was handsome, brilliant, witty, and generally the center of attention wherever he was.

MacLean was two people. Sober, he was hardworking, had a keen if not flashy mind, was a good family man and a valued employee in the Foreign Office. Drunk, he was aggressively and noisily anti-American, a trait not at all prized by his Foreign Office superiors, and was given to episodes of homosexuality, which he did not handle with the aplomb of Burgess.

During the last year or two before his defection, MacLean was losing control of these contradictions in his personality and was able to cope only with the aid of a bottle. Consequently his bouts of drunkenness were more and more frequent, and his behavior more and more bizarre, especially for a Foreign Service officer who was expected to be discreet.

Except for one period, the MacLean that Halperin knew in Moscow was the sober MacLean, a good colleague and steady worker at the institute, a good husband and father, and a good friend with no apparent

5. Kim Philby, a third member of this group, and the one who became the best known of all eventually, did not turn up in Moscow until 1963. When Halperin met MacLean in 1960, he had never heard of Philby.

antipathy toward Americans. The exception was a relapse into alcoholism that lasted for several weeks. Halperin, who is the prototype of the bourgeois family man, was appalled. Concerned for the health of his friend, he tried to persuade MacLean to take a drug called Antabuse. By itself the drug has no particular effect, but mixed with alcohol it makes one violently ill. It is intended to make the alcoholic stop drinking in order to end the vomiting that is wracking his body. Unfortunately, this "cure" breaks down on the fact that the true alcoholic does not want to feel better; he wants to feel drunk. He does not give up alcohol; he gives up Antabuse. In time MacLean regained control of himself, and Halperin never saw him like that again.

By the time Halperin got to know him, MacLean had been in the Soviet Union for nearly ten years, and he no longer viewed the world in quite the same black-and-white terms that had characterized his perceptions before he defected.

HALPERIN: It was sort of a painful thing. He wanted to justify what he had done, which means that he had to believe that what he had done would eventually be a contribution to the salvation of the world. Put it that way. It's a normal sort of thing, except that some people would also find it normal to say, "New information, new conclusions." His attitude toward the Soviet Union was somewhat critical, but with a different ultimate perspective on the thing. But he was quite intelligent about what was under his nose. He wasn't kidding himself to that extent, which made him very useful to me because he knew so much about the society, that I didn't know. He was the one who very immediately cleared up for me the fact that there were two parties in the ethical sense of the term. There were the Progressives and the Black Hundreds. And he was violently opposed to the Black Hundreds. And so many little things, you know. For example, he despised Gromyko, literally despised him. Saw him as an unimaginative bureaucrat holding on to his job and actually not above having people write articles for him for which he got the pay. I remember he referred to Gromyko as a "jumped-up peasant." Nice term, eh? Particularly British. Jumped up. There was a bit of snobbery in the term, and he was a little embarrassed by it. "I hate to say that but I don't know any other way to describe the fellow except as a jumped-up peasant." And I guess he was right about it. A very able, cleaver peasant, but fundamentally a peasant.

MacLean lived well in Moscow. He had a spacious apartment, a washing machine (but no dryer), a car, and outside of town, a *dacha*, or little holiday retreat. And he was generous with these things. On one occasion Halperin's daughter and her husband were visiting Moscow, and the MacLeans invited them all out for a picnic afternoon at the *dacha*. To save the MacLeans the trouble of driving into the center of the city, the Halperins were to take the subway to the end of the line, where Donald would pick them up and drive them the remaining twenty miles or so to the *dacha*. On the subway, it was obvious that the Halperins were not the average Russian family. Judith was six or seven months pregnant and wearing some stylish American maternity clothes, which made her stand out like a beacon. And they spoke English, which also drew attention to them. At the end of the line Donald, who was still Mark at the time, picked them up and headed out toward the *dacha*. Before long a truckload of army personnel passed them, and the soldiers were waving their arms quite vigorously for some reason. Then another passed with soldiers who were doing the same thing. Finally another truck cut them off while a car pulled in behind them, locking them in. They were stopped opposite a small airport of the sort that one might find outside a small city in the States for Piper and Cessna two- or four-seat private planes. They were informed that this tiny airport was a military installation and was off-limits to foreigners. They would have to turn back at once. MacLean argued but to no avail. Rules were rules. So he dropped the Halperins off a few miles back, then went ahead to the *dacha* for his wife and the food, and returned to the Halperins for the picnic.

What had happened? It seemed that several people had observed this woman in the flashy maternity clothes and her American companions on the subway. They followed them off at the end of the line, saw them get into an auto, took the license number, and called the authorities to report them. On this occasion the Russians proved to be quite efficient, and appropriate action was taken.

Apart from the liberating tendencies of the thaw, and the emergence of the progressives in public life, Maurice has few good things to say about Soviet life. If there is a theme in his discussions of Russia it is that all aspects of life there were hobbled by a system that simply did not work. That is a truism nowadays because the Russians themselves have been shouting it to the world. In 1960 it was not so clear, especially to people who wanted to sympathize. It was still possible to explain problems in terms of the devastation of the war or the Stalinist Terror. For many in the West it was easy enough simply to deny that any problems existed at all.

Halperin had no stars in his eyes on that score when he came over. He knew there were problems, but he believed that most of them were the products of external factors. What he saw everywhere and ceaselessly for three years convinced him that the cause was not external to the system; it was the system itself. He began to notice it almost immediately.

HALPERIN: You sensed you may be back in 1917 or something. The furnishings. . . . You go into a restaurant and the kind of service you get. A half hour before the waiter notices you even though the restaurant is half empty. I had never faced this sort of thing before. We spent the first three weeks in a hotel before the clearance came through—security clearance. They had to do some investigating. And I was given a formal appointment and also assigned an apartment. We took all our meals in the hotel and I was beginning to get a little annoyed. One of the things I noticed was that the chambermaids would do an awful shoddy job of cleaning and they couldn't make the beds properly. I didn't expect an affluent society, but this was not only not affluent, it was terribly shabby and there was a lot of carelessness about things too. My feeling was that there was something basic missing here—the spirit of moving ahead or something of that sort. Apathy, that's another word for it. And it gave me a clue from the beginning that there is something wrong here; something is not working.

His reminiscences are littered with examples of things that were in one way or another not right. When he first came over, for instance, he noticed a building near his apartment that had some scaffolding along the wall a few floors above the street. He felt good about this because it was a healthy sign that renovations were going on everywhere. When he left, more than three years later, the scaffold was exactly where it had been when he arrived. He had passed it almost every day, and not once in all his time there did he see anyone on it. Nobody even noticed it. It was part of the scenery. Perhaps it still is.

He discusses the food in much the same tone. Shortages existed in the stores, of course, but Edith managed to get by. At home they ate reasonably well, but eating out was something else. In most restaurants the food ranged from bad to inedible, and the service was worse. There were exceptions, usually ethnic restaurants from the other republics—a Georgian restaurant, an Armenian restaurant, an Azerbaijanian restaurant. The trouble was that they were expensive, and because they were good they were packed. The only way to get in without waiting forever was to bribe the captain, a system not unknown in our own large cities, of course. A few other attempts at upscale restaurants almost made it before falling victim to the system. Halperin recalls a time when the Russians refurbished an old hotel and renamed it the Budapest Hotel.

HALPERIN: And then in this hotel they opened up a Hungarian restaurant. How do they open a Hungarian restaurant? They imported the whole staff—cooks, waiters, maitre d'—the whole staff. And they imported a good deal of the food too. It was open to everybody who had the money. And the idea was that these Hungarians were going to be there for six months while they were training Russians to take over. Well, we went there several times and it was a delight. You know, it was just like leaving the country. Marvelous food, wines, service, everything. . . . And then the Hungarians moved out and the Russians took over. We went once and never came back. It was Russian again. They also had a Chinese restaurant which they had set up during the glorious period of collaboration. They took a hotel, the Peking Hotel, and brought in a Chinese staff to open the restaurant. I was told the same thing happened. Well, they still served Chinese food there after the Chinese had left, so we went there and everything tasted like borscht, no matter what they called it. It was borscht and so was the service.

Even Moscow's famous subway raised more questions than it answered for Halperin. The part that the world knows is a short line of only a few stations built in the 1930s, but what there is of it is magnificent, "a palace under the earth," Halperin calls it, with beautiful chandeliers and marble floors. The extensions from it, on the other hand, are ordinary stations. At first Halperin was stumped by the economic irrationality of the venture. How could the Russians have put such a huge sum of money into a mere showpiece when there was hunger abroad in the land? Then it occurred to him that what is economically irrational can make very good political sense. Maybe Stalin was trying to give the Russian people a vision of the future. Maybe he was saying, "Soon you are going to be living in palaces like this. Let us show you how it works underground."

HALPERIN: This reminds me that later on, after I began to think seriously about the construction of socialism in the Soviet Union, I had a conversation with a very sophisticated person, and I said, "You know, my impression is that you built socialism underground and you have built socialism under the sea. Your submarines are reputed to be first class. You built socialism in the air. I have been in your Aeroflot and it is very comfortable. But you haven't built any socialism on the ground."

After more than three years in Moscow, that was the impression of the Soviet Union he carried away with him. In the motherland of socialism, socialism did not work. But there was a new experiment in socialism going on much closer to America at the time. A few years earlier Fidel Castro had stunned the world by overthrowing the corrupt Batista regime in Cuba and installing a socialist system. Maybe in the hands of these Cuban idealists, Halperin thought, the system would finally be made to work the way it was supposed to. The Halperins would find out soon enough, for they were about to uproot themselves and fly to Havana, once again to start life anew.

7

Cuba Libre?

Accident, fate, the intervention of the supernatural—whatever we call it, we all reflect from time to time on how our lives are changed in important ways by contingency, by chance occurrences. If we had driven into the intersection five seconds later, our car would not have a bashed front end. If we had arrived at the party one hour later, we would never have met so-and-so.[1] And if Edith Halperin had been walking on the other side of the street one day in 1960, she would not have heard a small group of women speaking Spanish in the heart of Moscow, and the Halperins might never have gone to Cuba. But she did hear them, and Edith being Edith, she struck up a conversation with them in her singular version of the Spanish language. It turned out that they were wives of personnel from the Cuban embassy in Moscow, recently sent there by the new Castro government, and they were delighted to encounter a Westerner who spoke any kind of Spanish at all. In this way the Halperins entered into the social life of the Cuban diplomatic community in Moscow.

One of their friends at the embassy was particularly impressed with an article that Maurice had written at about that time on Latin American economic development.

HALPERIN: He was so happy with it because he, as it turned out, had no Marxist background at all. He didn't come from the Marxist

---

1. Many years ago a visiting student from Spain enrolled in my American history survey course because it fit her schedule better than the same course given by a different professor at a different time. We were married two years later.

*wing of the revolution but he was a nationalist anti-imperialist. And
he liked my article because there was no Marxist jargon in it; there
were no obstacles to understanding. The tendency in my article was to
deal with facts. Strange, you know. And he translated it into Spanish
and when I got to Cuba I found it. It was published in Spanish before
I got there.*

This was not merely courtesy on the part of the Cuban. He was
sufficiently impressed with Maurice to try to persuade him to leave
Moscow with Edith and go to Cuba. There was so much to do there,
and people like Maurice were badly needed. But the time was not
yet ripe.

It was Halperin's friendship with the Cubans that led to his meeting
with Che Guevara later that year.[2] Che was not yet in the pantheon
of revolutionaries, but he was already on his way to becoming a legend. Physically unprepossessing, this asthmatic Argentine physician-
intellectual-guerrilla had joined up with Castro in Mexico in 1956
and was one of the small band who survived the disastrous landing
in Cuba later that year. After the flight of the Batista government
at the beginning of 1959, it was Che, not Fidel, who led the first
band of tattered revolutionaries into Havana. Some months later, Fidel
sent Che on a high-profile world tour as a sort of roving ambassador
for the remarkable new revolutionary government at the doorstep of
the United States. It was not yet clear what direction this revolution
would take, but the strain of anti–Yankee-imperialism was already
quite audible, and no one gave clearer voice to it than Che.

Now Che was in Moscow, and one of the men at the embassy
arranged for him to visit Halperin's apartment that evening. Che, who
was a notorious night owl, showed up with two embassy officials
shortly after midnight, and he and Maurice talked through the night.
Che listened closely as Maurice spoke of his experience as a consultant to the Mexican government's industrial development bank, after

2. See Maurice Halperin, *The Taming of Fidel Castro* (Berkeley and Los Angeles:
University of California Press, 1981), 263–64, for his "reminiscence" of this meeting.

which the two engaged in a wide-ranging discussion of political and
ideological issues.

HALPERIN: What impressed me at the time, apart from his wide read-
ing and nimble intellect, was a questioning attitude toward prevailing
Marxist dogma and a genuine modesty concerning his own doubts and
speculations. I gathered that he was groping for a way to make a fresh
start in building a socialist society, perhaps on the order of what came
to be known during the "Prague spring" of 1968 as "socialism with a
human face." All in all, we seem to have hit it off fairly well, because,
before leaving, he invited me to come with my wife to Havana as guests
of the Cuban government. . . . [3]

Also, in a kind of moderate way he indicated his dissatisfaction with
what he had discovered about the Soviet Union. His first visit, you
see. And I know from speaking with his colleagues that he was really
indignant about the treatment that the elite received compared to the
situation that he saw of the great mass of people. Indignant about his
own luxurious quarters and the kind of fruits that were piled up on
his table which you couldn't find anywhere in Moscow. He was, as the
popular expression goes, sort of pissed off.

In the years that followed, Halperin watched, dismayed, as this
modest, searching young socialist shed his doubts and emerged a rigid
Marxist-Leninist, so pure in his commitment that he even doubted
occasionally whether Fidel was sufficiently committed to the true
course. Still, Che always retained a degree of liberal-humanism that
tempered his revolutionary zealotry.

HALPERIN: In Cuba he would intervene in the case of someone who
had expressed ideas that the government didn't like, and who was
immediately canned or put in jail. So he did keep a kind of liberal
approach with respect to the failings of the people around him. . . .
People knew that if you were in trouble and by any chance you knew

---

3. Halperin read this passage verbatim from his book into the tape machine.

Che, you would get out of trouble. That is, if Che had a good opinion of you even though he disagreed with you.

Fidel, who had a much more volatile temperament, was not known for such compassion toward dissenters.

When Che extended the invitation to come to Havana, Maurice filed it away for future reference. He had no intention of staying in Russia for the rest of his life, but he had no immediate plans to leave either. By 1962 the situation was entirely different. Halperin had soured completely on the Soviets, and the Soviets seem to have returned his sentiments. The Academy was in the process of organizing a new Latin American Institute, and Maurice was not invited to join it.[4] He was not being asked to leave the country, but he realized that if he stayed on he would be no more than a ward of the state without function, a prospect that held little appeal for him.

By spring it was clear that he would have to make a decision soon. He had three options before him, each of which posed a distinct problem. He could stay on in the Soviet Union with Edith; they could return to the United States; or they could accept Che's invitation and go to Havana. Remaining in the Soviet Union was the least attractive of these alternatives. They did not enjoy life there, and now that Maurice was to be deprived of feeling useful, there was absolutely nothing to hold them. Returning to the States was certainly more appealing. Their roots were there, as were their children; they had been away for more than eight years now, and they missed it. The problem was that Maurice had no job waiting for him there, and while the miasma of McCarthyism had dissipated by 1962, most American universities

---

4. The Halperins had amassed quite a lot of rubles in Russia, because there was almost nothing to buy, but they were not allowed to exchange them or take them west when they went to Cuba. In the summer of 1963, their son was planning to go to Europe with his bride, and it struck Maurice as a good opportunity to spend some of those rubles. They would all tour Russia together. The Russians, alas, had a different idea. They denied Maurice a visa. They had apparently found him more abrasive than they thought a guest ought to be, and the way he challenged authority, written or human, was not a prized quality there. As far as Halperin knows, the rubles are still there.

were still somewhat skittish about people like Halperin and unlikely to beat a path to his door. Nevertheless, he says, they went ahead and booked reservations to return to America.

As for Cuba, whatever attraction it held was marred by the almost daily rumors of an imminent American invasion. If it happened, it would not be left to a relative handful of Cuban adventurers this time, as had been the Bay of Pigs in 1961. The consensus in Moscow was that the Americans would go in with a full-scale military invasion. Still, the prospect of going to Cuba fascinated Halperin. This was not a revolution gone stale, like the one he was living in. It was young, idealistic, and not yet hardened. What direction would it take?

HALPERIN: I'd been reading the Cuban press and I was very well informed. I was relatively favorably impressed compared to what I had been living in for the last three years. There was lots of flexibility there, and you had, you might say, the Caribbean personality there. This was something that interested me intellectually. By the time I was thinking of going there Castro had already said he was a Marxist-Leninist, you know. It's clear that his society hadn't yet become Marxist-Leninist, though. And there were a lot of loose ends there, and a lot of Cubans themselves even called it "revolutionary cha-cha-cha." The drums were beating and they were dancing in the midst of all this. And I was curious about what was going to happen. What kind of Marxist-Leninism are you going to have with this new background? Is it the system or is it the inherited culture? Interesting question, right? I knew about Ivan the Terrible, and I could see that the Soviet Union was not completely Westernized at all. I could see a mixture, a blend. But Cuba is the West and I knew the history of Cuba. There's no tradition of Marx and Lenin there of any serious kind. The main revolutionary tradition is José Martí. It was an anti-imperialist tradition, but a bourgeois revolutionary tradition. It was not Marxist. Well, these were the thoughts in my mind as we were considering going or not going.

There was nothing equivocal in Halperin's views on the Soviet Union. As far as he was concerned, socialism did not work there or in the areas under its sway. As he weighed the opportunity of going to Cuba, he was asking a fundamental question. Why did socialism not work in Russia? Perhaps the problem was not with socialism as a system, but with Russia as a culture. If that were the case, then socialism might work in a different nation. And what nation could be more different from Russia than Cuba? Cuba's size, language, climate, history, culture, traditions, and people were all a world apart from what Halperin had observed in Russia. It was an intellectual problem, but it was one that had strong emotional resonance in Halperin's life. Could socialism work under the proper conditions? Maurice decided to go to Cuba to find out, and, as always, Edith went along with his decision. They canceled their plans to return home. His only reservation, given the tense international situation, was that "there was the possibility of getting killed."

The Cubans arranged for the trip, and they payed for it. Edith and Maurice made their way down to Odessa on the Black Sea, where they boarded a brand new, Japanese-built Soviet tanker bound for Cuba. They were the only passengers, and they were treated royally. They had a beautiful stateroom and ate lavishly at the officer's mess. Conditions for the seamen were first rate as well. They lived in clean, modern quarters and ate considerably better than they could have at home. In addition, they enjoyed the privilege of shopping in foreign ports for items that were unavailable in Moscow. Albert Maltz might have used these conditions to prove a case that socialism was a humane system even for common sailors. Halperin prefers to think that it was a good way to keep sailors from defecting. The only bad moment on the voyage came when Halperin played a game of chess with the young captain and lost.

In Cuba the Halperins were assigned a large and lovely apartment that "was almost still warm with the heat of the previous occupants," a Jewish family who had been allowed to leave with almost everything but their furniture. This illustrates a curious anomaly in Castro's policies at that time. By 1962 the government permitted a few Cubans to leave, and then only with the clothes on their backs and nothing else. Jews were the exception. They were allowed to leave in the name of "repatriation," that is, they were permitted to "return" to Israel. Where they might have gone from Israel was their own business.

So the Halperins found themselves in a nicely furnished, roomy, three-bedroom Havana beachfront apartment with cross-ventilation that caught the sea breezes and made their air conditioning almost superfluous. Cuban toilets flushed on call; the tap water was potable; the weather was balmy; and the people were cheerful. Compared to what they had left in Moscow, this was delightful. In fact, Halperin says, it was like going from the third world to a developed nation.

Indeed, in the early months, the only obstacle between Cuba and paradise appeared to be America. The hostile relations between the two nations that had worried Halperin in the first place continued through the summer, and they reached epic proportions in October, when President Kennedy informed the world that the Russians were installing missiles in Cuba.[5] Kennedy demanded that the missiles be removed and then announced that he was throwing up a "quarantine" around Cuba to prevent the arrival of further offensive weapons already on the high seas in Soviet vessels.[6]

The six-day missile crisis was perhaps the worst moment of the Cold War. The Soviet vessels were drawing ever closer to Cuba. What would happen if they challenged the American quarantine? Would the U.S. Navy board them on the high seas? Is it possible that they would have fired on the Soviets? For the first time, long-range nuclear war was not just a theoretical possibility; it appeared to be imminent. It is difficult to convey the mood of that weekend in the States; it was all that anyone could talk about, all that anyone could even think about. Secretary of Defense Robert McNamara remembers emerging from a harrowing, all-night session at the White House into a beautiful

5. Kennedy's people assumed that the missiles were being installed but were not yet operational. We have learned since then that twenty of the missiles were already armed with nuclear warheads and ready to be fired and that the Russians were within a whisker of arming another twenty.

6. There is more than a semantic difference between a "quarantine" and a "blockade." In international law, a blockade is technically an act of war. Kennedy did not want his action to be taken as an act of war, which would have painted the Russians into a corner and left them with no options between surrender and war.

autumn Saturday morning, and wondering if it would be the last one he would ever see. The previous day I was sitting with several of my students in the university cafeteria, all of us mute with despair. One of the students rose to leave, saying, "See you Monday." He took a few steps then turned back to us and added, "If there is one."

Halperin remembers quite a different mood in Cuba. There was no sense of proximity to a nuclear holocaust for the simple reason that the government had not said a word about the missile emplacements in Cuba or the forty thousand Russian troops then tucked away out of sight on the island. Maurice knew what was happening because he had a shortwave radio tuned in to Key West. The relatively few people with access to similar equipment were probably also aware of the crisis, but they were not trumpeting it in the streets. The average Cuban did not even know about the missiles until Castro denounced Khrushchev for removing them. Of course, everyone knew that something was up and that it involved Cuba, the Soviet Union, and the United States, but there was not the same doomsday sense in Cuba that was palpable in the United States.

What they expected was an American air strike to soften Cuban defenses, followed by the long-awaited Yankee invasion. In fact, this was one of the options given Kennedy by his military advisers during the crisis. The Cubans prepared for it by manning anti-aircraft batteries in the public squares of Havana, by setting up defenses on the beaches, and by arming themselves with pistols, machetes, and knives. As the tension increased, Maurice told Edith not to worry because their apartment was next to the archbishop's palace, and the American air strike was sure to spare that target. Halperin thus responded to the crisis with a blend of fatalism and cynicism, but he recalls that the Cuban people responded with a tremendous surge of patriotism. He discovered later that production even increased during this period, which is an interesting comment on the comparative emotional powers of nationalism and Marxist idealism.

And so, while many people elsewhere in the world were preparing for a premature departure from the Earth—perhaps even *of* the Earth—Cubans were preparing for hand-to-hand combat in the streets. Perhaps it is best explained in the pithy way that a Spanish Communist friend of Halperin summed up the Cuban character. "Cubans love to fight," said the Spaniard, "but they hate to work." Denied the chance to fight the Yankees, the Cubans felt betrayed by the Russians. It is not enough to explain this by saying that the common citizens did not really understand what was involved in atomic warfare, because the sense of let-down was not limited to the common people.

HALPERIN: I talked to a very important Cuban official immediately after the thing was announced. He knew about the missiles, and he talked about betrayal. The Soviets betrayed the Cubans. If they had the missiles, he said, they should have used them. What kind of madness is this? A person who otherwise is perfectly sane and sober. This was not an illiterate sugar-cane cutter. I'm positive he reflected the views of Che Guevara. He was very close to Che. It wasn't a question of ideology, but a question of fighting imperialism. It was suicidal.

There was a sense of unreality to the Cuban attitude that still amazes Halperin. In the end, however, the Cubans simply did not have the power to prevent sanity from prevailing between the Americans and Russians. As a quid pro quo for the Russians removing their missiles, Kennedy guaranteed that there would be no American invasion of Cuba. The world was spared the agony of a military confrontation between the superpowers, and Castro, Communism, and the island survived intact.

While all this was going on, the Halperins were establishing a social life for themselves, aided by their long-time accomplice in these affairs, Maurice's violin. The reader should understand at this point that amateur classical musicians make up a small international community of fanatics who somehow give off waves detectable to themselves and no one else. There is no other way to explain how they invariably find each other in the most improbable places and circumstances. So it was that the Halperins were soon hosting musical evenings peopled for the most part by foreigners who played in the city's symphony orchestra. For Maurice this was heaven because he had never played with so many first-rate musicians before. It probably did not hurt that as a foreign *técnico* he qualified for more and better rations than were available to most Cubans, including the musicians, who were not deemed essential to the revolution, and that he could thus host these musical evenings in style.

Altogether there were perhaps a half-dozen of these musicians, including a French cellist, an Argentine clarinetist, and an American violinist, who met every few weeks for music, food, drink, and conviviality. Halperin remembers in particular the cellist, a French Jew who had been a soldier when France fell and had been captured and placed in a military prisoner-of-war camp, thus escaping the fate of many French Jews who were eventually sent eastward to their deaths. Listening to the story, Maurice said, "Gee, how interesting." The Frenchman gazed at him for a moment and then said sharply, "It wasn't at all interesting." There are certain experiences that are simply beyond empathy.

A second group of friends were Cuban Jews who had long since emigrated from different parts of the world. Halperin's friends came primarily from the Ashkenasim, most of whom had come to Cuba between the wars when it was very difficult for Jews to get into the United States. The other Jews, who were less familiar to the Halperins, were Sephardim, who had come to Cuba before World War I, and were the descendants of those Jews who, along with the Moors, had been forced to leave Spain at the end of the fifteenth century. The common denominator of the Ashkenasim was Yiddish, a linguistic stew that is perhaps 80 percent German with a 20 percent leavening of Baltic, Slavic, Hebrew, and probably a few secret ingredients. Generally people who understand Yiddish can follow a conversation in German, though it does not necessarily work the other way around. More interesting to him was the language of the Sephardim, Ladino, which was remarkably faithful to fifteenth-century Spanish.[7] The Sephardic Cubans spoke a mixture of modern Spanish and Ladino that Halperin had no trouble following. The outsider might

---

7. My wife says that she can follow Ladino quite well if it is spoken slowly. It is still so close to its origins, she says, that scholars of medieval Spanish have studied spoken Ladino in order to recapture some of the sounds that have been lost to the Spanish language in the centuries since then.

have looked at these people and been struck by the fact that they were all Jews, struck, that is, by their similarity. Maurice, an insider, was struck by exactly the opposite, by how strong the differences among them were.

A third group of friends was made up mostly of people in the upper bureaucracy, most of whom were the embassy people the Halperins had first met in Moscow, along with some of the foreign technicians they had met since coming to Cuba, especially the Czechs. All of these people seemed more willing than the old Communists and the Soviets to take the billowing platitudes and shibboleths of the revolutionary vocabulary with a grain of salt and a knowing smile. Those in this particular circle all supported the revolution, but they were not blind to its flaws.

There was also the problem of earning a living, and here, as always, personal contacts played a major role. One of Halperin's Cuban friends from Moscow was a young journalist named Juan Arcocha. In Moscow, Arcocha had introduced Maurice to Enrique Oltuski, a young Cuban who was then visiting the Soviet Union. Through people like Arcocha and Oltuski, Maurice had already learned something about the complexities of Cuban politics while he was still in Moscow, and he began to get a sense of the different groupings during the early weeks in Havana.[8] Seen through the American popular press at the time, they were all just a bunch of bearded young revolutionaries taking their cue from the guy at the top who proclaimed himself to be a Marxist-Leninist.

Up close it was more complicated. There were the "old Communists," the Cuban equivalent of the American Communist party, who, like their comrades elsewhere, were in lockstep with Moscow's policies. They had opposed Castro when he and his handful of comrades

8. By mid-decade Arcocha had become disaffected with the Castro regime and left for Paris, where, among other things, he wrote a rather bad journalistic novel about his experiences with the Cuban delegation in Moscow. One of the characters in this novel was a middle-aged American named Sammy, a wise, charming, and increasingly disillusioned expatriate living in Moscow, who bore an uncanny resemblance to Maurice Halperin.

had made it ashore from *Granma*, the leaky vessel that had brought them to Cuba at the end of 1956, but they swung around behind him in June of 1958, when the leaky vessel suddenly began to look like a future ship of state. Then there were the Castro Communists, who were not devotees of the Moscow line. Many of them were, like their leader, recent converts to Communism who were suspicious and often contemptuous of the Moscow Communists. There were also other variants of socialists as well as some supporters in the Martí tradition, anti-Communists whose ardor was fueled more by anti-imperialism than by socialism.

In the beginning Oltuski was in this Martí tradition, a fervent anti-imperialist whose socialist credentials were suspect at best and who made no secret of his anti-Communist feelings. He had joined the movement as a member of Castro's underground before the revolution, and was soon converted by Che, who became his benefactor and protector during some troubled times ahead. Castro made him his first minister of communications after the revolution, apparently as a reward for his work in the underground. Unfortunately, Oltuski, who was still in his early twenties, did not even know what a ministry of communications did, as a result of which he did not have much to communicate there until some of the people who worked for him taught him what was going on. The old Communists in the ministry, however, were up in arms over having to work for this anti-Communist, so Castro fired him in order to keep the peace in the ministry. Both the hiring and firing of Oltuski were omens of the unpredictability that came to characterize the new regime.

By 1962, Castro, now more secure in power, was removing the old Communists from positions of authority and was thus able to bring Oltuski back into the government, this time as a vice minister in the Central Planning Commission, a vitally important government bureau charged with planning an economy that was beginning to falter. The commission needed all the help it could get, and if Halperin was a novice at planning, he was at least an educated novice who was familiar with Latin American affairs. So with the recommendation of Oltuski, he was taken on in the commission. That job lasted long enough to help the Halperins get on their feet and to familiarize Maurice with what he felt was the growing irrationality of the system.

HALPERIN: This was a very interesting experience with Oltuski and his Central Planning Commission. I didn't know anything about central planning, and I discovered they didn't either. I think I learned quite rapidly. There seemed to be a major irrationality about the whole thing, particularly without the proper statistics. They had mainly Czech advisers. Incidentally, we became very friendly with two Czech families. These were two Czech economists who had been assigned to the Cuban business, you know. They were actually Dubcekites [democratic socialists], although Dubcek wasn't known in the West yet. When the Dubcek thing emerged, I could see they had been thinking along those lines. And I tell you it was one of the useful experiences, because these sophisticated people knew what was wrong with the central planning thing in Czechoslovakia. And transporting it to Cuba, they could see, was a major blunder. They helped me understand the problems of Cuba attempting to create a socialist economy without having the basic means to do it, and the question of importing it.

Halperin remembers in particular a conversation he had with one of the Czechs about the merits of socialism and capitalism. The Czech admitted frankly that he believed capitalism would always outproduce socialism. But he did not want to judge a society primarily by the efficiency with which it produced material goods. He would still prefer socialism if only it would deliver the other things it promised. Unfortunately, he said, it didn't, or at least it hadn't so far. Halperin remembers these Czechs fondly, and in particular he recalls the large quantities of excellent Czech beer they supplied as they discussed these things.

Shortly after he started working at the Central Planning Commission, Maurice was invited to join the faculty at the University of Havana. There, too, there was a shortage of qualified personnel, especially in proportion to the rapidly expanding student body. He had his choice of teaching Marxism-Leninism or economic geography. He told his interviewer that if he taught the course in Marxism it would not be long before he would be denounced as a heretic, so he signed on as an economic geographer. He had no real expertise in that area, but he knew a bit of geography and a bit of economics, and he knew how to stay a few chapters ahead of his students while he acquired some seasoning in the field.

His job at the university turned out to be as sobering in its way as his job at the Central Planning Commission. In its endeavor to broaden the base of higher education in Cuba, the government had opened admissions into the university to virtually everyone. For Halperin this translated into a large class that ranged from nearly illiterate "riff-raff" (his characterization) to unemployed professionals nearing middle age and trying to build new careers under socialism.

As soon as he gave his first essay exam, the implications of this strange mixture emerged clearly. The answers fell primarily into two categories. The larger one consisted of students whose literacy was so fragile that their essays were almost incomprehensible. The rest consisted of literate answers that were characterized by what Halperin calls "ideological opportunism," by which he means essays that condemned capitalism, praised Marxism, and ignored the question. After that his exams consisted of true/false and multiple-choice questions. As much as he abhorred that sort of examination, it was the only way he could think of to avoid the pitfalls of ideological opportunism and semi-literacy at the same time.

That was not the only problem Halperin had with his students. Many of them felt that Cuba's new democracy should extend into the classroom with respect to such things as procedures and even course content. Halperin's commitment to democracy, on the other hand, stopped at the classroom door. Inside he was more committed to what Lenin called "democratic centralism," which, in Halperin's classroom, meant roughly that he would listen to what the students wanted and then tell them what they were going to do.

A showdown was inevitable, and it was not long in coming. It involved some question of procedure, which the more radical students wanted to settle by majority vote. Halperin was furious and said, "Look, I'm the boss here." But was he? The trouble was that many of these students were in the militia, and came to the class armed with pistols. As soon as he told them who was boss, he realized that he was a Yankee telling a bunch of angry, pistol-packing Cuban revolutionaries to go to hell. For a few nervous moments there was dead silence, and then one of the students rose and offered an olive branch, excusing the professor because he was a foreigner who could not really understand how things ought to be done in the new Cuba. In this way the students saved face but ceded control of the classroom to Halperin.

The other thing that nettled Halperin at the university was that he had to pass almost all of his students, even those who were demonstrably incompetent. One day, quite in jest, he proposed a solution to this problem to a university official. The university, he said, should award two types of diplomas. To the incompetents he would give gold star diplomas—a lot of fanfare, a lot of honor, and a one-way ticket to an unskilled job. To the 5 percent of the student body who really understood the material he would award bronze diplomas—not much honor but a tacit recommendation to good jobs in the government bureaucracy. Listening to Halperin describe the Cuban economy, one comes away with the feeling that the government got confused and gave the important policymaking jobs to the gold-star incompetents, while sending out the capable 5 percent to cut sugar cane.

Meanwhile, Oltuski told Maurice that he had been talking with his friend, the minister of foreign trade, and that they had decided that Maurice would be more useful in that ministry than in the Central Planning Commission. The ministry was in bad shape and needed help. Consequently, Halperin transferred to the Ministry of Foreign Trade as adviser to the minister. Shortly after that, Edith got a job in the same ministry teaching English to the Cuban personnel there. Maurice remained at the ministry, and at the university, for the remainder of his years in Cuba.

HALPERIN: The first thing that happened was I went in to see the minister, to get acquainted with him and arrange for my transfer. He was a nice fellow. We talked. That night he was fired. It was arbitrary. It was Castro who fired him, of course. Castro called him about two in the morning, as usual. This guy had no idea what was coming, no inkling. Maybe Castro thought he had mismanaged foreign currency or something, but he gave him a terrible threshing out. In Cuba, generally, when you have a top position like this and you're fired, you're s. o. l., if you know the expression. Because with very rare exceptions—and the only one I know was Oltuski himself—you go downhill. You're just simply out somewhere. This poor fellow, who just maybe two or three months before had gotten married and Castro had gone to his wedding—this poor fellow ended up by committing suicide. And there were a number of such cases, by the way.

The arbitrariness, the unpredictability, the fickleness with which things were done in Cuba were a constant source of anguish to Halperin. People and policies both were apt to appear, disappear, and reappear without explanation, without announcement, and sometimes without apparent reason. One day, for instance, the faculty members became aware that one of their colleagues, a woman, hadn't been seen at the university recently. With no forewarning she had simply dematerialized. Two or three months later, again without forewarning, she simply rematerialized—started teaching her classes again and attending faculty meetings as if nothing had ever happened. Nobody asked her any questions, and she did not volunteer any answers. Soon word got around that she had been arrested on suspicion, although no one seemed to know what she had been suspected of. She had been held in jail for those months and then released. Life went on.

As often as not, the whim and will of Fidel Castro himself were involved in some way. To illustrate, there was what we might call "The Case of the Missing Mangos." It concerned a young woman who was a student at the university and a research assistant for Maurice at the ministry. The woman was recently divorced, very pretty, and very bright. She was also fluent in English as the result of a boarding-school education in the States that her wealthy Cuban parents had given her before the revolution. And of course she was an ardent *Fidelista.* One day, as they worked together at the ministry, Maurice chided her about the fate of mangos in Cuba. They had been plentiful when he arrived, he told her, but now, perhaps two years later, they were almost impossible to find. That upset him because he was very partial to mangos.

HALPERIN: I told her that I was sorry to see that socialism and mangos were incompatible, but the fact is the mangos were disappearing. They were on the ground because there was no one there to pick them up. They had been growing in Cuba for centuries and now you couldn't find any. Well, one day she came to class and she said, "Yesterday a very wonderful thing happened. I was on a field trip with my economics class, and guess what—Fidel Castro appeared." Her eyes lit up, you know. This is a habit of Castro's. He'd show up anywhere at any time—whatever happened to strike his mind. You'd never find him in his office. He carried the government right in his pocket, the whole government in his side pocket. He had his fingers in everything, including this field trip. And she told me what a great thing it was. He was there and she talked to him. . . . The other part of the story is that shortly after this encounter with Castro she disappeared. No word. Disappeared from class; disappeared from her research. Nothing. Some time after that I was standing on the balcony of my apartment, and I noticed an army jeep coming up the driveway. The jeep stopped and a soldier got out with a very big sack. And lo and behold, he knocks on my door and he deposits the sack. It's a sack of mangos with a note from this young lady: "With my compliments," or something like that. She had become part of his household. She was his "companion." Castro only had one companion at a time. He was a serial monogamist and she was now the companion.

Well, I had forgotten about her, and some months later I was reading the daily paper, which I always read very thoroughly, almost every word, and I was clipping things out, getting ready to write a book when I left the country. And I read a small notice somewhere that a commission had left for North Korea to assist the North Koreans in cattle management. And sure enough, there was her name. She was being sent to North Korea. That means that her time was done and she got a nice reward and a job. And it also sent her ten thousand miles away where she wouldn't be bothering him for a while.

Amusing enough as an anecdote, the story emphasizes the capricious way of things at the time and the almost eerie manner in which people dropped from view in Cuba even when they were not in trouble. Rationality and, as far as possible, predictability are essential to economic efficiency, and Halperin was finding himself caught in a system with no rational boundaries at all.

That was certainly the case at the Ministry of Foreign Trade. By the time Maurice showed up for work, the new minister had been appointed, a very nice fellow named Marcelo Fernández, who, like Oltuski, had been an anti-Communist in Castro's underground before the revolution and had been converted to Communism afterward. "There were a lot of conversions there," Halperin observes. What amused Maurice was that Fernández had also been appointed to the Central Committee of the Communist Party, and he didn't know the first thing about Marxism. It became the source of a running joke between them, Maurice offering to tutor Fernández in Marxism and Fernández insisting on maintaining the purity of his ignorance.

After he settled into the job, Halperin was able to do some serious work at the ministry.

HALPERIN: I was put in charge of coordinating the information flow that was coming in. I had never done this particular thing before. I had had some experience in the U.S. Government with all kinds of information flows, however. So I had to improvise, but you don't have to be an intellectual giant to do it, and particularly when you're in the kingdom of the blind, if you have one eye, you're okay. And I had one eye. The minister wanted to see the total picture every month and at the end of the year. Nobody had prepared the total picture before. So I devised a reporting system by which they would know every month the basis of what's coming in and what's going out. And then at the end of the year I worked out an annual report of foreign trade information. What was sold and what was bought.

What is amazing, of course, is that nobody in the Ministry of Foreign Trade had thought to collect the most basic information on foreign trade before. They were trying to plan an economy without the information that is a prerequisite for planning. That is the sort of thing that had Maurice wringing his hands.

For a while Halperin hoped that Cuba would find its way to a more productive economy by seizing on an idea that was being debated at the time in much of the socialist world. The idea had originated with a Soviet economist named Yevgeny Lieberman, and it was keyed to the decentralization of decision making and the introduction of the profit motive into certain segments of the socialist economy. Halperin wrote an article defending Liebermanism in a foreign trade review, and quite a few people sought him out to tell him they agreed with him. Unfortunately Che Guevara didn't, and the idea never got off the ground. For Che, socialism was an ideal that was pure and whole and seamless. You could not amend it or augment it or diminish it. It was a noun that rejected all adjectives. You could only have socialism or non-socialism. Liebermanism was non-socialism. End of discussion.

Halperin watched as Cubans used up what he calls "the surplus they inherited from capitalism" and austerity became the rule of the day. In those days, there was never hunger or near-hunger in Cuba as there was in many other parts of Latin America, but foodstuffs that had been near-staples in the Cuban diet began to disappear. Meat was in short supply, citrus fruits and bananas were scarce (not to mention mangos), and coffee disappeared.

Halperin attributes this to the application of theories that often ignored the economic realities of Cuba. For example, sugar had long been the bedrock of the Cuban economy. Not long after the revolution, the government decided to plunge into economic diversification at the expense of some part of their sugar production. They decreed that cotton would play a major role in this diversification. But cotton does not grow by decree. Cubans knew sugar; they did not know cotton. The result was that sugar production dropped as predicted, while cotton production never grew as expected. It was a net loss for the economy.

A similar debacle occurred in connection with an ill-conceived venture into animal husbandry that was guided by the ideas of an obscure French agronomist named André Voisin.[9] The problem was that the Soviet Union was not able to provide enough feed grain to nourish Cuba's dairy cattle. Consequently Cuba had to purchase feed on the world market with hard currency, of which it had precious

9. The following account is adapted from Halperin, *Taming,* 134–40.

little to spare. Voisin's writing on the management of pasture lands suggested that the cattle could be fed efficiently on grass, thus saving the currency that would otherwise have to be diverted into the purchase of feed. Rationally applied, this approach might or might not have paid dividends to the Cuban economy.

Prudence would thus have dictated a meticulous investigation of its applicability in Cuba before heavy investment in it. But prudence was not the forte of Fidel Castro. He was given to great enthusiasms, and he proceeded to plunge ahead without doing any research into the feasibility of the program for Cuba. Eventually it became modestly productive but only after several failures and great cost. Discussing the program several years later, another French agronomist criticized Castro for following the plan too inflexibly, "without any consideration for differences of soil, moisture, and the varying capacities of unit heads to respond intelligently to local conditions."[10]

What is more, the economic situation was complicated by the constant meddling of Castro in relatively minor matters. One of the features of the system was its willingness to venture experimentally into special projects. The idea was not a bad one, but its execution left much to be desired. The heads of these projects were directly responsible to Castro, and Castro really liked to keep abreast of all of the projects. He also insisted that any change of plan made in one of these experiments be cleared with him first. No allowance was made for emergencies. This inflexibility proved to be costly in the long run.

The erratic fortunes of Enrique Oltuski again illustrate the problem. One of these experimental projects was a cattle-breeding farm near Havana. Oltuski was put in charge of the project. He knew nothing about cattle breeding, but he set out to learn quickly. Oltuski, remember, had been the victim earlier of a shift in power alignments, but in 1962, sponsored by his good friend Che Guevara, he was quietly restored to a position of authority. Now, in mid-decade, he was in charge of the cattle farm. The problem of distribution being what it was by then in Cuba, Oltuski was having trouble getting enough

10. René Dumont, *Cuba est-il socialiste?* (Paris: Seuil, 1970), 153.

feed for the cattle. It was precisely the sort of situation that the Voisin scheme was intended to prevent. So Oltuski decided to ship part of the herd out to where they could be fed on grass, which would then leave enough grain on hand at the farm to feed the remainder of the herd. Under the circumstances it seemed a reasonable solution to a difficult problem. When Castro learned that Oltuski had dared to move the cattle without first getting permission from him, he was furious. It made no difference that rapid action was necessary to save the entire herd from starving. To Castro it was an act of defiance that could not be tolerated.

HALPERIN: So this was a great crime. What happens in a case like this is that the person is sent to a work camp, to the gulag. So Castro gave Oltuski the choice: "You can go to the gulag and take your punishment or not. I'll leave it up to you. But you deserve punishment. You deserve six months in a gulag. I'll leave it up to you." Well, Oltuski is no fool, so he goes to the gulag. This was Castro's subtlety. They were actually prisons. I remember at the time everybody in the upper bureaucracy was talking about Oltuski going to the camp. I remember one top official saying, "Oltuski has been punished." And smiling because he knew what the situation was. No one had the slightest belief that Oltuski had committed a crime.

It does not take long for word of such an incident to spread, and for people in positions of responsibility to draw the obvious lesson from it and others like it: Do nothing until you are absolutely certain that it has been cleared at the top, and the top meant Castro. But Castro had more than cattle breeding on his mind. He was a world leader. He toured major capitals; he attended major conferences; he was already supporting Third World revolutions. Other things, like feeding cattle or, perhaps, harvesting mangos, had to wait until he had time to attend them because nobody wanted to take responsibility for them. It is not surprising that shortages appeared and austerity became the norm.

Sometimes the problems seemed impervious even to ardent supporters of the revolution who were prepared to make major sacrifices in its name. This was the case with a man named León, who was one of

Halperin's friends in the Jewish community. León had built a prosperous business manufacturing children's dresses over the years. He had a modern, mechanized factory and about twenty-five employees.

HALPERIN: Well, he belonged to the left-wing Zionist movement, the Zionist socialist movement. He was a socialist and he was a supporter of the revolution. Instead of leaving, as most of the rational Jews did, he stayed. And he tried to run his business for the benefit of the revolution and the people. Well, I wish I could remember all the details. First of all, the trade union took charge; production went down and quality went down. Also the government set up certain regulations, as a result of which everything was running down. He finally said, "Please, take my business." And they wouldn't because he was losing money all the time. He couldn't get them to take it over and he had a tremendous crisis. I guess what finally happened was he went bankrupt. It's a good example of the total lack of rationality, of realism. Here is a man producing something—good stuff—even exporting it. Leave him alone! Let him produce. He's willing; he's a patriot. He even cut his own salary in half. He was a great admirer of Che Guevara, and he simply wanted to help. He cut his own income. In the meantime they destroyed him. The lack of rationality and realism. And the almost inevitable confusion that happens under these circumstances.

What prevailed, then, was a system that often ignored Cuban realities in favor of theories that were devised for other conditions and that then pressed the logic of centralization to the absurd extreme of leaving virtually everything to the supreme leader. Meanwhile the leader rolled around in the system like a live grenade, threatening to go off at any moment, and thus introducing an element of instability into the system that was the very negation of the predictability that it depended upon. It was chaotic; it was contradictory; it was crazy.

Another feature of the early years was the strong emphasis on *trabajo voluntario*—voluntary work. More than anyone else, Che promoted this new ethic, according to which people were encouraged to do unpaid voluntary work on their days off. The work was not mandatory, but sometimes the pressures to do it could get pretty heavy-handed. In a country whose economy was reeling, it was, of course, an excellent way to get extra work from the workers without paying extra wages. For Che, however, the primary purpose was not economic as much as it was ideological. It was a way of achieving brotherhood through altruism, thereby realizing one of the ideals of socialism. And Che led the way by example.

HALPERIN: He would go and do the voluntary work. Unlike a lot of big shots. When Castro finally decided to do trabajo voluntario- *to get sugar cane cut—a big entourage went with him, interviewers and so forth. Not Che. Che went without any acclaim. The great mass of people who did participate did so because they were looked at as patriots. But I wasn't worried about that. And I was just a bit skeptical about the whole thing. One time I decided I was going to try it, like a sociological experiment. So I got up early and went off to join the group to do* trabajo voluntario *in a textile mill at the edge of town. We were there for four hours or so. What an experience! First of all, it was very clear that the voluntary workers didn't know beans about what was going on there. And to try to assimilate enough to do something useful was extraordinarily difficult. You just got in the way of the work. They'd show you how to do this, and you'd do it, and you wouldn't do it right. I came out with the conviction, based on empirical evidence, that this was not only a waste of time, but counter-productive from the point of view of production. Of course, this wouldn't be an important argument for Che.*

In Halperin's eyes, things were beginning to take on the appearance of the Soviet system laced with a dash of Cuban eccentricity to spice things up a bit. Perhaps that is what a colleague of mine had in mind when he returned from a two-month study tour of Cuba with a group of students at the end of the 1980s. He was still sympathetic with the revolution, but he was not oblivious to its defects. I asked him what his dominant impression of Cuba was. He thought for a moment and then said, "Picture Prussia run by Latin Americans." Now, that is quite a picture.

As the Cuban economy deteriorated in the 1960s, so did the cultural climate. When Halperin arrived it was still relatively open and in many ways quite vibrant. The higher bureaucrats were aware of breaches of civil liberties, but these were not yet extensive. Debate about the system and criticism of its flaws were still tolerated, although one had to be careful about directing that criticism toward Castro. There were problems for dissenters, but, then, Halperin could relate a few tales about problems for dissenters in the America he had left in 1953. And compared to the Soviet Union, this was heaven. Unfortunately it did not last.

What happened to the press offers one example of the changing cultural climate.[11] From the outset the official voice of the Castro movement was *Revolución*, a flamboyant tabloid that unblushingly cranked out cheesecake and radicalism in roughly equal proportions for Cuba's revolutionary masses. It stood in sharp contrast to the organ of Cuba's Communist party, *Hoy*, which, in format, tone, ideology, and language was cut from the same pattern as *Pravda*.

Though impeccably radical, *Revolución*, unlike *Hoy*, was not at all predictable, except perhaps for its hostility to the old Communists themselves. This was particularly true of its weekly literary supplement, which mirrored the anti-Stalinism of the parent journal, and which Halperin characterizes as "eclectic and antidogmatic within a wide leftist spectrum," as its inclusion of such writers as Albert Camus, Leon Trotsky, and various experimental Cuban poets and novelists seems to prove. By 1961 the battle between the literary supplement and the old Communists was spinning out of control, which was something that Cuba's insecure regime did not really need at that moment. So Castro intervened and acted according to a new principle in revolutionary Cuba: "For those within the Revolution, full freedom; for those opposed to the Revolution, no freedom." Loosely

---

11. Some of the discussion that follows is adapted from the taped interviews with Halperin, and some of it is from his two books on Cuba. See especially Maurice Halperin, *The Rise and Decline of Fidel Castro* (Berkeley and Los Angeles: University of California Press, 1972), 247–53.

interpreted, this means that one had complete freedom to agree with Castro and none at all to disagree with him. George Orwell could not have done better.

The supplement was suppressed from that moment, but the parent journal, *Revolución*, continued with its freewheeling ways and did not try to conceal its glee when the old Communists fell from grace in 1962. By the following year, however, the balance of forces had shifted again, as Castro drew closer to the Soviet Union and therefore to the old Communists. In particular, what seems to have incurred Castro's wrath was the way that *Revolución* reported his visit to Moscow in the spring.

The reporter was Maurice's friend Juan Arcocha, and at first glance, it is difficult to see how his reporting could have upset Castro. The message throughout was that Fidel had been a tremendous popular success and an object of adulation by the Russian masses. Arcocha related how Castro, in his usual informal and impromptu fashion, decided one night to take a stroll in Red Square with some of his Cuban friends. The Soviet hosts, however, were not programmed for informal and impromptu, especially by a visiting head of state. They went into a frenzy trying to draw Castro back into the Kremlin, but to no avail. Word spread quickly, and in a few moments Fidel was surrounded by a huge crowd of admiring locals.

The next day Fidel was leaving from his visit to Lenin's tomb when he noticed in the distance a throng in Red Square held back by police barricades. Before anyone could stop him he strode over to the barricades, and the delirious crowd pressed forward, shouting "Fee-del, Fee-del!" Fidel reprimanded the police for trying to manhandle the mass of people, and when the message was translated for them, Arcocha reported that "the police looked at Fidel as if they were seeing visions."

Some days later Arcocha summarized Fidel's impact in the Soviet Union, contrasting his "simple and amiable manner" and "his interest in human problems" with the stuffy formality of the chiefs of state who usually visit the Soviet Union, "people of a different type, solemn and governed by protocol, who [are] driven from place to place at high speeds in black automobiles with curtains drawn."[12]

It was not what Arcocha said about Castro that got him into trouble. It was what he left unsaid, but clearly implied. Decoded, his articles said that while Fidel was warm and informal, the Russians were cold and bureaucratic; Fidel was a man of the people, even the Russian people, but the Russian leaders were afraid even to approach their own citizens. Of course, it was not the first time *Revolución* had printed articles that reflected an anti-Stalinist bias, but it was certainly an unwise move at this particular moment, when Castro was mending his fences and trying to build up goodwill with the Soviets.

Fidel revealed his displeasure in a television speech after he returned, when he digressed from his subject in order to censure the newspaper for the embarrassing way it had overpraised his actions in Moscow. Castro had never objected to inflated praise before, but he could not risk alienating his Cuban audience in this case by trying to repolish the Russian image that Arcocha had so jubilantly tarnished. This attack on *Revolución* astounded the audience, because *Revolución* was his own creation, the official organ of his movement from the beginning. Such digressions during Castro's speeches often carried a covert message, and in this case the message was made clear. Both Arcocha and the editor were fired.[13]

Castro had already hinted at the direction his discussion of the press would take earlier in this speech, when he lavished praise on *Pravda*. He was impressed, he said, by the way it could compress all the important news into four pages, a triumph that he attributed to Russia's "magnificent editors," who managed to "collect and synthesize the most important things." He scarcely needed to add that Cuban papers customarily sprawled over sixteen pages or more. The difference in the cost of newsprint alone was huge, and this was doubly important in a country like Cuba, which, unlike the Soviet Union, had no forests of its own from which to process pulp.

12. Halperin translates and quotes this from *Revolución*, May 10, 1963.
13. Arcocha left Cuba for Europe in 1964 and went to work at the Paris headquarters of UNESCO. He broke with Castro in 1971.

Castro's message was that *Revolución* should mute its anti-Stalinism and declare some sort of truce with *Hoy*. It did little good. The two papers continued to snipe at each other until Castro had had enough. In October 1965, he closed them both and replaced them with a new journal, *Granma*, symbolically named after the yacht that had launched the revolution nearly ten years earlier. It would have been interesting if *Granma* had preserved *Revolución's* cheeky tone in *Hoy's* sober format. What it preserved, however, was *Hoy's* stuffy content in *Revolución's* florid format. It looked like the *National Enquirer* and sounded like *Pravda*.

In his second book on Castro, Halperin offers another perspective on the constricting cultural tolerance of Cuba when he discusses the case of Oscar Lewis, an anthropologist who had published landmark studies in the 1960s of poverty in Mexico and Puerto Rico.[14] Lewis proposed to add a dimension to those works by studying the poor in socialist Cuba. After ten revolutionary years, he wanted to know, how had socialist values affected the "culture of poverty," which had been the dominant concept in his earlier works.

Maurice took an interest in the project from the beginning because he and Edith had become close friends of the Lewises when Oscar and Ruth were doing their research some years earlier in Mexico City. He had run into Lewis while vacationing in Montreal at "Expo 67," had listened to his enthusiastic outline of the project, and had predicted that Oscar would never get permission to do the study, because it "was incompatible with the rigid controls maintained by any Marxist-Leninist state, including Cuba." But Lewis was not to be dissuaded. He came to Havana early in 1968 and persuaded Castro to endorse the project, which was to begin in a year. The Lewises and the Halperins enjoyed a happy reunion, and Oscar was ecstatic as he outlined his plans to Maurice.

To guarantee the integrity of the project, Lewis insisted on certain ground rules in a meeting he had with Castro. He required complete

---

14. Halperin evaluates the case of Oscar Lewis in *Taming*, 141–51. My own discussion is adapted from these pages.

control over the project without government interference or censorship of any sort; he wanted Castro's word that he would be allowed to take all materials of the study, including taped interviews, out of Cuba without government inspection, because taped interviews were central to his methodology, and the need to protect them from meddling or editing was crucial; and he wanted assurance that no harm would come to any individual who cooperated with the study. Castro accepted all the conditions.

Early in 1969 the Lewises launched the project, assuming that it would take about three years to complete. The research went smoothly for more than a year, and then, without warning, the authorities terminated the project and confiscated its files in June 1970. At that time, according to Halperin, the files contained about half the materials already collected. Fortunately the other half, more than twenty thousand pages of transcript, had already been sent to the States. Two years later, Raúl Castro explained that the government had acted because Lewis was engaging in deceit and espionage. Unfortunately Oscar Lewis could not answer these charges. He had died of a heart attack some months after being forced to leave Cuba in 1970.

The charges of deceit and espionage were absurd, of course. The real reason was transparent. Oscar's digging was unearthing material that did not flatter the regime. To be sure, his purpose was to dig up information, not flattery, but he assumed that an honest study that spoke openly of problems in the new Cuba could only foster a positive image. In a story that is filled with ironies, perhaps the most poignant is that the Lewises themselves were longtime leftists and enthusiastic supporters of Castro's revolution. Their confidence in Fidel soared when he told Oscar in 1968 that Cuba was probably the only socialist country in the world that would authorize an outsider to do a study of its own poverty with no strings attached. He probably even meant it when he said it, but Oscar learned, as Maurice had learned before him, that Fidel was a fickle person for whom yesterday's promises applied only to yesterday's conditions. And yesterday's conditions no longer applied, because for several months the Lewises had been turning up material that the government considered completely unacceptable, in particular (but not exclusively) the sharply critical views of one man who was bitterly hostile to the regime and its leader. The Lewises learned of the cruelest irony after they were safely back home. Shortly after their departure, the government had arrested the hostile informant and thrown him into prison. They felt personally responsible and were dismayed.

Halperin analyzes many of the Cuban conditions and attitudes that were discussed in the three volumes of this study that eventually did come out in the late 1970s under Ruth Lewis's guidance, and in the process, he reveals his own hardening attitude toward Castro and toward socialism in general. For example, he chastises Ruth for conceding the government's "right" to do what it did and for diluting her discussion of Castro's role in the affair. The government unilaterally violated the conditions it had accepted, and in particular, he says, stands condemned for imprisoning a man who was assured he had immunity to speak his mind openly. Moreover, the government in this case could only mean Castro, since only Castro had the authority to revoke a decision that he had made in the first place.

He attributes Ruth's feeble explanation to "an unwillingness to shed some of the naivete about socialism in general, and Castro in particular, that had led Oscar into the fatal trap." But he praises Oscar for maintaining "his integrity as a scholar" when controversial material began to appear. "Instead of self-censorship, which a firm commitment to Castro's Cuba would require," Halperin says, "he continued to do whatever was possible to meet his commitment to professional probity, never suspecting that Castro himself would betray him."[15]

Halperin is being generous with Lewis here, for Lewis did not really have to make such a choice between his data and his commitment as long as he believed that Castro supported him. Halperin's own discussion of Lewis's motives leads one to feel that the anthropologist was not expecting to find utopia in Cuba and would have had no difficulty insulating his faith in the revolution from information and attitudes that were hostile to it. Certainly Castro's generous role in encouraging the project must have persuaded Lewis that here at last

15. Halperin, *Taming,* 145.

was the "socialism with a human face" that had so tragically been wiped out in Prague just two years earlier. That admiration for Castro would surely have survived the tales of a dissident. In Ruth, at least, it seemed almost to have survived the crushing action of Castro himself.

Halperin's wrath is really aimed at Castro, for it is Castro who was unable to reconcile scholarly integrity with a commitment to the regime. It is Castro for whom self-censorship should have followed from a "firm commitment" to the regime. Halperin characterizes the attitude of both Lewises toward socialism and toward Castro as "naivete," while he uses such words and expressions as *betray, double-crossed, quixotic impulse, congenital urge*, and *boast* to describe Castro's role in the affair. This is the sort of charged language that was unwelcome in R&A during the war, but that is not to say that it was inappropriate in this instance. Judging from Halperin's discussion of the Lewis affair, it is a reasonable evaluation. The point is that it *is* an evaluation, not merely a description, and it says as much about Maurice Halperin as it does about Oscar Lewis or Fidel Castro.

Maurice had come to Cuba in 1962 in part to answer a question. Was the failure of socialism in Eastern Europe the fault of socialism or of Eastern Europe? Might it take root and flourish in more fertile soil, or was it doomed everywhere? By the time he left in 1968, he had his answer. Socialism was not likely to work anywhere.

What did he mean by "socialism"? The word has been so loosely used in recent decades that it is losing contact with its origins. In common usage it has become almost synonymous with welfare capitalism of the sort practiced in varying degrees by most of the Western industrial nations. But that is really inadequate. Any serious definition of socialism must include public ownership and control of all the major means of production and distribution—for practical purposes, all property—which precludes all Western nations. On closer inspection it becomes clear that Halperin's discussion of socialism is far more specific than this dictionary definition. He is really talking about a system with highly centralized planning and decision-making and no democratic controls. It was the only form of true socialism practiced in the postwar years, and it was the one he came to know intimately during his tour in Moscow. And as he judged it, it had failed on both economic and humanistic terms.

That is why he turned so hopefully to Cuba in the early 1960s. This was not socialism imposed on a sullen population by the Red Army, as it was, for instance, in Czechoslovakia. It was the result of a popular, homegrown revolution. Nothing was imposed on it by a foreign nation. Everything was fluid. Why, for instance, shouldn't something like Liebermanism work? What was wrong with decentralized decision-making? Why shouldn't Enrique Oltuski be permitted to save the lives of a herd of experimental cattle rather than having to wait for permission from the top while the cattle died? And why shouldn't there be some profit motive in a generally socialistic economy, if that would increase the production and distribution of goods? Was there something intrinsically incompatible between democratic controls and socialist economics?

In six years Halperin watched as Cuba appeared to come up with the wrong answers to all of these questions. The leaders were young, impatient, and increasingly dogmatic. It is not that they were unwilling to experiment, but the experiments they were willing to try all seemed to be devised for someplace else. Or they were applied without the information needed to proceed. Or they were applied by people who did not have the credentials to apply them. The more each trial proved to be an error, the more tightly they insisted on controlling the next one. The more they were questioned, the more efficiently they silenced the questioners. By the end of the decade they had an economic system that did not work and a political system that did not permit anyone to say that it did not work. In those spheres, at least, they had managed to emulate the Soviet Union.

The only significant difference from Russia, as Halperin describes it, involves the person of Fidel Castro himself. Few would dispute that his leadership of the revolution was remarkable, but serious questions must be raised about the way he ran the country, for run it he did. He seems to have made the leap from believing that he had led the revolution, which he had, to believing that he *was* the revolution, which he was not. Proceeding from this self-exaltation, he made sure that no plan was shaped and no decision made without his personal involvement. Unhappily, his temperament was mercurial and his decisions often whimsical. It is, as they say, a helluva way to run a store.

HALPERIN: As for the answer to the question of whether the failures are due to the historic heritage or to the system, I came away with the belief that—of course the historical heritage always plays a role—but mainly responsible was the system. . . . And I would apply that to the Soviet Union too. It's true that Stalin created the system basically, but you had the background of Ivan the Terrible and you had the background of atrocities in tsarism. It's true that in Cuba you didn't have by any means a pure democratic background. But you had a lot of Western background there, and you had Martí, not Ivan the Terrible, as the progenitor of a lot of Cuban culture. So I think my answer would be, in terms of what I understand from my experience, that the system finally decides about the failures, and not history. It's a failed system. I'm not saying anything new now. Gorbachev is saying it, right? And Deng in China.

It is best not to overdo this. Maurice was disappointed, but he remembers Cuba more fondly than he recalls Moscow. For all the failures of the economy, great strides were made in the fields of literacy and medical care. And the suppression of dissent was never as severe as in Eastern Europe, if only because the climate wouldn't permit it. A work camp in Cuba is not the same thing as a work camp in Siberia. Moreover, there was a certain joy and vibrancy in the Cuban people that made daily life pleasant in spite of shortages, in contrast to Moscow, where a pessimistic population helped to make daily life unpleasant. At any rate, the shortages never affected the Halperins seriously in Havana, because they continued to receive privileged rations. That, along with the balmy climate, lovely apartment, and abundance of friends made their personal lives quite comfortable.

Nevertheless, Maurice decided to leave. He was beginning to find it impossible to reconcile his material comfort with his moral discomfort in Cuba. And whenever he begins to feel morally or intellectually uncomfortable, he begins to let people know about it. Word of his discomfort always gets around to the people who are responsible for it, and they are usually unhappy at having it brought to their attention. Then things happen.

The Halperins had already begun to plan their departure when a good friend in the Ministry of Foreign Trade approached Maurice in the fall of 1967, and said, "You know, we have a lot of fire-eaters around here now. I think you ought to be careful." This was not an idle observation; it was a warning that Halperin was making the wrong people angry. Then, toward the end of the year, the minister himself, a good friend, took Halperin aside and said that he was very sorry, but as of the New Year they would no longer be allowed to employ foreigners in positions of influence in the ministry. Maurice was fired. He still had his job at the university, at least for the time being, and he and Edith had accumulated a large reserve of pesos that they hadn't been able to spend, so there was as yet no crisis. But it was clear by now that their horizons in Cuba were strictly limited. So they planned to leave in the next few months. Fortunately, the political climate in the United States had lightened, and Maurice was hopeful of landing a job back there once again in academia.

The supernatural had other ideas, however.

8

The Great White North

The Halperins planned to return to the United States in September 1968. Edith's brother, a physician, had a summer house at Martha's Vineyard where they could live the following year, rent free. In addition, they had saved a reasonable sum of money while they were in Cuba. From the beginning, 10 percent of their pay had been in convertible currency, which was a perk available only to foreign technicians. They had squirreled quite a bit of that away in a Canadian bank over the years (American banks, of course, could not conduct business in Cuba), and now had enough saved to get them through the year with no problem.

Maurice planned to write his book while they were in Martha's Vineyard. He had been preparing for it ever since he first arrived in Havana by quietly, almost furtively, clipping material he could use from newspapers and magazines. He did not want to take a chance with notes, he says, because "you never know when you might have trouble." It was a wise decision. Then, with things loosening up in the academic world for people like himself, and with a book in the hopper, he hoped to land a job at a decent university by the following September, although he was already past sixty. That was the plan, but it didn't work out that way at all.

The reason was the intervention of a friend whom the Halperins had met at one of Havana's finer watering places, a hotel with grand facilities that was reserved for Soviets and East Europeans and was open for food and drinks to other foreigners like the Halperins but was closed to Cubans. Halperin remembers its clientele as one of the most interesting international communities in the city. Among them, for instance, was an Argentine named Ernesto Bravo, a Communist who had been beaten to within an inch of his life by the Perón regime, and then fled to Russia where he recovered his health before coming to Cuba to teach biology at the university. Bravo's wife, Estelle, was a young woman from Brooklyn who has become quite prominent in recent years as a producer of documentary films in Cuba. Known as Estella Bravo, her Latin name gives no hint today of her Brooklyn origins.

And then there were the Browns. Fred Brown was a direct descendant of John Brown of Harper's Ferry.[1] Like his ancestor, he was one of society's natural mavericks. He had moved to Canada many years earlier, become a Canadian citizen, taught at a native community school in Northern British Columbia for a while, and lived in various communal settlements before coming to Cuba to teach philosophy at the university.

HALPERIN: Fred was a very devoted follower of John Dewey. He was a pragmatist philosophically, a true believer as far as Dewey was concerned. Well, that's a kind of true belief I could accept. It's a true belief that negates true believism, so to speak. Anti-true believer. And he knew all of Dewey's writings very well.

So here was Fred Brown, inheritor of a maverick gene, the kind of person who is anti-Establishment no matter what or where the Establishment is. And he was a pragmatist, a disciple of John Dewey, teaching philosophy at a university where Marxism-Leninism was the preferred way of thinking about things. In fact, he had great hopes for Cuba and was trying to reconcile Marx with Dewey in his own mind, which is no mean trick. Inevitably, he was getting into trouble at the university.

---

1. John Brown, of course, was the abolitionist whose raid on the federal arsenal at Harper's Ferry, Virginia, in 1859 was intended to trigger a slave revolt in the South. The raid failed in its immediate purpose, but its consequences certainly increased the tensions that led to the Civil War. Brown was captured, tried, and executed.

HALPERIN: So he came to me and I still remember it very clearly. We went into my study and had a long talk. He asked me what I thought and I said, "Fred, I think it is hopeless. You are not going to move this monolith here. It is moving only in one direction and it is not your direction, Fred. It isn't my direction either and I don't think there is much hope here." So he asked me whether he should stay on and fight or leave. I said, "Fred, leave." And he did. He left.

Sometime in 1967 the Browns returned to Canada, where Fred accepted a job at Simon Fraser University. Maurice had all but forgotten them when he received a call from Fred, who was in Vancouver, inviting him to come up and participate in a two-week conference on Latin America at SFU. The university would pay for the trip and take care of expenses while he was there. For Maurice this came as a welcome relief from tedium now that he was no longer working at the ministry, and he jumped at the offer.

Then he learned that there would be a small logistical problem. At the time there were no direct flights from Cuba to Canada and of course none to the States. Moreover, the Mexican government was making it difficult to fly from Havana to Canada via Mexico City, so in order to fly to the West Coast of Canada, he booked a route from Havana to Madrid to Montreal to Vancouver.

Halperin remembers the journey in detail. After running a gauntlet of bureaucratic nitpickers at the Havana airport, he finally made it to the waiting room, where there were three or four people, foreigners like himself, sitting quietly as departure time approached. Finally they were told to board, and as soon as they left the waiting room they were joined by enough Cubans to fill the entire plane. Why the Cubans had been kept in another waiting room until boarding time was a mystery.

HALPERIN: Well, we were on the plane and these Cubans wore poker faces. Made a big impression on me—even the children, subdued, quiet faces. Plane left, still poker faces. Then at one point we reached the point of no return. If something happens you go on to Madrid, not back.

*You're closer to Madrid so you are surely not going back to Cuba what-
ever happens. So the crew—this was a Spanish plane, Iberia—told the
Cubans, "Well, we have now reached the point of no return." Bedlam
broke loose. These people started dancing in the aisles and it was very
touching. Such a wonderful thing, you know. Such a marvelous thing
to see them. Hopping up and down, talking, lively—what a business.*

There was more bureaucratic red tape at the airport in Madrid and
more waiting in Montreal before Halperin finally arrived in Vancouver,
by which time his eyes were spinning in their sockets. Brown met
Halperin at the airport, put him up in a motel and left. Halperin slept
the night through and went up to the campus the following morning,
refreshed and prepared for a conference on Latin America. But he was
not prepared for what he found.

Simon Fraser was Canada's "instant university." It opened its doors
in 1965 atop a mountain where, a year-and-a-half earlier, there had
been nothing but trees and deer. From the beginning until institutional sclerosis began to set in a few years later, chaos was king. A
conservative administrative structure sat uncomfortably upon a wildly
diverse faculty and a seething student body, many of whom had been
drawn by the promise of small classes and an innovative learning
environment. In addition, there was a significant number of American
draft resisters, most of whom were politically radical and many of
whom were emotionally alienated as well.

Now, all of this may begin to sound like just another variant of
what was happening at many American universities at the time. But
this was not America. It was Canada, and Canadian universities were
only mildly affected by the ferment of the 1960s. Simon Fraser was
one of two or three exceptions. In addition to the predictable chaos of a
brand new university, one found the same sorts of cultural and political
radicalism there that one found in the States. And there seemed to be
an organization for every impulse. The first thing I saw when I arrived
in 1967 at this futuristic, concrete campus on a mountaintop was a
huge banner opposite the library that commanded, "ANARCHISTS—
ORGANIZE!" If it is possible to capture the spirit of any institution
in two words, that banner did it.

Halperin at that time was coming from quite a different environment. He had spent almost ten years in Moscow and Havana, where radicalism—that is, Marxism-Leninism—was the orthodoxy, and political and social eccentricity were "discouraged." Except for the standard military fatigues of the revolutionary elite in Cuba, for example, the clothes in neither country warranted a second look. As a result, Halperin's first visit to the campus left him stunned.

HALPERIN: I took a cab up to the campus the next morning. I got into the mall and I was amazed. Great throngs of people in various strange costumes. A lot of bearded people and people with odd gowns, and I decided, "Well, they must be making a movie here somewhere." Literally. I had missed the '60s, the whole business, and when I saw it I decided they were making a movie and these people were the cast.

His first day on campus, Maurice was taken to lunch by Tom Brose, a politically radical faculty member whose field was Latin American politics. The cafeteria they went to had recently been part of a faculty lounge. But the students decided that faculty lounges were elitist (which they are, of course), so they "liberated" it. For some years thereafter it was known as Liberated Zone Number One. As a radical, Brose was fully sympathetic with the liberation of the cafeteria, but as a gourmet, he had no patience at all for the food they served in it. As they were eating, he apologized to Maurice. "We have to eat the garbage they serve here, but what can we do?" Maurice looked at him in amazement. He had just come from Cuba and to him this food seemed almost heaven-sent. "What are you talking about," he said. "This is great." "Terrible, terrible," muttered Brose. "It's swill."

Halperin had only been on the campus for a few hours, and already he was beginning to feel as if he were "through the looking glass." He had left oppression and come to chaos. It had him reeling briefly, but then he settled back and enjoyed it. "I flourish in chaos," he says.

Indeed, he flourished so much that when the conference was winding down, the head of the Behavioral Sciences Foundation wanted to take him on as a faculty member. Nobody knew exactly what he would do there, because nobody knew exactly what the Behavioral

Sciences Foundation was supposed to do, except innovate. The university had given itself a mandate to move in new directions, and this was part of it. That was the essence of the interview Halperin had with the president. "Are you sure you are qualified?" the president asked. "I'm as qualified as anyone else in it," Halperin answered. The president agreed.

By the time Maurice left the office he had a job in Canada at a university that was unlike anything he had ever experienced. He had spent nearly a decade living and working in stifling political atmospheres and rigidly bureaucratized societies, and now he was about to join an institution that had the politics of Babel and no apparent intellectual guidelines at all. He never even returned to Cuba. He phoned Edith and told her to pack everything the Cubans would let her take along and ship out to Montreal, where he would meet her. She finally arrived in June, and the Halperins began the last phase of their lives together.

Maurice settled into his job quickly. He spent the summer reading everything available on comparative education, which he was to teach in the fall semester. When classes began in September, he found that he was almost overprepared for undergraduate seminars that were limited to twelve to fifteen students. In Havana he had been lecturing to fifty or sixty at a time, and a class that size leaves no room for discussion. "It was the first time I had been in this new atmosphere, you know, with a lot of gab going on," says Halperin. "I discovered that basically you didn't have to do much talking. The students did the talking."

While Halperin was settling quietly into the education faculty, a different department was settling noisily into the arts faculty. This was the Department of Political Science, Sociology, and Anthropology (PSA), and there was nothing else like it in North America at the time. The man who built the department was Tom Bottomore, an English Marxist scholar who had come over to help establish the new university. Bottomore followed two principles in shaping his department. First of all, he wanted to break through the barriers of specialization that he felt were balkanizing Western education. In fusing the three disciplines that made up his new department, he wanted to emphasize what they shared intellectually. Its focus would be an interdisciplinary approach to the study of society. It was one of the university's high-profile innovations. Within a short time the profile was to be higher than anyone ever dreamed.

The second mandate that Bottomore gave himself proved to be far more provocative. He wanted to create a department that would emphasize radical scholarship. Since there were few people available in Canada at the time who qualified, Bottomore searched for young radical professors from American universities. He had no difficulty finding them either, but he discovered almost immediately that they had a very different agenda from his own. What he hired were a number of Marxists whose primary commitment was to activism. As they saw it, theory was empty without practice, and they planned to fuse the two. Basically, they saw the department as a forum for changing the university, and the university as a forum for changing the society around it. That was the 1960s.

Initially these young professors were enthusiastic about the appointment of Halperin. His years in Moscow meant nothing to them, because the New Left of the 1960s held the Soviet Union in contempt. But Havana was something else. Fidel Castro and especially Che Guevara were icons to them. While they had been dallying with theory, Halperin had been immersed in revolutionary reality, and they intended to tap into his experience and expertise at once. Even before he received his appointment he was invited to give a lecture on Cuba to the PSA people.

HALPERIN: I used to say that the first time I ever really ran into Marxists was right here at Simon Fraser. I never met any in the Soviet Union or Cuba. Real true believers. Well, I was sort of greeted as someone who had come straight from the Elysian Fields. You can imagine. Coming right from Cuba—my God, six years in Cuba! Like a disciple, a direct disciple of the sacred word. Well, there was a terrible disappointment after I made my first speech, a very big let down. A few people asked questions. I shot them down and there was a great puzzlement. "This guy from Cuba, we thought we had something." I had no further contact with these people, except for a few of them on a personal level. Brose was a gourmet. We had that much in common.

Chinese food—he introduced me to the Chinese restaurants in Vancouver, and he was a nice guy. I enjoyed his company when we didn't talk politics.

The situation on the mountain really began to warm up in the summer of 1968, less than three years after the university opened, when the entire faculty launched a frontal assault on the authoritarian administrative structure of the university. The format was the "joint faculty" meeting. The arena was a large auditorium. Students were admitted as spectators and immediately became participants. There was no time limit on the meetings and no limit to their number. There was a tacit understanding that no blood would be shed, but otherwise the rules were what might generously be called flexible, bent often on a meeting-to-meeting basis by whichever faction could sit tight until the enemy got hungry and went home for dinner.

This went on for the better part of the summer, two or three times a week, four, five, or six hours a session, beginning in mid-afternoon. As the hysteria mounted, heads began to roll. The president resigned, then his successor resigned, and then *his* successor resigned as well. The university went through four presidents that summer, and the fourth one survived largely, it seemed, because he knew how to use Roberts Rules of Order.

By the end of the summer, when the adrenalin and the decibels had returned to normal, the administrative procedures of the university had been significantly altered. Before, power had flowed from the top down. The president had been responsible to a Board of Governors but otherwise free to do pretty much as he wished. Department heads had been tsars in their own domains, free to hire and fire at will, to shape the curriculum according to their own whims, and to grant or deny tenure and promotions as they saw fit. Afterward, power appeared to flow from the bottom up. The authority of the president was trimmed; the system of appointed, autocratic headships was replaced by elected chairs; and many departments allowed student representation at their meetings. Somewhat later the faculty discovered that when push came to shove—and push did come to shove—the administration still cracked the whip, but until then it was an exhilarating adventure.

Thinking back on it, Halperin smiles and says, "I lived three years in Moscow and six years in Havana, but I had to come to Canada to see the revolution." For most of us the revolution ended that summer. For Maurice the worst of it was still ahead.

Most of the departments in the university had few if any radicals, as a result of which the procedures they established for themselves were relatively moderate. In PSA, however, the radicals were an absolute majority, and this was reflected in the way they restructured their department. One of the most divisive issues was the matter of student participation in departmental decision making. How many students should there be? Should they be allowed to vote? In the history department, for example, three students were added to the two dozen faculty members at department meetings. They were allowed to vote on curriculum matters, but not on such matters as faculty promotion and tenure. The PSA faculty went much further because they had a different view of what a university was. They tended to see faculty and students as equal partners in learning and action. Quite logically, then, they insisted on granting students parity with faculty at department meetings, and giving them an equal vote on all matters, including promotions and tenure for faculty, and in the election of the chair.

This was too much for the chairman, who was not one of the radicals, and he resigned. When the department, including its student representatives, elected one of the militants to replace him, confrontation with the recently liberalized administration was inevitable, and it came almost immediately. In July 1969, the dean of arts, who had been a radical himself a year earlier, rejected the election and placed the PSA department into trusteeship, which meant that a committee from outside the department was appointed to run it. In effect, he trashed the department's procedures and reasserted the administration's authority. Push had come to shove.

The response was postponed until after classes resumed in September, but when it came, it was explosive. The radicals called a strike, apparently believing that the administration's reversion to authoritarianism had so alienated students and moderate faculty that the strike would shut down the entire university. Most of the radicals walked out (thus defaulting on their contractual obligations) and then discovered that they had overestimated their support elsewhere in the university. Student support, which was significant at the outset, quickly faded and became inconsequential. Many faculty members did not like the way the administration had acted, but were not willing to go to the wall for individuals who were ideologically hostile toward them, and often personally contemptuous as well.

In addition, the rest of the faculty had a better understanding of the probable consequences of the strike than did the radicals. Some years later I asked one of the radicals who survived why he did not join his comrades on strike. He said, "Because they had absolutely no sense of the power realities of the situation—who held it and how they would use it. All the strike did was give the administration the pretext to wipe them out. I warned them at the time and was attacked as an administration stooge for my trouble. They really thought the revolution was at hand. My God, they were living on another planet." That effectively sums up the situation. They overestimated their strength and underestimated their opponents'.

The strike was a dismal failure and ended officially six weeks after it began. The aftermath was a catastrophe for the radicals. By the time everything was settled, six of them had been dismissed outright, and in the next few years, several others without tenure simply did not receive new contracts when theirs expired. The aftermath was no picnic for the university either. The Canadian Association of University Teachers (CAUT)—the Canadian equivalent of the American Association of University Professors—investigated the affair and determined that SFU's president had not followed due process in the dismissals. It censured the university, which amounted to a request that academics everywhere boycott SFU.[2]

It was during this period that the Behavioral Sciences Foundation was disbanded and its faculty scattered elsewhere in the university. This proved to be serendipitous for Halperin, because one of the professors whose contract was allowed to run out was Tom Brose,

---

2. The president, upset at this prospect, called the dean of arts and asked how he should respond to the CAUT. The dean, a published poet, told him to send the CAUT a wire saying, "Fuck you. Nasty letter follows."

the specialist in Latin American politics. Maurice replaced him, moving from the education faculty into the bloodied and depleted PSA department to begin teaching in a field where he had some authority. It was the ultimate irony. After decades on the Left, he ended up a scab, a strikebreaker.

Fortunately he was not received that way in the department. The faculty saw him as someone who could talk to both radicals and moderates, and perhaps bridge the gap between them. And for the students he was, for a while, the "Hero of Havana," the man who had known Che and aided Fidel. They were even prepared to anoint him as a cultural rebel, a slight misunderstanding that occurred when Maurice, a veteran pipe smoker, heard about a tobacco-substitute made of finely shredded lettuce.

HALPERIN: I had my office there and I usually kept my door open and I began smoking this stuff. And of course the odor spread throughout the corridor. First thing I know students came running up with a kind of admiration in their eyes. "So you are smoking pot. How wonderful. We have a man that will just open the door and smoke pot." My reputation went way up. Well, I had to calm them down and explain that I was smoking lettuce.

Maurice entered PSA in the fall semester of 1971. He had not been in the department at the time of the strike and had made no enemies over it. Thus he built up a reservoir of goodwill during his first two semesters in the department, and seemed a reasonable choice when the members elected him to serve as acting chair for the summer semester. A new permanent chair was to be brought in from the outside in time for the fall semester, so Halperin's tenure was to be little more than a holding action. Since he agreed that he would make no significant decisions without consulting with the rest of the department, nobody was worried about the summer. But controversy has a way of stalking Maurice, as we have seen, and there were enough radicals left in the department to make sure that it would not be long in surfacing. Still, they did not initiate the conflict; Halperin himself did that.

The trouble started because Maurice has no patience for what he calls nonsense. According to the department's constitution there was to be a regular department meeting every two weeks. Maurice considered that to be nonsense. There should be a meeting whenever there was enough business to justify a meeting, and he would determine when that was. Meanwhile, he would be able to carry on the day-to-day routine more efficiently himself.

HALPERIN: So I sent a memorandum to the members of the department that said something to the effect that it's summertime and there isn't much business. We're waiting for a new chairman, so let's not hold these regular meetings. If there is some business to be discussed, let me know and I'll call a meeting. Lo and behold, we had a whole summer without meetings. The first fundamental change up there.

It was not only fundamental, it was illicit, because the department's constitution specified that there be a meeting every two weeks. And it was unilateral, in spite of Halperin's agreement to take no significant action without consulting his colleagues. Still, he got away with it. There was some grumbling, but it was summer, and things really were slow. They did not stay slow for long, however.

As it turned out, the appointment of the new chair fell through, and the department found itself facing a new semester with no one in charge. Pressed for time, the administration extended Halperin's tenure as acting chair for another semester. It appointed him in spite of the fact that the department's constitution specified that the chair must be elected by the faculty.

One can argue that the administration technically had the authority to override the department on this issue—it had done so, after all, with the trusteeship—but it is difficult to see the wisdom in Halperin's accepting the offer, no matter who had what authority. There was an uproar in the department, but if he had handled things prudently after that, he might still have made it through the fall semester without incident. Far from letting things simmer down, however, Halperin continued to act in violation of his agreement and began to meddle arbitrarily in substantive matters.

The first serious explosion came in mid-summer when the professors began to send in their course outlines for the fall semester.

HALPERIN: I hadn't looked at these things before. Now I looked at them and I saw some extraordinary things. Self-advertising of the grossest sort. And no kind of uniformity. From course to course there has to be a structure somewhere. I'm thinking about the OSS, about Boston University. . . . I couldn't see any structure there, you know. Some people would turn in two paragraphs, some would turn in three pages, and some of the stuff sounded so stupid and was such a bunch of crap. So the next thing I did was to do some editing. I don't have to go into the details. Censorship! So I was already becoming a bad egg before the real big scandal broke.

It is amazing that a man who had paid a price in the past for speaking his mind, and who had read a ringing defense of academic freedom into the proceedings of a U.S. Senate committee, should have been so insensitive on this issue where it affected his colleagues. He did not simply *edit* these outlines; that is a misleading euphemism he uses from time to time. He censored them, and he should have expected a hostile response. If it was too late to systematize course outlines for the fall semester, Halperin should have left them alone and raised the issue at the first meeting of the new term. Then the entire department could have worked out a policy on course outlines to put in place for the spring semester. Under those conditions, even dissenting faculty would probably have gone along with a majority decision to systematize course outlines, assuming, of course, that systematizing did not mean ideological tampering. As it was, Halperin's action provoked such a reaction that he backed off and let the original outlines go through. There is much to be said for experience, but Halperin's experience with the OSS and Boston University served him badly in this instance, as it did when the big scandal broke at the end of the summer term.

It involved what Maurice felt to be an unsavory situation centering on the departmental assistant (DA). This is an administrative, not a faculty, position, and every department in the university has one. When Halperin took over he very quickly sensed that his DA was not just administering but was making her office the hub of radical activity in the department. Moreover, he suspected that she was leaking information to radical faculty and students, a suspicion that was recently confirmed to me by one of the faculty members from that era.

Halperin decided to see just what was going on, so he came up to the department on a weekend when the halls were deserted, entered her office (he had a key), and proceeded to go through her files. To put the best face on it, this was a totally unethical venture. What he found, he says, were files that were complete chaos; two-thirds of them were simply useless and could just as well have been thrown out. He concluded that there was no reason to pay such a high salary for so little work and so much disruption. Not only did the department not need the DA it had, it didn't need any DA.

He checked with the administration, which gave him the green light, and he checked with the personnel office to make sure that the woman would be placed in a similar position elsewhere in the university. After reassuring himself on both counts, he declared her position "redundant," which allowed him to get rid of her without actually firing her. As in the OSS, she was "traded around." All that remained now was to parcel out her duties to himself and to the stenographers in the office. There would probably be some flack from the departmental malcontents, but since he had the administration behind him he was not worried about it.

The flack turned out to be more than he had bargained for. The PSA students were up in arms, which did not surprise him. The student newspaper was up in arms, which did not surprise him. The departmental radicals were up in arms, and that did not surprise him either. But the opposition included some of the moderate faculty members as well, and that did catch him by surprise. The following day, nine members of the department signed a letter to the administration saying that the removal of the DA was "strongly disruptive of the day-to-day administrative workings of the Department" and accusing Halperin of actions that were "directly in contradiction to the manner in which he agreed to administer the Department" when he was first elected acting chair. They requested his resignation and asked that they be allowed to recommend an acting chair for the coming semester. Summer classes were over when Halperin acted, and many faculty members were already out of town. Subsequently six of the PSA faculty sent up a letter in support of Halperin's action, but the damage was done.

The letter of reproof itself did not ruffle Halperin. Indeed, he seems to have welcomed the hostility of the radicals. But he was clearly distressed that moderates should have attached their names to it. He assumed that, as friends, they must have known that his actions were appropriate to the problem, and thus he is forced to look for some other explanation for their behavior. He attributes it to fear. "These were people who could easily have avoided voting against me," he says. "Very good, close friends, you know, and I credited it to fear of the other faculty people."

One signature in particular upset Halperin. It was that of Ernest Becker, who, like Halperin, had come to SFU in the late 1960s as a member of the Behavioral Sciences Foundation, and like Halperin had moved over into PSA when the foundation was closed down. Becker was a man of very broad learning and had become one of Halperin's closest friends in the few years they had been together at the university. That was what confounded Halperin. How could this man have turned on a close friend?

Becker tried to explain in a letter he wrote to Maurice a few days after the incident. It is a murky letter, but in the end his meaning is clear enough. He is convinced, he says, that the administration is consciously seeking "to completely possess the PSA department" and to "abrogate the autonomy of the professors" in it. But he is also convinced that the course of action that Maurice has chosen is—unwittingly, he emphasizes—helping the administration to do it. He is "shocked" at Halperin's intransigence in the affair, and reminds him that he—Halperin—had told Becker many times, that "this is an imperfect world; one lives in it by compromise, getting along with all points of view, in fact, accomplishing little or nothing of what one truly believes in."[3]

Halperin did not answer the letter. A week or two later he encountered Becker in the hallway. Becker stopped to talk to him, but Maurice cut him off, saying, "Ernest, I don't want to talk to you." He

3. Ernest Becker, letter to Maurice Halperin, August 23, 1972.

also broke off relations with the other moderate who signed the letter. Sometime later Becker entered the hospital. Maurice found out that the diagnosis was cancer and that there was no hope. At such times the differences that destroy friendships fade before a more profound reality. Maurice went to the hospital and realized almost immediately that Becker knew he was dying. The two old friends passed some time talking about everything but what had driven them apart at the university. When it was time to leave, Maurice rose and they shook hands. Halperin groped for something to say, for some formula, but all that came out was, "Goodbye, Ernest." Not long after that Becker died. A few months later his last book, published as he was dying, won the Pulitzer Prize. Written before he knew he was ill, its title was *Denial of Death.*

This whole affair suggests an explanation for what had happened to Halperin. Becker saw him as a man of reason, a man of compromise, and was "shocked" to see him behaving in an authoritarian manner. It was not all that shocking, however. On those occasions in the past when Halperin had been in charge—in the OSS and at Boston University—he had not been responsible to a constituency that could vote him out of power. He had authority and he was willing to use it. He did not have to accept counsel or even listen to it. He could rule by fiat if he wished. Yet the impression one gets from his subordinates in the OSS, at least, was that, on the whole, he did listen to counsel and try to reach some sort of consensus on the issues that occupied them. He was willing to compromise in an imperfect world. This is not to say that he bent to the prevailing winds. He was decisive but he was reasonable.

Why then did he abandon his tendency to compromise during his brief tenure as acting chair of PSA? He had been around long enough to witness the university-wide struggle to get rid of authoritarian headships, and to know that of all departments in the university his was the one most likely to respond with fury at any effort to return to that system. To be sure, he had the blessing of the administration, but he must have known that in pursuing an authoritarian path he would precipitate another crisis in a department that really did not need another crisis. That is what Becker was trying to tell him.

I think his actions make some sense if they are seen as a reflex of his experiences in the 1960s. His three years in Moscow left him with a very bitter taste from Soviet socialism, which he saw as economically lame, intellectually arid, and politically repressive. He went to Cuba with hopes that a more benign climate would permit socialism to take root there and bear the fruit of its promise. For six years he watched as, in his eyes, it increasingly took on all of the worst traits of Soviet socialism. By the time he left Havana he was cynical about the promise and sick to death of the slogans. He was not only drained of socialism; he was disgusted with it.

To come to Canada with those views, and then to find himself on a campus that was seething with socialist chiliasm and socialist slogans, must have been, at the very least, a disheartening experience. For three years the relative quiescence of the education faculty permitted him to ignore campus unrest. But his transfer to PSA thrust him into the middle of it. Marxist dogmatics had become his nemesis in Moscow and again in Havana, and he despised its more rigorous practitioners. Now, even though their ranks had been decimated in the aftermath of the strike, there were still enough radicals in PSA to raise his hackles. He felt that they were mischief-makers of the worst sort, and that the center of their activities was the DA's office. His suspicion that she was leaking confidential information to them would explain why he rifled her files. Short of firing the remaining radicals, which he could not do, firing her seemed as good a way as any to clip their wings for the time being.

What he did not count on was the opposition of the moderates. When pressed, he is not able to give a convincing explanation for their opposition, so he attributes it to weakness and personal betrayal. He expected them to support him, or at least to abstain—even "when the actions are wrong," as Becker put it—out of friendship.

All of these tortured rationalizations dissolve before the only reasonable explanation for the opposition of the moderates. Halperin had agreed to certain conditions about how he would administer the department, and then proceeded to violate that agreement repeatedly. That he could not, and still cannot, see that this behavior was in any way improper is a measure of his implacable hostility toward the remaining radicals, and no doubt as well of a latent streak of authoritarianism that the situation activated. That he could not concede principled motives to the moderates is a measure of how much he misread the events at SFU since his arrival, for without the support of the moderates there would have been no liberalization of procedures in any department. The moderates in his department who opposed him demanded his scalp because they refused to let him wipe out their hard-won gains.

That Halperin could only explain this "betrayal" as weakness should not be surprising, because his entire public life had been keyed to friendship, personal loyalties, and "connections." He was hired by the OSS because an Oklahoma friend had gotten through to William Langer about him. And he had a really good look at networking as an outsider in the Ivy League clique that dominated the R&A branch. He continued to learn about this process during the war as he and his Washington friends got rid of troublemakers and incompetents by "trading them around." They took a "You take my headache, and I'll take yours" approach. The people he added to his department at BU were not hired after an academic search, which is customary, but because he knew them in one capacity or another in the Boston area. His jobs in Mexico came through personal contacts, and his position in Moscow through the recommendation of Lombardo. This is not to say that these appointments—both the ones he received and the ones he made—were in any way tainted or undeserved. Halperin was prominent in his field and an effective administrator who did not have to apologize to anyone for the positions he held. And the people he hired at BU were certainly capable. Yet the whole process bespeaks a habit of mind that verges on cronyism. Thus it was quite natural for him to cast the drama at SFU in terms of friends and enemies, and therefore to interpret the opposition of friends as weakness and personal betrayal.

Maurice Halperin sees himself as a child of the Enlightenment who was shaped by two dominant influences. The first of these was the late nineteenth-century intellectual renaissance that took place among East-European Jews. His father, a man with little formal education, made the atmosphere of this renaissance a part of his household, and Maurice flourished in it as a youth. The second was his formal education, beginning with the rigorous classical curriculum of the Latin School, continuing with the impact of such thinkers as Montaigne and Voltaire during his undergraduate training at Harvard, and culminating with his doctoral work at the Sorbonne. Given this background, it is not surprising that he believes in the perfectibility, or at least the improvability, of humankind and its society, and therefore in progress; that he bristles at injustice, but never speaks of sin or evil; and that his keen mind excels at rational analysis and the problems that lend themselves to rational analysis.

At the same time, the realm of feeling seems almost foreign to him. He can analyze a person, group, or culture more persuasively than he can empathize with it. And passion, either in himself or in others, seems almost to embarrass him. This is a man who has been through some pretty distressing experiences in his life. Yet when I asked him pointedly on two or three occasions how he *felt* about some of his experiences he generally answered with what he *thought* about them. When there is no hard evidence to explain a person's behavior, he is likely to ignore it altogether.

On one occasion I asked him why he thought Bentley had lied about him; I even offered a possible explanation. He dismissed my hypothesis almost impatiently, saying, "That's just speculation." Indeed! If the lady's lies had destroyed *my* life for no discernible reason, I would have plunged into a veritable sea of speculation. I would have agonized over it. I would have clutched at any hint of an answer. I would not have been merely angry, I would have been apoplectic. And I would have let the world know what I thought of this miserable creature. Here was a woman and an event that had the most profound personal consequences for Halperin. How strange (it seemed to me) to dismiss them because there was no hard evidence to weigh and measure.

Perhaps this was just a modern expression of the Enlightenment mentality: no evidence, no issue; next case. There is not even a hint of frustration that no evidence existed. It is as if feeling and thought occupy mutually exclusive categories for Halperin. Those questions that cannot be answered by one method are not even eligible for consideration by the other. They cease to exist as questions.

Although a maverick in his public life, Halperin had a normal, even traditional, personal life from the beginning. When he speaks of his childhood his conversation turns warmly to the influence his father had in shaping him. But he rarely speaks of his mother at all. It is not that there is any hostility toward her, but simply that she was part of the domestic landscape.

He conveys the impression that the household he helped create as an adult was not unlike the one he grew up in. It seemed to turn largely on his needs, and his needs, as it turned out, were exceptional. Not many men have to break camp under duress in their lives. Halperin had to do it repeatedly, and each time his wife, Edith, was completely supportive. This speaks of a loving relationship between them, but also of a very traditional one in which she deferred each time to his needs. It is important to note here that Edith was a remarkable woman. Warm, attractive, professionally trained, and extremely intelligent, she could at any time have said, "Enough. I don't want to leave this place for a strange land. Good school teachers are in short supply in America and if I have to, I will build my own life. Don't go, or go without me." They always talked things over, but the result was always the same; Maurice made the decision, and Edith went along with it.

This is not to say that he ever demeaned her in our conversations. On the contrary, when he spoke of her, one sensed immediately the strength of the bond between them. It is just that he spoke of her infrequently. In fact, Edith played a surprisingly small role in the dozens of hours that Maurice spent reminiscing on tape with me about his life. One comes away feeling that, like his mother, Edith fulfilled some undefined woman's role. And like his mother, she was more or less taken for granted.

For a while I wondered if I did not exaggerate the significance of this apparent gap in Halperin's recollections. Then his daughter, Judith, came out to visit her father in Vancouver, and while there she read over the transcripts of the many sessions we had already completed. She said that she had things to add, so the three of us then taped a conversation together. It soon became clear to me that Judith, too, felt her mother had not been given her due in Maurice's sessions. She took some trouble to emphasize Edith's strong influence in the home and her unusual capacities and accomplishments outside of it. Judith filled in some of the gaps, but in the end she confirmed my impression that Edith had settled for a very conventional role in a household that clearly revolved around Maurice.

In important and obvious ways Maurice Halperin left Cuba in 1968 a different man from the one who arrived in 1935. The young Halperin was just becoming aware of squalor and exploitation, and of injustice and oppression, and he felt impelled to act against them. If there was a public ethos in the 1930s, it was bound up with those perceptions. Social and economic conservatives were on the defensive in those years, and especially among intellectuals there was an exhilarating belief that everything was possible and commitment was imperative. The question for them was not whether to act, but how to act. Was the millennium at hand or still off in the future? To put it a bit differently, do we go for it all now, or do we approach it piecemeal over a longer period of time? In the political environment of the time the alternatives lay to the left of center, especially for intellectuals.

Maurice made his life in that political environment. He was increasingly drawn toward socialism as an ideal, but he was apparently under no illusions about its prospects in America for the near future. He supported New Deal liberalism at home and looked hopefully toward the Soviet "experiment" abroad, and even more basically, of course, toward Soviet foreign policy. Except for the period of the Stalin-Hitler Pact, he did not really depart much from those commitments for the next twenty years.

The big change for Halperin came after the mid-1950s, beginning with the Khrushchev "revelations" about Stalinism, and concluding with almost ten years of life in the socialist world. He says that when he first went to the Soviet Union he carried the usual left-wing bias against the consumer society. "Ads, ads, ads; buy, buy, buy; consume, consume, consume. Well, let me tell you," he says now, "there's nothing like living in a society where there's nothing to consume to make you appreciate the consumer society. I'm all for it." By the time he arrived in Canada, he still supported social welfare measures, and he still operated within a framework of Enlightenment values. One might classify him, still today, as a New Deal liberal. But he is immovably hostile to any variant of socialism. He does not reject its humanistic vision; he just does not think that socialism can bring it about, ever. And to that extent he is a very different person from the fellow-traveling Halperin of the depression and war years.

After Maurice left Oklahoma University in 1941, his boss, Roy Temple House, told a colleague, "You know, Halperin is not a trouble-maker; trouble came to him." In other words, he was just a bystander in life to whom things somehow happened. His daughter follows a more literary approach to the same general appraisal. She sees him as a modern-day Candide, a primal innocent caught up in a nasty and capricious world. Both views share the common assumption that Maurice was never really the agent of his own destiny. He does not chase trouble; trouble chases him. It is clearly a portrayal of himself that he cherishes. And to my mind it misses something elemental in his character that better explains the swerving course his life has followed.

Whatever Maurice Halperin is, he is not a Candide. Although he encountered misadventures in his life, and eventually retired from the fray, he has never really been an innocent who naively believed that this was the best of all possible worlds. If he believed that, he would never have lifted a finger to change it. But he did perceive injustice, and when he saw it, he fought it. In pursuing a course of activism he inevitably made enemies, many of whom, whether Oklahoma oil men or Bolshevik bureaucrats, were exceedingly powerful.

When he was a boy, he interpreted injustice in personal terms, most often in the context of anti-Semitism. He heard about it constantly at home, and he encountered it often in school, until one day he decided to do something about it. He took on a big Sicilian kid at school who had been abusing him about his Jewishness, and to his surprise, "knocked the hell out of him." It is interesting that in a completely unstructured interview his mind should reach back more than seventy years and fix on that incident as something significant in his life. Obviously it made quite an impression on him. It didn't end anti-Semitism in the world, but it did put a stop to the badgering he was taking at school. It was his first encounter with injustice, and it had a most satisfactory ending.

Justice, injustice—that incident and what it signified to young Maurice echoed throughout his adult life. Recall the old man he met years later in a Mexican sanitarium, Lenin's first minister of justice, who confronted his leader with the injustice in the new Bolshevik regime. That man, too, took a stand against injustice, such as he could, and it made an impression on Halperin. Like the fight in the schoolyard, it was an isolated encounter (he never saw the man again) that reached something very basic in him. When he encountered something he felt was wrong, he stood up against it without calculating odds that were often against him. For example, it was no big deal for people in New York City to fight for the Scottsboro Boys during the depression, because the political culture of New York at the time was receptive to such a stance,[4] but it was a different matter in those years to fight against lynching in Jim Crow Oklahoma. Urban liberals could safely defend Steinbeck's *The Grapes of Wrath* and applaud the Mexican government for taking control of its own oil resources in the 1930s, but Halperin was courting disaster by doing those things in a state whose legislature was dominated by the banks that were tractoring the "Okies" off the land and the oil companies that were being expropriated in Mexico.

Years later he alone savagely attacked the incompetence (a different species of wrong) of one of his Moscow colleagues, and thereby implicitly questioned either the competence or the courage of the rest of the crowd there. It was an injudicious act for a man in his precarious circumstances. Still later, when he began to express the same open contempt for the authorities and their system in Cuba, his friends there tried to warn him that he was heading for trouble.

---

4. The case refers to a group of young black men who were falsely accused of raping two white women in Alabama. They were tried, convicted, and sentenced to death. After several appeals and retrials, the death sentences were commuted as part of a compromise with the defense. In the end, several of the men served long prison sentences for a crime they did not commit.

In some ways his misadventure at SFU was an expression of the same impulse. Rightly or wrongly, he perceived malice, dishonesty, and plain wrong-mindedness in the radicals, and he moved against them. His motives might have been pure, as Ernest Becker tried to tell him, but that did not excuse his behavior. Specifically, the means he employed were ill-chosen. They went against the grain of everything that had been happening at the university in the three preceding years. And in the end he accomplished nothing, because the position of DA was soon restored.

In adopting authoritarian means, Halperin followed the policy that he was most familiar and comfortable with. He had been on both ends of authoritarian structures at different times in the past with mixed results. At Oklahoma University before the war he had been the victim of a power play by the legislature. Given due process, he could never have been fired without cause, as he was. From there he moved to the OSS and flourished in a situation where he took orders from those above and gave orders to those below. He sought consensus, but he had the authority to act in its absence. At Boston University he tailored a department to his own specifications. He got along well there not because the structure was democratic, but because the personnel he hired were congenial. Thus his authoritarianism, like his hostility toward radicals, was nourished by personal experience. Once he possessed power at SFU the outcome was almost predictable. Of course, that is the advantage of the historian. With hindsight everything in the past becomes predictable in the present.

No, Maurice Halperin was not simply a passive object to whom things just happened. His adventures and misadventures were not random but recurrent over the years. There was a pattern to them. Put bluntly, Halperin could not keep his mouth shut in the face of any wrong that he deemed correctable. At times during our interviews he acknowledged as much, although it is not clear that he really recognized the role this trait played in his life, or how incompatible it was with the image of a passive innocent. "I was sometimes rather imprudent about a lot of things," he said on one occasion, "and also maybe a little playful, just wanting to stir things up a little sometimes. It is part of my bio-chemistry, I guess." He repeated this biochemical metaphor weeks later, when he was talking about his increasing troubles in Cuba. It is not misplaced. He had a constitutional inability to pass a moral problem without jumping in with both feet. If we want a literary counterpart to Maurice Halperin, we should look not to Candide, but to a creature who would fuse the moral fervor of Don Quixote and the earthy realism of Sancho Panza.

Halperin retired late in the 1970s. In 1988, Edith, his wife and companion of more than sixty years, died. He was awarded an honorary (LL.D.) degree by Simon Fraser University in 1992. He still writes;[5] he still teaches a course every semester on the Cuban revolution; and he hasn't been in trouble for years.

5. His most recent book is *Return to Havana: The Decline of Cuban Society under Castro* (Nashville, Tenn.: Vanderbilt University Press, 1994).

9

The Lady or the Tiger?

There remains one huge unsettled issue in the Halperin story, and it is necessary to bring Elizabeth Bentley back at this point in order to explore it. To reduce a complicated tale to its simplest form, Bentley accused Halperin of committing espionage, and he denied (and continues to deny) it. Their stories are flatly contradictory. One of them is lying, but which one? The answer to this question is important for three reasons.

First of all, Bentley's accusation was the pivotal event in Halperin's life. Because of it, he lost his job at Boston University and spent years of exile in Mexico, the Soviet Union, and Cuba, before settling in Canada.

Second, our answer must shape the way we perceive Halperin. If Bentley lied, then he was the victim of a terrible injustice that altered and nearly ruined his life in mid-passage. On the other hand, if she told the truth, then Halperin has escaped justice for crimes committed against his country a half-century ago.

Third, it has an important bearing on how we apprehend the wider historical currents of the era. If Bentley was telling the truth about Halperin, she becomes a more credible witness against the others she accused. But if she was lying about Halperin, it almost had to be with the complicity of the FBI, and specifically of J. Edgar Hoover, since nobody at the Bureau would have dared such a venture without his approval. Moreover, it could cast doubt on the rest of her accusations. In other words, the credibility of her testimony about Halperin has a bearing on the controversy over the postwar congressional investigations into alleged subversive activities. Was the government really honeycombed with Soviet spies? If so, does liberal tender-mindedness bear any share of the blame? Did it put America at any disadvantage in the Cold War? And if not, were all the allegations just a nasty scheme of conservatives to discredit the New Deal and the postwar Democratic party?

There are also possible variations on these themes. For instance, Bentley might have lied about some of those she accused, and told the truth about others. If so, then perhaps there was some espionage going on, but nothing like what is implied in Bentley's charges, and certainly not enough to justify the extensive "witch hunts" after the war. But if that was the case, why would she give such curiously erratic testimony? Are we dealing with a disturbed mind here? Any effort to clarify these matters must start with Bentley herself.

Who Was Elizabeth Bentley?

Elizabeth Bentley was the product of a middle-class New England background and a Vassar education.[1] Like many people horrified by domestic depression and international fascism in the 1930s, she drifted into the Communist party and then, late in the decade, into its underground apparatus in New York. Her immediate superior and lover was a man named Jacob Golos, a Russian-born naturalized American citizen, who was an important operative in the NKVD, a forerunner of the Soviet KGB.

During the war she was put in touch with a number of people who worked for various agencies of the government in Washington. She usually introduced herself as "Helen," a research aid to Earl Browder, who was at the time head of the American Communist party. She then asked these friends in government to bring information to her from their agencies that would be of interest to the party. Having established

---

1. Bentley published her autobiography in 1951. It is a somewhat sanitized and romanticized account of her trials and tribulations as a Communist. It was reissued in 1988 with a long "Afterword" by Hayden Peake, who painstakingly evaluates her account. See Elizabeth Bentley, *Out of Bondage* (New York: Ivy Books, 1988).

these contacts, she traveled to Washington every two weeks to pick up material from them, then returned to New York and turned over the material to Golos, who, in turn, relayed it to his superiors in the Soviet espionage network. According to her account, these contacts in Washington were all either party members or reliable fellow travelers and were thoroughly sounded out before they were asked to turn over any material to her.

Golos died late in 1943. Increasingly frightened both by her new superiors in the NKVD and at the prospect of being caught by the FBI, Bentley turned herself in to the FBI in the fall of 1945. Only after several sessions with her did the Bureau believe her. She testified behind closed doors for a grand jury in 1947 and before two congressional committees (including HUAC) in July 1948, when her revelations became public knowledge for the first time. Eventually she named more than one hundred people, but subsequent investigations focused primarily on the more than two dozen who were still employed by the federal government when she began to talk to the FBI in 1945. One of them was Maurice Halperin. Her deposition to the FBI, which ran to around one hundred single-spaced pages, was signed on November 30, 1945. Of her various accounts this was the one closest in time to the events she discusses, and is the basis for most of the discussion that follows.

What Did Bentley Say about Halperin?

Bentley's allegations about Halperin fell into two categories: there were those things she claimed to have heard about him from others; and there were those things she claimed to know firsthand because she took part in them. The more damaging statements, of course, were of the second category.

Bentley said that she "learned" (how? from whom?) that Halperin had been a Communist party member in Oklahoma but that he had lost contact with the party when he came to Washington. Sometime after his arrival, he and Willard Park, a former colleague at Oklahoma University, got in touch with Bruce Minton of the *New Masses*, a left-wing journal, and told him that "they desired to be placed in contact with some Communist in the East." Minton "apparently" relayed the information to Golos, who then arranged for them to meet Bentley. Her first meeting with Halperin took place, she says, "in the latter part of 1942" at Park's Maryland residence, at which time she "arranged to collect Communist Party dues" from him. Not long after that, Golos went to Washington, "and apparently made arrangements with them on that occasion to be supplied . . . with certain information to which they had access in their respective offices." For the next few months, according to Bentley, they passed the information along to Mary Price, who had recently been Walter Lippmann's private secretary, and Price gave it to Bentley. Up to this point in her account Halperin had given nothing directly to Bentley; she had no firsthand knowledge that the material was actually coming from him. It was OSS material, but it could conceivably have come from another source. Then Price became ill, and Halperin and Park began to give the material directly to Bentley. After that, her contact with Halperin was personal, and her allegations take on added weight because they did not involve intermediaries.

Golos was not impressed with Park's material, which Bentley characterized as "throw-aways and rather inconsequential data." But that was not the case with Halperin, who, she says, passed along "mimeographed bulletins and reports prepared by OSS on a variety of topics and also supplied excerpts from State Department cables to which he evidently had access." Elsewhere in the FBI files there is an internal (Bureau) letter to Hoover that discusses these materials in greater detail. It says that in Bentley's early contacts with Halperin "he had apparently unlimited access to what she describes as daily cabled intelligence summaries compiled by the State Department." On her biweekly visits to Washington, the letter continued, "HALPERIN would have a two-weeks accumulation of such summaries and sometimes would turn them over physically to her, while at other times he would perhaps clip out a pertinent paragraph or two and hand it over to her." Bentley said that security measures at the OSS tightened up later on, and Halperin had to be more careful. After that, he "adopted the practice of personally typing digests of such information as he thought of interest."[2]

How valuable was Halperin's information? Bentley herself was not qualified to judge it, but in her deposition, she said that "Halperin's contributions were gratefully received by Golos, who appeared to attach considerable importance to them." She also said that Halperin came to New York occasionally, where she and Golos would take him out to dinner or to a show. Never, she says, did Halperin indicate that he knew who or what Golos really was. He and several others were "told that such information that they supplied was being transmitted to Earl Browder," and she had no idea whether he knew or suspected that it was really going to the Soviet Union through the NKVD. Perhaps this was to give these people what nowadays is called "credible deniability." Or perhaps it was for the squeamish among them who were willing enough to give information to the American Communist party, but might balk at the prospect of passing it along to the Soviet Union.

As far as the law was concerned, it made no difference whether they passed it to the party or to the Soviet Union. Much of the now-declassified OSS material that I examined in the National Archives was clearly stamped with the following warning: "This document contains information affecting the national defense of the United States within the meaning of the Espionage Act. . . . Its transmission or the revelation of its contents in any manner to an unauthorized person is prohibited by law." Thus Bentley's contacts could believe whatever they wanted about where such material was going, but if they were indeed passing it along to her they must have known that they were violating the Espionage Act in giving it to her, or even discussing it with her, no matter what its destination. Sometime after her last meeting with Halperin, Bentley says, her new Russian contact told

2. Letter addressed to "Director, FBI" (Hoover), dated January 27, 1947. The letter is on an FBI letterhead, but I do not have the final page with the author's signature. It was probably from D. M. Ladd, the assistant director of the Bureau, who was apparently sending summaries of the Bentley information to Hoover at that time. The FBI file number on the letter is NY 65-14603.

her that Donovan had accused Halperin of being a Soviet agent, and that Halperin had then failed to meet his contact on several occasions. That was the last she heard about Maurice Halperin.

So Bentley's statement comes down to this: she had firsthand knowledge that Halperin was a member of the Communist party; that he paid party dues to her; that he passed along printed material from the OSS and the State Department from late 1942 or early 1943 until late 1944, approximately two years; and that he occasionally met her and her superior in New York City. She had hearsay information that it was he who had initiated the contact with Communists in Washington; that the material he gave to her was prized by the NKVD; and that Donovan was aware of Halperin's activities by 1945, and had confronted him with them. She also knew that Halperin had been at Oklahoma University, that Willard Park had been there with him, and that Park was now employed in Washington. When Halperin was called before the Senate Internal Security Subcommittee, these allegations were potentially devastating. How does he respond to them?

What Is Halperin's Response to Bentley's Charges?

Halperin is careful to establish a sense of the political climate in Washington during the war as a preface to his discussion of Bentley. There was what he calls a "culture of indiscretion" in the capital that was characterized by loose political gossip and almost daily leaks to the press. One example was that the columnist Drew Pearson was often fed information by Hoover, and he rarely thought twice about publishing it.

HALPERIN: Now you recall that Hoover and Donovan were not fond of each other. That's putting it a little mildly and, as a result, Donovan was one of Pearson's favorite targets. I remember one case that was spectacular. Pearson published information from a secret OSS document revealing that Donovan was backing, or had decided to back, Tito rather than Mihajlovich in the Balkans. The purpose of the leak was obvious—to discredit Donovan. Here he was supporting a declared Communist rather than a supposedly democratic resistance leader.

I remember at the time I felt that this kind of leak could be of use to the enemy in military operations. One would imagine that Drew should immediately have been called up, you know. The FBI should have banged on his door. But of course he got the information from the FBI; that was the problem. Nothing happened to him. I remember that Donovan was furious about this and wanted to make a tremendous issue. He traced the leak back to the FBI. But basically he was helpless. Edgar Hoover was a tremendous power. Washington was teeming with journalists looking for scoops or maybe leads, checking out rumors, picking up what scraps of information they could, or maybe just using expense accounts to invite officials out and eat well.

After he became chief of the Latin America Division, Halperin was one of the people the journalists invited out on occasion. "The journalists discovered me," he says, and he accepted. It was a welcome break from the hard-driving work of the division: the meals were good, and he was flattered to discover that some journalists thought he was important. He had lunches with a stringer from the *St. Louis Post-Dispatch* and a staff member of the *New Republic*, and he had breakfasts with a man from the Jewish Telegraphic Agency. He describes these people as "left of center" liberals (but no more than that) with whom he was ideologically congenial.

HALPERIN: Well, we chatted about some of the jurisdictional scuttlebutt floating around, but mainly about Latin America. I was very careful not to reveal classified information, though naturally my views and opinions were enriched by my knowledge of classified material. But this was being done and there was no, what shall I say—it didn't contravene the rules. I want to again emphasize that there was a line I never crossed—out of prudence, perhaps. I mean, I did have some prudence at times.

There was a second and quite different factor in the wartime climate of Washington, which Halperin characterizes as the "several wars" that were being fought. There was, of course, the war against the Axis, the "declared war." But there was also a jurisdictional war between governmental agencies, which, in Halperin's world, meant the war between the FBI and the OSS. And there was an ideological war under way that contained the seedlings of the Cold War.

The FBI/OSS war went back to the 1941 struggle between the two agencies over dominion in Latin America, a struggle in which, as I have said before, Halperin had unwittingly played a significant role. Donovan lost that battle but continued to operate unofficially in Latin America, and Halperin was delighted to supply him with ammunition when he could.

HALPERIN: From time to time we would get reports from the FBI claiming to be secret information from some Latin American country. In at least two instances that I recall we—that is, my staff and I—were able to identify the purportedly secret source of information. It was, in both cases, none other than an item taken verbatim from a Latin American newspaper. [Woodrow Borah corroborates this.] *Hoover was passing these things on as information that his secret agents were bringing up to Washington. Well, obviously I sent the evidence to Donovan and I am sure he knew what to do with it.*

Evidently FBI agents in Latin America were fobbing material off on Hoover that they claimed was confidential information they had been able to get by covert means, when, in fact, it was material they had cribbed from local newspapers that were available to anyone. The Bureau then routinely, and perhaps even triumphantly, passed the "confidential" material along to the OSS, where Halperin and his crew tracked it down and informed Donovan, who then used it to embarrass Hoover. It gave Hoover one more reason to remember Halperin.

The third war involved the question of who really was the ultimate enemy in Europe. Officially, of course, it was Germany, but there were what Halperin calls "people in high places," especially in the State Department, but also in the OSS and elsewhere in Washington as well, who saw Soviet Russia as the ultimate enemy. This is not to say that they minimized the threat of the Nazis, but they anticipated a war with Russia after the Germans were defeated. What distressed Halperin about this is that these people felt that an alliance with Germany would be a crucial element in such a war. That prospect was dampened by the official policy of "unconditional surrender," which would almost certainly eliminate Germany's capacity to take part in such a war. What this faction wanted was a negotiated surrender that would crush the Nazis without destroying Germany. The Allies never abandoned the policy of unconditional surrender, but their devotion to it was considered by many to be suspect.

Halperin was completely opposed to a negotiated peace. As a Jew, he had strong personal feelings against the Nazis, and, like many people at the time, he was probably not inclined to make fine distinctions between Nazis and other Germans. He believed that a negotiated peace that left Germany intact would not destroy Nazism, but only leave it dormant, and would certainly not affect the German presence in Latin America. He was committed to the official policy of unconditional surrender, and he admits that he "did what (he) could to supply information, orientation and whatnot that would block a negotiated peace." No doubt there was more than a touch of malice in his views too. It became clear with the fierce German resistance after D-Day that unconditional surrender meant the destruction of Germany. Halperin shed no tears at the prospect. Indeed, he was a supporter of the Morgenthau Plan, which called for the destruction of industry and the pastoralization of Germany after the war, a plan which he now concedes was "utopian." These things help explain the direction and strength of his commitment during the war, and give added meaning to his OSS sponsorship of a military invasion of Argentina, and his emphasis in the Latin America Division on the "importance of the Nazi presence in . . . Argentina, Chile and Bolivia."

Another factor in the ideological war, and in Halperin's response to it, was the perception in Washington of the Communist party at the time. The party threw itself passionately into the war effort and was willing to commit heresy against socialism to do it. It opposed all strikes and worked actively to suppress them in unions where the Communists were strong. On the international scene it supported any regime, no matter how reactionary, that opposed the Nazis, which explains its support for the more conservative alternative in the Bolivia coup. In the spring of 1944 the party even dissolved into the

Communist Political Association, which permitted it to work actively for Roosevelt's reelection without the embarrassment of also supporting Communist candidates for office before a skeptical public. All of this seemed to support its claim that Communism was just "twentieth-century Americanism." The party hid its work clothes, put on a suit and tie, and went respectable for the duration. And it was accepted on those terms by more and more people during the war. All of these things contributed to the backdrop for Halperin's encounter with Elizabeth Bentley.

Halperin says he was introduced to Bentley not by Bruce Minton, but by a relative of Minton, whom he does not want to identify in order not to embarrass his family. As far as Halperin knew, the man was not a Communist, but because of his connection with Minton, Halperin had no reason to doubt his description of Bentley as a research assistant to Browder. Bentley introduced herself to Halperin as "Helen," and said something to the effect that "I understand you are an expert in Latin American affairs. Could I come and talk to you about Latin American affairs for background information for Earl Browder?" Halperin agreed. Bentley says this was late 1942. Halperin thinks it might have been early 1943, but he is not sure. He does recall that in the context of wartime Washington described above, her request, and his response to it, seemed perfectly normal. Halperin suggested they meet over lunch, but she said she arrived from New York too late for lunch and asked if they could meet at his house. Again he agreed.

HALPERIN: Well, she came twice, I am pretty sure of that, and possibly a third time. Everything was perfectly normal. She came in, I introduced her to Edith and the kids and we sat down. She talked to the kids, you know, in a normal way as an adult would. Talked to Edith about the weather and then we moved into a corner of the living room. She had a notebook and she began asking questions about Latin America. I told her I wanted her to understand that I would not be able to give her classified information, and also explained that actually the main source of my understanding of what was going on came from perfectly open sources. Now, whether or not she was disappointed I have no way of saying. She came and we talked Latin America—Chile, Argentina, the Nazi business, the parties there, the economic situation—an intelligent, what shall I say, approach that she had. She was obviously no dope in that respect. She took some notes. There was, as I look back at it, there was something totally normal about her. I mean, it never occurred to me that there was anything odd or fishy about her. . . . It had all of the feeling of being very normal. The blinds were open, we were sitting there with the kids, the mother-in-law, chatting. Never any documents involved of any kind, ever. Well, let's say she came twice, anyway, at an interval of maybe a month, six weeks, I forget. And possibly there was a third time. But not too long after we had begun she said she had to have an operation and she didn't know when she would be able to come back again. I wasn't disturbed by that in any way. "Good luck with your operation," I said. And that's the end of it. Never saw her again. I gave it no further thought.

Halperin says he never met Mary Price or Jacob Golos; that he never paid party dues to Bentley or anyone else because he was never a member of the party; that he never gave her money in any other context; and that he never saw her in New York or had dinner with her or Golos (under any name) anywhere. Furthermore, he says, he never discussed classified information with her and never so much as gave her a scrap of paper—nothing written, printed, or mimeoed. There was no contact with another Russian or party "contact" after her "operation," and Donovan never accused him of being a Soviet agent or anything remotely like that. He is at a loss to explain why she said what she said about him. "I can't figure out her motives or why she would distort the thing to this extent."

Bentley and Halperin are not far apart on the Minton connection or on his acquaintance with Park. She also knew about his time at Oklahoma, but, according to Halperin, is wrong about his membership in the party there, although he concedes that his activism did bring him into contact with people from the party in Norman. What it all boils down to is that Halperin admits having known Bentley and having talked to her two or three times over perhaps six weeks early in 1943, but he claims that he transmitted absolutely no classified material to her, either orally or printed.

The gap between these two accounts is too wide to explain simply in terms of blurred memories, either his now or hers then. So which one of them is lying? The answer is obscured by the fact that Bentley turned herself in to the FBI without one sliver of evidence to support her allegations. Of course, even solid evidence can be dismissed by the credulous. The will to believe can be a powerful hallucinogen. Whittaker Chambers fled from his underground life in 1938 with enough evidence to choke a horse, yet in the face of this mountain of evidence, there are still some who believe Alger Hiss's persisting claim that he was innocent. In Hiss's behalf, of course, it must be said that he does not have to prove his innocence, which is just as well for him because, as we know, it is almost impossible to prove that you did *not* do such-and-such. The same is true for Halperin. He cannot prove that he was not a member of the party, or that he did not pass important information to Bentley, nor does he have to. The burden of proof lies with Bentley, and she had no proof to offer. We are left with an unsupported allegation.

That brings the reader face to face with a problem the historian has to cope with all the time. How do you solve a problem when there is no hard evidence available, and when the circumstantial evidence might even support contradictory conclusions? Fortunately historians do not operate in a court of law, and do not have to prove a case beyond the shadow of a doubt. They operate very much in doubt's shadows and deal with probabilities more often than with certainties. They examine shards of evidence in some larger context, they consider alternative explanations, and then they come to a conclusion. Moreover, different historians can examine much the same evidence in different contexts and come to different conclusions. For example, I place Halperin's tenure as chair of PSA in the context of university-wide trends, and judge him harshly for his actions. Another historian might prefer to view him in the narrower context of a department that was overstocked with obstructionist radicals and praise him for the courage to stand up to them, in spite of university-wide pressures to proceed democratically. With that understood, we may return to the matter at hand.

What Do We Know about Halperin That Might Lend Credence to Bentley's Story?

We know from Halperin himself, of course, that he was a fellow traveler for many years after 1936, with two years off for the Stalin-Hitler Pact. We know that he was involved in various left-wing causes in Norman, but we must be careful here, because left-wing causes at the time were often liberal causes also, and so his involvement does not necessarily tell us much at all. Communists and liberals both supported industrial unionization, for instance, and opposed racial segregation.

More significant is an open letter that Halperin signed in 1939, which was published in *Soviet Russia Today*, a journal of the era that was extremely friendly to the Soviet Union. The letter was released on August 14 and published in the September issue of the journal. The dates are important here, because it means that Halperin signed the letter at the height of his early venture in fellow traveling just *before* the Stalin-Hitler Pact. The September publication date—after the pact was concluded—should therefore be ignored. The letter was signed by "400 leading Americans," including (by my recognition) party members and fellow travelers, along with a much larger group of names—some familiar to me, others not—to which I am unable to pin any political label.

The purpose of the letter was to strike back at the anti-Soviet propaganda put out, so it said, by "the Fascists and their friends" and to enlighten those misguided liberals who had been duped into supporting the attack on the Soviet Union, especially those who had "carelessly lent their signatures" to a recent manifesto of John Dewey's Committee for Cultural Freedom attacking all forms of dictatorship and asserting that "the Fascist states and Soviet Russia equally menace American institutions and the democratic way of life." Among the duped liberals who carelessly signed the manifesto were John Dewey, Sidney Hook, Sherwood Anderson, Sinclair Lewis, John Haynes Holmes, Norman Thomas, and Oswald Garrison Villard. The letter then went on to list ten points intended to bathe the Soviet Union in a flattering light, and thus to discredit the calumny that mentioned it in the same breath with Nazi Germany. Thus the letter contrasted Nazi book burning with the Soviet Union's making available the best of world literature and thought to the Soviet masses. It said nothing, of course, about how the "best" literature was determined, nor about what happened to literature and thought not judged the best. It also asserted that there had been "a steadily expanding democracy in every sphere," and gave special emphasis to the recent Soviet constitution, which guaranteed, among other things, universal suffrage and civil liberties, but did not mention that there was only one legal party to vote for. It pointed proudly to the rise of trade unions without mentioning that they did not have the right to strike. It also praised some very real accomplishments—the improving status of women, the spread of modern child care, universal access to free education and medical care, and the rapid spread of literacy. While some of these benefits might not have been very high in quality, they were generally a great improvement over what had prevailed under the tsars.

In short, the letter was a mixed bag. It praised the legitimate achievements of the Soviet regime, but it failed to question demonstrably absurd claims about democracy, civil liberties, and open access to world literature and thought. And it completely ignored the monstrosities of Stalinism—most obviously, the massive purge trials and the elimination of an entire class of peasants. The result was a work of propaganda that was thoroughly compatible with the party line of the United Front period. That Halperin signed the letter is an indication of how strongly he supported Soviet international objectives at the time, but it also suggests that his support for Soviet domestic policies might have had a stronger ideological element than he is willing to admit. Still, it may only document what he has already told us about himself: he was a fellow traveler prior to the Stalin-Hitler Pact.

We also know that the FBI had a file on Halperin from 1940 until at least 1949.[3] Unfortunately it is not much help, because most of it is not

3. I am obligated to Barnett Kalikow, who first secured this file in 1983 under the Freedom of Information Act, and to Maurice Halperin for turning it over to me.

available. Only about two-thirds of the pages have been released, and most of those are almost entirely inked out. What remains does nothing to support Bentley. As early as May 1940, an anonymous source in Norman reported Halperin as a suspect in "espionage and Communistic activities," although it is not clear what sort of espionage he was able to carry on in Oklahoma in 1940. The reports from Norman—still mostly inked out—continued periodically for the rest of the year and into 1941, but they remained inconclusive. In April 1941, a report said, "Investigation failed to reveal radical or subversive tendencies reflected in class room." Another report that year appeared to cite people who knew nothing about "seditious or subversive" activities on Halperin's part, but still another cited someone who had heard of Halperin vaguely "as a person with Communistic sympathies."

If the information from these reports seems vague, let me quote one entire page to give the reader a taste: "[Several lines inked out] A review of [inked out] failed to reflect [inked out] by Dr. MAURICE HALPERIN [5 lines inked out] . . . had heard of no [inked out] and had never heard of Dr. HALPERIN. [3 lines inked out] failed to reflect any information concerning [inked out] or of any [inked out] by Dr. MAURICE HALPERIN. [Rest of page inked out]." The page *appears* to say that there is no negative information on Halperin, a supposition that is supported shortly thereafter in a memo that recommends dropping the case: "A review of the file indicates that no further investigation appears to be desirable at this time, and this case is therefore being closed subject to being reopened upon the receipt of any additional information which would warrant further investigation."

By November, Halperin has joined COI in Washington, and Hoover himself is interested. Hoover informs the Oklahoma City office of the Bureau that Halperin is now with the federal government. He notes that Halperin's file indicates that he had been a member of the Oklahoma Federation for Constitutional Rights and that several people in Norman said that he had "Communist leanings." Hoover then instructs the agent to conduct a careful investigation into alleged subversive activities by Halperin, with emphasis on the "evidence gathered by the Oklahoma State Legislature on which was based its recommendation that Dr. Halperin be dismissed from the University of

Oklahoma by reason of his Communist tendencies."[4] The investigation dragged on into 1942. In mid-January, the Oklahoma City office, in a heavily inked-out memo, concluded that Halperin was "not believed to be member of Communist Party or any front organizations but is believed [inked out] to have communistic sympathies." By February, the investigation had been turned over to the Washington office of the Bureau, which called Halperin in and, with his consent, questioned him under oath. The entire transcript, mercifully uncensored, is included, but it is summarized in a brief synopsis that says,

> On February 12, 1942, Dr. HALPERIN was interviewed under oath and stated that he is not now or never has been a member of the Communist Party or the Young Communist League, nor does he advocate the overthrow of the present form of government. He stated that he was a member of the Oklahoma Federation for Constitutional Liberties, but that it was not affiliated with the National Federation for Constitutional Liberties.

In fact, when he was asked if the Oklahoma Federation was affiliated with the National Federation, Halperin replied, "Not to my knowledge," which is not the flat denial that appears in the synopsis. The National Federation for Constitutional Liberties was affiliated with the Communist party and was probably organized in response to a resolution by the American Civil Liberties Union, which effectively barred Communists from its governing committees. Halperin's organization was the Oklahoma Federation for Constitutional *Rights* (not Liberties). The timing of the two coincides, and the names are strikingly similar, but whether they were actually related in any way remains moot. More important was Halperin's sworn testimony that he had never belonged to the party or engaged in subversive activities, which repeated his sworn testimony before the Oklahoma legislative committee a year earlier. In March, Hoover sent all the material from Washington and Oklahoma to the COI for Donovan's action, and COI responded that,

---

4. Letter from J. Edgar Hoover, November 6, 1941. Actually, no specific reason was given for Halperin's dismissal, except that it was deemed to be for the good of the university.

after reviewing the material, it had decided to take no administrative action. Apparently not happy that Halperin was getting off the hook, Hoover then informed Donovan of the 1935 trip to Cuba. There the matter ends in the file. It is fair to assume that Donovan was not terribly put out by news of the Cuban caper, because he still refused to take any action against Halperin, who stayed on with the OSS for another four years.

There are a few conclusions we can draw from this FBI material. The Bureau had a line on Halperin as early as 1940, and Hoover soon took a personal interest in the matter. There were allegations originating in Oklahoma about Halperin, but there was no evidence to support them. Despite the lack of evidence, Hoover remained suspicious, but he was unable to persuade Donovan to take "appropriate" action. Finally, Halperin did what he refused to do years later before the Jenner Committee: he swore under oath that he had never been a member of the Communist party, thus opening himself to a charge of perjury if evidence to the contrary ever turned up. It is possible, of course, that Halperin had never been a party member before this time, that he joined some time after it while he was in Washington. In that case, both his sworn testimony of early 1942 and Bentley's sworn deposition to the FBI in 1945 would have been accurate.

Meanwhile, Army Intelligence was carrying on its own investigation of Halperin as part of the routine security check required for personnel in sensitive positions. Among others it interviewed a Laura Schutte, who had lived in Norman before coming to work in Washington in 1939. She had apparently known of Halperin in Norman and was aware of his dismissal from the university, although she was already in Washington when that occurred. She had learned, apparently while still in Norman, that Halperin "was actively connected with all civic matters, a student union and the welfare association, and was interested in the above groups primarily to carry on subversive activities." She also informed her CIC (Army Counter-Intelligence) interviewer that Edith "was active in similar groups, including the girl scouts, and was believed also to be carrying on subversive activities." The interviewer did not comment on the value of this information, nor shall I.

CIC also interviewed Halperin's COI boss, Preston James, who characterized Halperin as "a typical academic liberal who has advanced notions on liberalism." James was aware of the dismissal from Oklahoma University, of the Soviet bond, and of the trip to Cuba in 1935, but he was convinced that Halperin was "a sincere, open minded, loyal person who is eager to do something for his country," and was not a Communist. The file also contains a long letter from former Oklahoma University president Bizzell, who went over much of the same material, noting that he had read Halperin's articles and found nothing objectionable in them, yet concluding that he agreed with the dismissal because he had been "convinced for some time that his connection with the University was detrimental."

Thus, apart from Edith's effort to subvert the Girl Scouts, CIC did not turn up anything that the FBI had not already uncovered. There were deeds in Halperin's past that made some people suspicious, but no evidence of anything more than the "advanced notions on liberalism" that Preston James described. Ten years later, of course, that sort of advanced liberalism would undoubtedly have been considered sufficient grounds to deny Halperin security clearance. But this was 1942, when Nazi Germany was the enemy and Soviet Russia the ally. Donovan had no illusions about the Soviet Union, but he obviously saw nothing in the reports on Halperin that alerted him to subversion. And he needed the man's skills. As a result, Halperin finally received his security clearance.

Thus far we have turned up nothing more than a collection of oddments that can be read either way. On the one hand, there are the duck theorists who will say that if he walks like a duck, and quacks like a duck, and swims with other ducks, then he probably is a duck. On the other, there will be those who insist that an attraction to ducks does not prove duckness. He had denied party membership and subversive activities under oath and was otherwise quite willing to admit to fellow traveling, which could explain his general affinity for Communists. There is enough here to put the historian on guard against efforts simply to dismiss it all as a bunch of red-baiting (which Halperin does not do, by the way), but there is not enough to make a firm case against Halperin for anything. And, all of this taking place before Halperin even met Bentley, the question of espionage is not yet even relevant.

Halperin's departure from Boston University is not so easy to explain. The president, an honorable man by all accounts, including Halperin's, had assured Maurice, and had told the university community, that there would be no dismissal without evidence of wrongdoing. According to several of Halperin's former colleagues at BU, most members of the university community, and especially most of those who were on the committee that would hear his case, were sympathetic to him and felt that he was the victim of a witch hunt. These colleagues agree that his "prospects for weathering the storm were quite good," as one of them put it.

Since his prospects were good, and since he was still on full pay, why did he leave for Mexico? In particular, why did he leave in the manner he did? It is curious, to say the least. Halperin says there was nothing precipitous about his departure, that he and Edith took several days to drive rather casually to Mexico, and even stopped on the way to spend the night with an old friend in Washington. The chronology of events and the story told by Halperin's former colleagues all suggest otherwise.

Halperin left without even giving the faculty committee a chance to hear him out. President Case was trying to give Maurice every opportunity to deny the charges formally and save his job. Common courtesy, if nothing else, required that Halperin call Case and say, "Look, I've talked it over with my wife, and we've decided that these bastards have set their sights on me, and one way or another they're going to get me. I can make a living in Mexico, and there's no sense prolonging the agony. Thanks for all you've done for me, and so long."

Why did Halperin decide not to face the university community? What did he have to lose? After all, faculty hearings of this sort do not require sworn testimony and are not carried on under formal judicial procedures. Halperin could have chosen to answer some questions and not others, which was not a privilege he had in the more daunting arena of a Senate inquiry. He could have testified about himself, for instance, without answering questions about anyone else. He could even have answered the faculty committee's questions and then explained to them why he would have to "take the Fifth" on those same questions if called before a congressional committee again. For that matter, he could have told the committee a string of bald-faced lies without opening himself up to a charge of perjury, which was another luxury he did not have with the Jenner Committee.

He says he left basically because there were enormous pressures on President Case, as a result of which he (Maurice) didn't have a chance. But is that really so? As long as he continued to plead the Fifth Amendment, the Jenner Committee would be stymied. It could hear from Bentley about Halperin, but it would never hear from Halperin about Bentley. There would be accusations against Halperin but no case against him, just as there was no case against the others she accused without supporting evidence or corroboration of any kind. And as long as there was no evidence against Halperin, President Case had no grounds to move against him. Whether the regents would have forced Case to fire Halperin remains an unknown, because Halperin did not wait around to find out. Certainly his former friends and colleagues at BU feel that he had more than an even chance of surviving the ordeal with his job at the university intact.

Halperin is nothing if not a fighter. He had often fought against the odds in the past; why not this time? Even if he was correct in feeling that "they" were out to get him, it is difficult to understand why he chose not to fight. At worst, he had nothing more to lose than was lost by his sudden departure anyway. There are signs of undue haste in his behavior that have not been explained yet. His credibility in the BU affair is definitely shaky. We shall return to this point shortly.

Two later developments in Halperin's life also raise questions about the way he has portrayed himself. The first of these was his departure from Mexico, which also had more than a touch of panic about it. At the end of 1958, remember, Halperin was tipped off that the Mexican police were rounding up American leftists and deporting them to the United States. Halperin then went into hiding and negotiated a deal with the Mexican authorities that gave him a short period of grace during which he was able to arrange to leave with Edith for the Soviet Union, rather than the United States. Compared to his expatriation to Mexico, this was a really drastic move. He knew

Mexico very well, spoke the language fluently, and had both Mexican and American friends there. When he went there he could look forward to an emotionally comfortable situation. In contrast, he had never been close to the Soviet Union, did not know a soul there, and could not speak the language or even read the alphabet.

To be sure, the political situation in the States was still unpleasant for people like Halperin, but the worst was over. McCarthy himself was dead; the Supreme Court had gutted the Smith Act; and Senate investigating committees had fallen into relative quiescence. HUAC was still active, but it was becoming more of a nuisance than a threat. If, after a time, Halperin had been unable to land a university job, he could probably have worked in a bookstore until things improved or used his many contacts to find him some other job. And if all else failed, he could still have used his Mexican contacts to arrange something for him in Eastern Europe at a later date. It is odd that Halperin did not even return to see his parents before leaving for Russia.

The second development involves his entire situation in the Soviet Union. He arrived in 1959, which was still a very tense time in the Cold War, was accepted not as a tourist but as a resident, given an apartment that most Russians would have envied, and put to work in what must have been a fairly sensitive research institute. It is a fair assumption that before the Soviets opened the gates to him they put him through at least as tough a security check as the Americans had when he went to work for the OSS, and it is likely that he never would have gotten in unless people like Lombardo and Bassols testified that he was politically safe. Once again, this proves absolutely nothing about espionage, but it does add to the questions about Halperin's commitments, or at least about how the Soviets perceived them.

How Credible Was Bentley's Testimony?

In the end, the burden of proof—or in our case, the burden of probability—falls on Bentley. Since she produced no evidence implicating Halperin in espionage, and since no one else has ever corroborated that charge, it becomes a difficult matter to settle with any confidence. For that reason the question of her general credibility is crucial. Has anything turned up since 1945 to verify the statements she made about any of the accused in her deposition? Fortunately, Hayden Peake goes over this matter with great care in his "Afterword" to the reissue of Bentley's *Out of Bondage*. Peake demonstrates that Bentley did indeed tell some self-serving lies and that she made occasional errors of fact in one or another of her statements over the years. He concludes, however, that there is no pattern to these misstatements, and, more important, that not one of them has any bearing on the charges she made. They do not affect the substance of her story.

Peake then discusses several developments over the years that do lend credence to her tale. For instance, she accused William Remington of being a party member, of knowing Golos, and of having passed information to her on occasion in Washington until he went into the Navy in 1944. Remington admitted having met with her from time to time while he was with the War Production Board, of having given her *unclassified* information, and of having known Golos. But he denied under oath that he was ever a party member, and claimed he thought Bentley was just some sort of journalist, although he admitted buying copies of the *Daily Worker* from her. He also said he had no idea that Golos was a Communist, although he had been introduced to Golos by a Communist friend of his Communist mother-in-law. He was tried for perjury about his party membership and convicted on the testimony of several people, including his former wife.

Bentley also said she had been a contact for Hazen Sise, a "Canadian Communist" employed by the Canadian Film Bureau in Washington. She made no claim of espionage involving Sise, but she did provide intimate information to the FBI in 1945 about his marital, health, and psychiatric problems, all of which were corroborated many years later by Canadian historian James Barros, who had access to Sise's private papers.

Bentley also identified Abe Brothman as a contact who turned information over to her before the war, and CBS correspondent Winston Burdett as a Communist who was in contact with Golos in 1939. Both men eventually verified these allegations, although Brothman claimed that the blueprints he gave to Golos were his own property, that they were not classified, and, therefore, no breach of security or illegal act was committed. Nevertheless, his testimony corroborates her claim that she was collecting sensitive information. Similar corroboration came from Rose Arenal, the sister-in-law of one of the Mexicans who was apparently in on the plot to assassinate Trotsky.

One of the more interesting examples involved Duncan Lee, a direct descendant of Robert E. Lee, and a member of Donovan's Wall Street law firm before joining the OSS as Donovan's assistant. Bentley claims to have met Lee through Mary Price, to have collected valuable material from him regularly on her trips to Washington, and to have gone out to dinner with him and Golos in New York on one occasion. She said that Lee became increasingly nervous about his involvement, and eventually broke off his contacts with the Soviets. Lee's story is that he and his wife met Bentley at Mary Price's home and saw her occasionally because they found her interesting. After a while, however, she began to grate on them and they stopped seeing her. On one occasion he admits having had an innocent dinner with Bentley and her friend, Golos. And that was all. He had nothing to do with Communism and passed no information to her.

All of this is evidence that corroborates parts of Bentley's story, and therefore tends to make the rest of it that much more credible. But it is necessary to point out that none of it supports a charge of espionage against anyone. Still, it is amazing how many sophisticated people, who were engaged in highly sensitive war work, admit to having had totally innocent friendships with Bentley, and to having chatted casually with her about their work, or to just having passed the time of day socially with her in Washington, although her only apparent purpose for visiting the capital every two weeks was to gather as much information for the NKVD as possible and then return immediately to New York. What are the probabilities of all *that* being the case? Something is very much awry here.

Still, it is just possible that all of these meetings were quite innocent, and that Bentley's whole story was part of a huge, carefully crafted conspiracy to discredit the Left, as some have argued from the beginning. For this argument to stand up, Peake replies, one must recognize that Bentley, with or without helpers, had to conceive and commit to memory a story of great magnitude and complexity such that most of the people targeted would not have alibis for the actions charged. . . . In her preparation, she would have to have had access to United States intelligence data and that of the Soviet Union. She would be required to create, memorize, and recall code names, multiple meetings, places, times of events that never occurred, many involving people she didn't know. She would, on demand, have to describe their homes, life-styles, personal attributes, education, professional experience, and families. . . . And then, for whatever reason, the conspiracy would have to account for Bentley's going to the FBI to tell her story with no substantiating evidence.[5]

As if that were not enough, further corroboration for Bentley's story has now turned up in an entirely unexpected quarter. A. S. Feklisov, a retired KGB colonel, recently published an article in a Soviet journal of military history on the espionage "achievements" of Klaus Fuchs. Fuchs, remember, was one of the nuclear physicists employed on the Manhattan Project to build the first atomic bomb, and had secretly provided information on the bomb to the Soviet Union while he was still in New Mexico during the war. After the war, he returned to England, where he continued to pass information along to the Soviets until just a few months before he was tracked down and uncovered late in 1949. Feklisov was one of his contacts in England. In discussing the eventual imprisonment of Fuchs for providing nuclear information to Soviet intelligence, Feklisov describes a chain of circumstances that started with the 1945 defection in Canada of Igor Gouzenko, an obscure cipher clerk with the Soviet embassy in Ottawa, and led eventually to Fuchs and Harry Gold, his American contact. Feklisov refers to "the Gouzenko treachery" and then mentions that "another traitor, Elizabeth Bentley, gave evidence that [Gold] was connected with the Soviet intelligence service."[6]

5. Bentley, *Out of Bondage*, 266.
6. Col. A. S. Feklisov, "Heroic Achievements of Klaus Fuchs," *Voenno-istoricheskii zhurnal*, issue no. 1, 1991, 34–43. The reference to Bentley is on page 37. I want to acknowledge Owen Lock and Hayden Peake, who steered me to this article, and especially to thank my colleague, Richard Debo, who translated it for me.

There is really only one way to understand this reference to Bentley as "another traitor": In Feklisov's eyes, she, like Gouzenko, was a traitor to the Soviet Union because she defected and snitched. In other words, Bentley was exactly what she said she was—an espionage agent for the NKVD. Although it is only a clause of a sentence in an article about someone else, this is a stunning bit of information. It is the first time in almost fifty years that anyone has stepped forward with direct evidence to corroborate Bentley's story.

Anything is possible, of course, but not everything is probable. To swallow the great conspiracy theory at this point—to really believe it—calls for an act of heroic credulity. Among other things, the theory would now have to include the KGB as a co-conspirator with the FBI, which is really a bit much. No, after we discount for possible lies, distortions, fantasies, and even the possibility of FBI "coaching," it is still much easier to believe that most of Bentley's story is legitimate than it is to believe that most of it is a lie. Let us face it. There were confessed and convicted Soviet espionage agents in England and Canada, including, by the way, Klaus Fuchs. Are we expected to believe that there were none in the United States, or that, if there were, the FBI always got the wrong people? To ask that question is to answer it.

At the same time, we have to guard against blind acceptance of every charge that Bentley made. It is possible, for instance, that most of her accusations were valid, but that some, for whatever reasons, were not—that some were, in fact, lies. It is possible that this NKVD agent lied about Halperin violating the Espionage Act by passing classified information to her. Which brings us to the final pair of questions. Why would Bentley lie? Why would Halperin lie?

Why Would Halperin Lie?

It is important to emphasize once again that Halperin was not being hounded simply because he was a Communist but because he was alleged to have committed espionage. The question of his membership in the Communist party is really unimportant, except as it related to his sworn testimony in early 1942 that he was not a member and never had been. Anyhow, by the time he appeared before the Jenner Committee the statute of limitations had run out on any perjury that he might have committed more than ten years earlier.

To raise the question of possible espionage, however, is to plunge us back into the anxiety-ridden 1950s. Between the spring, when Halperin "took the Fifth" before the Jenner Committee, and the fall, when he drove to Mexico, one terrifying affair had taken place: Julius and Ethel Rosenberg were executed after being convicted under the Espionage Act of 1917, the same act that Halperin would have violated if he had given classified material to Bentley during the war.

The question here is not why did Halperin lie, for he never even testified. When things began to heat up for him in the fall he left for Mexico. The proper question then is, Why did he leave? If he was guilty, the answer is easy. He left because he did not know what kind of evidence the government had, and he was not willing to risk execution to find out. But one can rephrase pretty much the same argument to explain why even an innocent Maurice Halperin would leave: He had had nothing more than a few casual talks with Bentley, during which he had been careful not to discuss any classified material. At worst, he had been indiscreet, and now the politicians were out to capitalize on his indiscretion at any cost. They were out to nail him and, for all he knew, some of them might be prepared to fabricate the evidence necessary to do it. Given that perception of the situation, even an innocent Halperin would have been justified in bolting for Mexico. He had learned as a boy in that Boston schoolyard that there is a time to fight and a time to cut and run. It is one thing to bet against honest odds; it is quite another to bet when the house uses a stacked deck. And Halperin had no desire to be a martyr. At least that would explain the otherwise inexplicable departure from Boston. Thus the Rosenberg execution and the general hysteria of the era can be used to explain Halperin's behavior, whether he lied or told the truth.

Why Would Bentley Lie?

Guilty or innocent, it is easy to understand why Halperin would lie. But why on earth would Bentley lie? Remember that her initial deposition to the FBI was made in the fall of 1945, almost three years before the general public learned about her. There was no Red Scare then at all. True, there were signs of strain between Moscow and Washington, but most people still looked confidently to the Grand Alliance and the UN to carry the world forward into a new era of peace, prosperity, and international goodwill. In those circumstances Bentley could not possibly have expected to cash in on some great fiction, or to receive public acclaim and glory for it. Anyhow, we have already seen that the great-fiction theory does not stand up well to our test of probability. We have also seen that there is verification by now for significant portions of her testimony, which makes it all the more difficult to understand why she would lie only about a few of the people she accused.

Specifically, we still cannot explain why she would lie about Halperin. Nothing in her account about him, or in his about her, indicates that she had any personal animus toward him. On the contrary, she speaks quite warmly about him and Edith in her book. (Halperin says, "You'll pardon me if I don't return her warmth.") There is really only one convincing way to make a case that Bentley lied about Halperin, and that is to look for some sort of conspiracy—not the kind of grand conspiracy that Peake demolishes, but a conspiracy against this one man, Maurice Halperin. To come up with a conspiracy theory that is in any way plausible, it is necessary to make the FBI, and specifically J. Edgar Hoover, the architect. This may seem farfetched, but that is not necessarily so.

We know that the FBI was on Halperin's case before he ever came to Washington and that Hoover had taken a personal interest in it by the time Halperin joined the COI. We know also that Halperin indirectly discredited the FBI's activities in Mexico shortly after Pearl Harbor, and that the memo he wrote about it was forwarded to the White House right in the middle of a bitter squabble between Donovan and Hoover over whose agency would have jurisdiction in Latin America. We know also that Halperin and the Latin America Division embarrassed the FBI during the war over phony reports that were coming from the Bureau's agents in Latin America. It is also fairly common knowledge that Hoover had a thin skin and a long memory. If there is any doubt about that, recall that he was involved in, and ultimately responsible for, the FBI effort to destroy the career of David Halperin, whose only sin was that he had the wrong father. The attack on David nearly a decade after his father had left the country was really part of Hoover's vendetta against Maurice, against this so-and-so who took on the FBI and came up with "a handful of diamonds." This FBI episode with David is the one fact that supports the mini-conspiracy hypothesis.

Proceeding from this hypothesis we can now imagine a situation in which Bentley might have lied. She turns herself in to the FBI in October of 1945. The FBI debriefs her in October and November (before the deposition), meticulously checks her story and concludes that she is telling the truth in all important matters they can check. During the debriefing she discusses her acquaintance with Halperin, and the story she tells is basically the same story that Halperin himself tells, that is, she saw him two or three times in his house and he chatted with her in very general terms about Latin American affairs. After that she never saw him again.

Hoover hears about this and finally sees a way to skewer Halperin. Bentley has already admitted to spying, and she has agreed to talk without receiving immunity from prosecution. Indeed, in the introductory paragraph to her deposition she even states that "this statement may be used against me in court." This clearly puts her in jeopardy, and Hoover has no difficulty persuading her to embroider a bit on the brief acquaintance with Halperin. And so, coached by Bureau agents, she fabricates the tale about Halperin that she finally sets down in her deposition. This is not a case of memorizing hundreds of lies about dozens of people. All she has to do is go along with a few lies about one man whose whole family, residence and lifestyle she knows well enough to discuss comfortably, if she ever has to testify about them. In this explanation of the affair, Hoover is the villain, Bentley a pawn, and Halperin the victim. Of course, the Hoover-vendetta theory fits equally well with a guilty Halperin, the only difference being that Hoover would not have needed to coerce Bentley into lying.

The only other way to explain why Bentley was lying is to suggest that she was engaged in a neurotic fantasy that was centered on, and limited to, Maurice Halperin. In view of the neurotic and alcoholic behavior that she displayed in the later years of her life, this is not outside the realm of possibility. But there were no signs of this sort of behavior when she turned herself in or for several years thereafter. Halperin, himself, describes her as perfectly normal. Anyhow, why Halperin and no one else? To answer that, one would have to fabricate a whole fantasy life for Bentley, which would be no more than a fantasy about a fantasy. It is really a much less plausible answer to our question than the Hoover hypothesis, however plausible that might be.

Many years ago Frank Stockton wrote a charming story called "The Lady or the Tiger?" It tells of a "semi-barbaric king" in olden times who settled the guilt or innocence of accused criminals in a most unusual fashion. He would place the accused before two identical doors in a vast and crowded amphitheater. Behind one of the doors lurked the fiercest tiger in the kingdom; behind the other, the fairest damsel in the realm. The accused then had to walk up to one of the doors and open it. If he chose the tiger he was immediately torn to pieces, which settled the questions of guilt and punishment at the same time. If he chose the one that hid the maiden, his innocence was proven, and he was rewarded on the spot with her hand in marriage and no doubt a future of wealth and bliss. (The modern reader will note that there were apparently no female offenders in the realm.) In this manner justice was meted out with complete impartiality, and the public was entertained with great frequency.

Now, it happened that the semi-barbaric king had a semi-barbaric daughter, beautiful and passionate, and that the daughter was deeply, secretly and, alas, apparently quite physically in love with one of the king's lesser young courtiers. Before long the king found out about the illicit affair, as kings will in these fables, and there was nothing for it but to put the young man to trial. Into the amphitheater he went, and before the two doors he was placed. Behind one waited a ferocious tiger. Behind the other waited a beautiful maiden. And directly above him sat the king and the king's daughter. Passionately involved as she was in the case of the accused, the princess had, through great effort and massive bribes, found out the secret of the doors. She knew which one hid the tiger and which one hid the lady. She knew that if her lover chose one door he would be ripped apart before her semi-barbaric eyes. She knew that if he chose the other he would be married on the spot to a beautiful maiden—also before her semi-barbaric eyes. When the accused bowed to the royal box his eyes met hers, and he knew instantly that she held the secret, which she confirmed in that moment by moving her arm imperceptibly toward the door on the right. Confident in the depth of their love, the young man walked without hesitation to the door on the right and opened it.

At that point Stockton abandons the story and asks the reader to consider the situation very carefully before providing his or her own ending. In one sense, the key lies in the psychology of the princess. Is her love deep enough to permit her lover to spend the rest of his life in the arms of another woman? Or is it so fierce that she would rather see him torn to shreds than yield him up to another woman? In a more subtle sense, however, the key lies in the psychology of the reader, for what reader would be able to suppress his or her own psyche in order to ponder that of the princess? Stockton makes an equally strong case for either decision by the young lass—that she would sacrifice her own happiness to save him for another woman, and that she would yield to jealous rage and destroy him first. Remember, she was only semi-barbaric. Did the "semi" prevail, or did the barbaric? In trying to answer how the lady responded, the reader, consciously or otherwise, is also asking, How would *I* have responded?

Of course, the analogy between Stockton's story and Halperin's story does not stand up to really close scrutiny. But there is a similarity in that you, the reader, have a story with two possible endings, and you can make a pretty good case for either one. That is the predicament of the historian without (and often even with) solid evidence. You now have essentially the same information that I have. I can only proceed with my understanding of the probabilities. If you are going to provide a conclusion to this episode, you must do as I had to do. You must plunge into the evidence with all of your biases, prejudices, predilections, and wishes at work. If you do that you will not just passively find an answer; you will become a part of it. There is no "objective" way to settle this matter.

Remember that your decision not only directs you toward a judgment of Halperin, but also helps to shape your understanding of an era. In terms of our story then, and not Stockton's, which one was it, the lady or the tiger? Bentley or Halperin?

Epilogue

Having come this far, the reader may be a bit put off by my lady-or-tiger gambit. Just how does the historian take odds and ends from the past and make them into history? Specifically, how does this historian, without any hard, documentary evidence, do it with these particular odds and ends? "If you leave it to the reader, Kirschner, it's a cop-out," said one recent critic. "Was it the lady or the tiger?" A reasonable question.

First of all, let me return to the best case I can make for Halperin. Remember that the FBI was onto Halperin before he ever left Oklahoma and that he had insulted FBI intelligence activities in Mexico at a particularly sensitive moment of intra-governmental tension at the end of 1941. During the war, Halperin obviously enjoyed spreading the word that FBI agents in Latin America were putting something over on Hoover with some phony reporting, and Hoover was not a man to forget such humiliation. Ever. Thus, when Elizabeth Bentley turned herself in to the FBI in 1945, Hoover was no doubt delighted to hear whatever she had to say about Maurice Halperin. And from the astonishing effort made to destroy Halperin by destroying the career of his son almost twenty years later we know that Hoover was capable of carrying on a vendetta of Sicilian dimensions. All of this might well justify the assertion that Hoover and his agents "coached" Bentley to lie about Halperin. It is clearly a possibility.

But is it probable? Let us suppose for a moment that Hoover did induce Bentley to lie under oath about Halperin. If he did, surely Halperin's case was not unique. If Hoover suborned perjury in the Halperin affair, it would be reasonable to assume that he did so in others as well. It would be reasonable to assume that the commission of felonies was a standard procedure for him. But if that was the case, why did he back off from David Halperin years later? He apparently did try unsuccessfully to induce David's mentor at the hospital to fire David as an incompetent, but that is a far cry from suborning perjury. If he was unable to find anything legitimate on David, all he had to do was fabricate a little evidence—perhaps produce some latter-day Bentley to commit perjury about David's politics. It would have ruined David and satisfied Hoover's lust for vengeance against Halperin. But he didn't. We have to assume either that he underwent a remarkable change of methods and character between 1945 and 1962 or that he never suborned perjury with Bentley in the first place. While perjury remains a possibility, it seems improbable when one considers the case against Halperin.

What is that case? It is purely circumstantial; it is based more on the cumulative effect of many little things than on the heavy impact of any large one; it is *my* construction of the case, and it can be countered at every step of the way with an alternative explanation of those "little things." In fact, to help the reader do just that, I have included Maurice Halperin's own response to many of the points I raise, although I have exercised the privilege of commenting on some of his responses.

First of all, there is the matter of Halperin's political views. He describes himself as an issues-oriented fellow traveler. That is, he was never committed to the party line on ideological grounds but was drawn to support the Soviet Union on specific issues, above all on its call for collective action against the threat of Nazi Germany in the mid-1930s.

Actually there are hints throughout Halperin's reminiscences that there was much more commitment to ideology in his stance than he cares to admit. For instance, in his 1934 analysis of the Mexican situation, he threw a gratuitous barb at New Deal domestic affairs that was plainly congenial to the "Third-Period" line of the Communist party at the time, when FDR was still labeled a "social fascist." This had absolutely nothing to do with Soviet foreign policy or action against the rise of fascism. It is a small thing, but it sets off a small alarm.

It is also odd that when the party engineered the journey to Cuba in 1935 it could find no one between New York and Oklahoma who knew more about Cuba than Halperin. Halperin says that his name came to the attention of the organizers when *Time* magazine cited his 1934 article on Mexico. But knowledge of Mexican affairs does not qualify one as an expert on Cuba any more than knowledge of Canadian affairs qualifies one as an expert on Australia, simply because they share a common language. To me it seems odd that the organizers searched him out at a distance of two thousand miles—not decisive, but odd. (MAURICE: "There were very few specialists in the U.S. on Cuba at the time. One of them, Carleton Beals, spoke at the public meeting the night before we left. Going to Cuba to investigate human rights violations by Batista was risky. This could explain why Beals chose to lambaste Batista from New York rather than in Havana. Mexico and Cuba share certain Latin American characteristics. I was a Mexico specialist, but also a Latin Americanist. I was one of only two people in our group who were fluent in Spanish. . . . The leftist orientation of my article on Mexico would make me compatible with the purpose of the expedition. My being invited—and we don't know whether one or more others had turned down the invitation—seems reasonable, not 'odd.' ")

Then there is the matter of Halperin's signature on that open letter about the Soviet Union in 1939. It is a far more incriminating sign of belief than the voyage to Cuba, for this had absolutely nothing to do with issues, either with Soviet foreign policy or Latin American affairs. It was a hymn of praise to Soviet democracy that was clearly defined by party ideology. It is hard to see how anyone could have signed it who did not believe it. Halperin could easily have supported Soviet policy without praising Soviet domestic affairs. Why did he endorse the statement if he did not believe it? (MAURICE: "Explicitly the statement had nothing to do with Soviet foreign policy. But *implicitly* it had everything to do with it. At the moment it was support for the only major power with a militant anti-Nazi policy." DON: There were plenty of people at the time who supported Soviet foreign policy without feeling compelled to endorse some fantasy about Soviet democracy. That was the very purpose of the Popular Front, after all.)

This statement was followed almost immediately by the Nazi-Soviet Pact. For an issues-oriented man, here was an issue—*the* issue, in fact—which he says had engaged him as a fellow traveler in the first place. His weekly column in the university newspaper gave him a

forum, one which he had often used to comment on foreign affairs
and on the domestic affairs of foreign nations. He was free to write
on anything he wished, yet at this world-shaking event he fell mute;
not a word about a Soviet action that freed Hitler to start World War
II; not a word about the Soviet invasion of Poland a few weeks after
the war started; not a word about the Soviet invasion of Finland at
the end of November. He may have been dismayed by the pact, as he
says, but the sale of his Soviet bond does not speak louder than his
silence in these matters. Stalin was in bed with Hitler, yet this didn't
arouse Maurice's anti-fascist impulse at all. His silence, in fact, seems
to excuse Soviet aggression. He was obviously not prepared to weigh
the sins of Stalin on the same scale that he used to weigh the sins
of Hitler—not even after the war started—and the only explanation is
that a powerful ideological residue remained to keep him silent.

The little hints continue to accumulate in his recollections of postwar
events. For instance, very early in our conversations, he told me that he
voted for Harry Truman in 1948, because he feared that a Republican
president would trash the entire New Deal. It was only later, when he
told me he had been inclined to blame the Americans for the Cold
War, that the 1948 election popped back into my mind. That was the
election in which Henry Wallace bolted from the Democratic party
and ran on a third-party ticket for the presidency with the blessing
and support of the Communist party.

The overriding issue for Wallace's Progressive party was the Cold
War, and its analysis of the Cold War followed the Communist party
line very closely: America was entirely to blame, not the Soviet Union.
The election took place right in the middle of the Berlin blockade and
airlift, which was one of the defining moments of the Cold War, a
moment of terror that lasted almost a year, an event that many feared
would start World War III. At precisely that time Henry Wallace was
offering an alternative to Truman's abrasive anti-Soviet posture, and
by his own admission, Halperin was then still a fellow traveler. The
election was almost a litmus test of beliefs. Those who followed the
Soviet line on the Cold War voted for Wallace. If Maurice voted for
Truman in 1948, he was the only fellow traveler in the United States
who did. If he voted for Wallace, however, it certainly makes him

sound less ideological to say he voted for Truman. (MAURICE: "The only period I fully supported Soviet foreign policy was *prior* to the Cold War. . . . I did not want to see the Cold War intensified. The dangers of a hot war were too great. Privately I felt the Soviet slogan 'peaceful coexistence' pointed in the right direction. Publicly I took no stand on this issue." DON: In an earlier taped interview with me, Halperin said that he had placed *primary* blame for the Cold War on the Americans until he was "200 percent disabused" of this belief by Russian liberals *during his tenure in Moscow years later*. And by the way, how one votes is not a matter of public stance.)

Then there is the discrepancy between what Halperin first told me about his response to Khrushchev's speech at the Twentieth Party Congress in 1956 and his daughter's recollection of his response. Maurice said that the most surprising thing about the speech was that it was made at all, and he added that the nature and extent of "Stalin's criminality" were shocking. But otherwise, he said, the substance of the speech did not particularly surprise him because of reservations he had harbored about Soviet domestic affairs since the purge trials of the 1930s. He was not really disillusioned by it all, because he had never held any illusions in the first place. But Judith said that the speech had had a "profound influence" on her father. Unlike most other academicians in his position, she continued, "my father was absorbing this information and was changing his mind." Changing his mind from what? If the speech had that *profound* an influence on him, it calls into question his professed doubts about the purges of the 1930s. The only people who were shocked by the revelations of 1956 were those who had never seriously questioned reports about the purges in the first place. In fact, by 1956 they were the only people for whom these were revelations at all, since, in broad outline, the information had been in the public domain for twenty years. It took an act of will to ignore it. (MAURICE asserts that "most politically sophisticate[d] people in the West were astounded" at the time. Don: In 1956? The only thing astounding about the speech was that it was made at all. I knew and read a lot of politically sophisticated people at the time, and not one of them—not one—was surprised at its substance. The only people who expressed surprise were people who were still to some degree apologists for the Soviet Union. Are those the 1956 political sophisticates Maurice was talking about?)

There is another factor, and it involves something that came to my attention only very recently—in fact, only after I had finished a preliminary draft of this epilogue. At this point it is necessary to return to the allegations of Nathaniel Weyl. Recall the situation. Weyl had appeared before SISS almost immediately after Halperin did in March 1953. In his testimony, Weyl said he had heard from Homer Brooks, the party organizer for Texas and Oklahoma, that Halperin was a Communist, and that this information was confirmed for him a short time later by Valentín Campa in Mexico. Halperin says he has never heard of Homer Brooks and that he was already known to party people in Mexico, but only as a fellow traveler.

Because of the serious discrepancy in these two accounts, I had tried to track down Weyl but had long since abandoned the search as a lost cause. Now, thanks to a very recent tip, I have been able to contact Weyl, and he has added some vital information to that long-ago Senate testimony. The primary source for that testimony was actually Weyl's wife, who had been a party member with him at the time, and who broke from the party when he did over the Stalin-Hitler Pact. When Weyl first spoke to the FBI after the outbreak of the Korean War, he told them that he did not want to involve his wife, Sylvia, and would not discuss her publicly. The Bureau accepted his decision and did not press him on the matter. However, since his wife died several years ago, he feels there is no longer any need to protect her. The information he adds now is so important that I think it is necessary to quote him precisely on his major point:

> When I came to Houston, Sylvia accepted the job of organization secretary (the no. 2 spot) of the Texas-Oklahoma district of the CP. When we went down to Mexico, Homer told her to take over Halperin's job as rep to the Mexican Party. She met with Halperin at our hotel. I seem to recall meeting him then, but was not present at her talk with him. She told me that he had been uncooperative and resentful at having been replaced.[1]

1. Nathaniel Weyl, letter to author, August 7, 1993.

Not long after this letter, I spoke with Weyl over the telephone to clarify a few points, and he said that this meeting would have taken place some time in 1936 or 1937, when he and his wife were in Mexico together for the first time. He added that his wife had asked Halperin for whatever records he had of his affairs with the Mexican party but that Halperin had only turned over some clippings, probably from the Mexican CP newspaper. It is worth noting that Halperin is an inveterate newspaper clipper, which I did not mention to Weyl. Bentley confirms this as well. Weyl repeated that Halperin seemed to be very unhappy with the situation. Weyl could not explain why Brooks had made this decision, but he assumed that it was simply because Brooks had more confidence in his wife than in Halperin.[2]

So Weyl, himself an expert in Mexican affairs, an admitted former Communist, and a man of apparent integrity, clearly implicates Halperin as a Communist party member in the 1930s. In his letter to me Weyl observes that "the criterion for the communist movement at that time was not whether one carried a membership card (neither Sylvia nor I did), but whether or not one accepted the discipline of the party and understood its ideology and line. If Dr. Halperin says he was never a party member, this may be a semantic issue without too much substance."

Is Weyl lying? If so, we must add one more participant to the plot against Halperin. Like Bentley, he would have been a perjurer, coached either by the FBI or by SISS itself. But if that had been the case, why should he have limited his perjury to mere hearsay? By Halperin's own account the two had met in the 1930s. So if Weyl was prepared to lie at all, why not really do a job of it and say that Maurice himself had revealed his party membership when they met?

Then there is the matter of motive. What earthly reason would Weyl have for lying? To be sure, Weyl's information is only hearsay, but hearsay from three different sources, including his wife, cannot be ignored. Or are we to believe that his wife lied to him? (MAURICE: "Let me state for the record that while I do remember meeting Weyl once and very briefly at the Mexican CP where I was doing research

2. Nathaniel Weyl, telephone conversation with author, August 20, 1993.

on an article, I did not meet his wife, much less alone in a hotel room. I was never anybody's 'rep' to the Mexican CP, so I couldn't lose a job I didn't have." DON: For the record, in an earlier taped interview with me, Halperin clearly stated that he had met Weyl's wife in Mexico at the time.)

It is important to emphasize that none of this implicates Halperin in espionage or even identifies him positively as a member of the party. Nor does any one of these factors prove anything by itself. Taken together, however, they suggest a pattern of dissembling on Halperin's part that was intended to obscure the degree of his commitment to the Soviet Union over a twenty-year period. The evidence suggests—to me at least—that this was not just a matter of anti-fascist foreign policy, but that he *believed* in the Soviet Union and in the Communist party as well. Since that was not at all uncommon in the era, and certainly not illegal, one has to wonder why he has not been more forthcoming about it.

The developments in Boston, in 1953, were something else. If earlier discrepancies set off a small alarm in my ear, these set off fire bells and sirens. There was, for instance, Halperin's springtime compromise with the university committee that was looking into his appearance before SISS. He agreed to issue a statement that he had never been a party member while he was at BU, but he told the committee that he would continue to take the Fifth Amendment before SISS on all questions pertaining to his beliefs and affiliations. When he explained to the Senate committee that its investigation was an unacceptable threat to the principle of academic freedom, he implied that this was an important reason for his refusal to cooperate. In light of that statement, it is difficult to understand why Halperin did not see a challenge to the same principle when the university committee pried into his beliefs and affiliations. If academic freedom was really the issue, then Halperin should never have told the committee that he had not been a member of the Communist party during his tenure at Boston University. He should have told them that he could not, in good conscience, make any kind of statement to them about party membership at any point in his life. He should have told the university committee exactly what he had told SISS, i.e., that they had no right to pry into his political beliefs.

But this was not really a matter of principle; academic freedom was not the issue at all. The only convincing reason for Halperin's silence before the Jenner Committee was that he did not want to deny his affiliation under oath.

The situation became much more serious the following November, when the Halperins left for Mexico after Maurice was publicly accused of having committed espionage for the Soviet Union. He says that he and Edith simply appraised the situation and decided to leave because no good could come of it in the growing climate of repression. There was no panic, no flight; they just left, knowing that Maurice could make a living in Mexico. Except for Halperin's own recollection, however, all the evidence indicates that he did not just leave, he fled. He did not wait to defend himself at the impending university hearing, and he did not tell a soul in the university community that he was departing. A man who always observed the common courtesies, he did not even call the president of BU to tell him that he was leaving.

There are implications in this situation that raise serious doubts. The Halperins have always been a close-knit family. Maurice and Edith were certainly loving and caring parents. Nevertheless, they left David behind to finish his school year when they went to Mexico in November. This is not to say that they abandoned David. On the contrary, he was left in the care of Maurice's parents, which must certainly have minimized worry. Still, one feels that there had to be a powerful reason for them to leave without him, especially when one remembers that Halperin had a hearing pending at the university and that he had been suspended with pay and had a contractual commitment from the university for at least that academic year. Even if the university had dismissed him after his hearing, it would doubtless have paid him the balance of his salary for the year, and Edith could have continued with her job teaching school.[3] There was simply no economic reason for them to leave. They could have waited for David

---

3. The consequences for Fifth Amendment professors were mixed. HUAC indicted some of them but sent none to prison; SISS did not indict any of them. Some universities fired their silent professors; others did not. See especially chapter 7 of Schrecker's *No Ivory Tower*.

to finish his school year, and left for Mexico together if the hearing at BU resulted in dismissal. For that matter, anxiety about making a living beyond that year scarcely explains so sudden a move to a foreign country. The teacher shortage was just becoming a matter of concern at the time, and there were jobs available for someone with Edith's credentials and experience.

Thus "making a living" does not explain the Halperins' decampment from Boston. It might explain why they chose Mexico, but it does not explain why they left in the first place. This only emphasizes the significance of leaving David behind and supports the contention of Maurice's colleagues at the university that there was a shocking haste in their departure.

There is still more reason to question Halperin's version of the Boston affair. Maurice claims a memory lapse in his original account. The six weeks he remembered when the matter first came up turned out to be only a few days. Well, he said, one's memory sometimes does strange things after forty years. It is a reasonable explanation. My memory often does strange things after forty days. But that is not the way he told it to a visiting professor from Latin America in the early 1970s. According to a friend of mine (who prefers to remain anonymous), this professor said that Halperin had described the departure from Boston in terms that could only be summed up as fear and flight. Moreover, at about the same time, Edith Halperin told a similar tale to a local faculty wife. So Halperin's memory was quite accurate for at least twenty years after the event.

To me, Halperin's account of the Boston affair simply does not make sense. The most persuasive conclusion is that he cobbled together a misleading story about his departure because the truth would appear incriminating. He tried to convey the impression that he did not run, that he had no reason to do so. But he did run, and he must have believed it was necessary. This does not necessarily indicate panic. The departure could very well have been part of a contingency plan; nonetheless, it was precipitate. In the end, it is not only his flight that is suspicious, but the tale he created to disguise that flight. (MAURICE: "What were [we] fleeing from? The implication is from possible arrest. This meant getting out of the jurisdiction of the U.S. *promptly.*

Does traveling 6 days on main highways in broad daylight in an easily identified Studebaker to cross into Mexico, past U.S. border surveillance, constitute 'flight'? If flight were our motive, it would have made much more sense to drive to Canada in a matter of a few hours." DON: Halperin was not under arrest, indictment, or subpoena. Except for his brother and his parents, not a soul even knew he had left Boston. He could have taken six days or sixteen or twenty-six, and he could have done cartwheels across the border without raising suspicion, *because no one was looking for him.* He knew he could make a living in Mexico but not in Canada, because Canada did not have the welcome mat out for alleged American "subversives" at the time. Several of his former colleagues at BU believe that he ran, and two people in Vancouver claim to have heard *from him and Edith personally* that they ran. Certainly his behavior—not waiting for his hearing or even to find out when it would take place and not informing president Case of his departure—suggests that he was fleeing. But why did he do it? Maybe it was because he was guilty and afraid that the government would produce evidence against him. Maybe it was because he was innocent and afraid the government would fabricate evidence against him. What intrigues me is that he insists he did not run when everything suggests that he did.)

Unfortunately, Halperin's memory of the BU situation is still doing strange things, and apparently no amount of prodding or evidence to the contrary can set it straight, even now. In his recent book on Cuba, written *after* he had read my account of the BU affair, he says, "My conduct before the Jenner Committee led to a protracted and disagreeable ordeal of questioning by Boston University, under strong outside pressure and with a frightened faculty and passive student body. The result was at first suspension and then dismissal. Thus in late 1953, Edith and I drove to Mexico City to begin a new chapter in our lives."[4]

But the faculty, according to some surviving members of it, was not frightened, and the questioning by BU leading up to Halperin's

4. Maurice Halperin, *Return to Havana: The Decline of Cuban Society under Castro* (Nashville: Vanderbilt University Press, 1994), 10.

departure was neither protracted nor disagreeable, because it never happened. He and Edith left before the university had a chance to do any questioning at all. Moreover, he clearly implies that he left for Mexico because he was fired. But we have seen that it was the other way around; he was fired only after he had fled to Mexico and refused BU's renewed offer of due process, its offer to fly him back for a hearing at the university's expense.

Halperin's departure from Mexico five years later is also curious. It is clear that if the police had found him they would have returned him to the United States, but why did he go into hiding so that he could arrange to go to the Soviet Union in preference to returning to America? The most likely answer is fear, just as fear had driven him to Mexico in the first place. But fear of what? Did he worry about not being able to make a living? It is not likely. The teacher shortage in the States was critical by then, and Edith could probably have had her pick of jobs. For that matter, Maurice could surely have found some sort of job himself, if not one commensurate with his training, experience, and ability. He had contacts all over the country, and there were publishing houses, obscure trade journals, and bookstores everywhere. Even Alger Hiss, notorious, rightly or wrongly, as a one-time Soviet spy and by then an ex-convict, found work after his release from prison. The Halperins could surely have lived in at least modest comfort in the States. (MAURICE: "Had they found us, we would have been deported, as others were, to the U.S. Not a desirable thing to have on one's C. V., and complicating our return to Mexico where we both had jobs, our apartment and all our possessions. . . . Then again, nothing attractive waiting for us in the U.S. More bad publicity, negative effect on uncertain job situation [your optimism unfounded] and great likelihood that the kind of job I wanted would not be available. On the other hand, if I could go to the Soviet Union I had nothing to lose and an extraordinary new experience to gain. [And this is exactly the way it turned out.]" DON: What "return to Mexico"? The Halperins were being thrown out of the country. They were given three months to wrap up their affairs [apartment, possessions], whether their destination was America or the USSR. This had nothing to do with their choice not to return to the

United States. And how did Maurice think opting for the Soviet Union would look on his C. V.? What kind of publicity did he think would come of that? Arthur Schlesinger, Jr., for instance, took it as evidence that Halperin was indeed a Communist. Perhaps that was an incorrect inference, but it was a reasonable one.)

Was Halperin afraid that he, an innocent man, might be sent to prison? That is certainly a possibility, but it is one that must be appraised cautiously. By the end of 1958, when the situation in Mexico had turned sour for Maurice, the political atmosphere back home was beginning to clear. The Supreme Court had rediscovered the First Amendment when it severely trimmed the Smith Act in 1957. It was moving carefully, but it was moving.

More directly relevant to Halperin's situation was the example of Owen Lattimore. Lattimore, whose own credentials as a fellow traveler in the late 1930s were substantial, and who was sympathetic to the emergent Communist regime in China after the war, chose, nevertheless, to return from Afghanistan in 1950 to defend himself from Senator McCarthy's slanderous charge that he was the "top" Soviet espionage agent in the United States. A one-time fellow traveler publicly accused of espionage for the Soviet Union, his situation was not unlike the one facing Halperin a few years later in Boston. But Lattimore fought Senator McCarthy; he fought Senator McCarran and SISS later on; and eventually he fought the Justice Department on a perjury charge. (They came up with perjury because there was no Elizabeth Bentley in his background to lend even faint credibility to the charge of espionage.) And he did it all without taking the Fifth Amendment. It took more than five years, but he was exonerated in 1955, when a federal judge dismissed the charges against him and the Justice Department chose not to pursue the matter any further. The precedent having been set by Lattimore in the worst part of the 1950s, an innocent Halperin could almost surely have faced down the Justice Department in 1959, if it had ever come to that. Instead, he chose to go to Moscow. Was he afraid the government might actually produce some sort of evidence after all this time? If not, why else did he hide in Mexico rather than return? (MAURICE: "re Owen Lattimore. His ordeal was exactly what I wanted to avoid—an expensive, all consuming affair, a career in itself. I had absolutely no interest in being a hero or a martyr. I just wanted to get on with a normal life, or something close to it." DON: My point is that Lattimore made it possible for other unjustly accused people to challenge their accusers *without* having to make a career of it. And just how normal did Maurice expect life to be in Moscow?)

His relatively easy acceptance by the Soviets is also problematic. Maurice had to clear a KGB security check that must have looked, among other things, for some assurance of ideological collegiality. This does not necessarily mean that the KGB gave him sanctuary as a former agent, as they did with Donald MacLean, but at the very least, it does reveal that they found nothing at all worrisome about him.

Even after he came to live in Canada, Maurice continued to avoid the United States. He did not even cross the nearby border for something like twenty years. During that period, he had children and grandchildren living in various American locales from Seattle to Maine. As a semiretired professor he had more time than they to go visiting, but instead they always came up to Vancouver. The impression is that his fear of entering the United States persisted until the late 1980s, when he finally did venture across the border. (MAURICE: "Edith developed a persecution complex, something like paranoia, with respect to returning to the U.S. She also had heart trouble, with frequent anginas. I could have insisted, but didn't want to trigger a heart attack.")

Maurice may be the only person left in North America who really knows the truth about Bentley's charges against him, but beyond the continent there is one other place where the truth is probably recorded. The KGB, remember, did a thorough security check on Halperin when he arrived in Moscow. If he had done any work for the Soviets during the war, his KGB file might well mention it. If it is not in that file, then it is surely either in Bentley's file, if she has her own, or in the file of one of her controls, who undoubtedly have their own. And if it is not in any of those places, then in all likelihood Halperin is telling the truth.

Obviously I was aware of this from the beginning, but I paid no attention to it because I knew that not even *glasnost* would open the files of the KGB for me. And then, startlingly, the situation in the Soviet Union changed so rapidly that there no longer was a Soviet Union and no longer a KGB; there was a Russia and a Russian Intelligence Service. Soon the word came out that the RIS was opening some of the KGB files to a select few Western scholars. Why not me, I wondered. That summer I told Maurice that I was going to contact the former KGB to see if I could arrange to go to Moscow and search the relevant files. What did he think of the idea? His spontaneous response was, "Well, you know, you can't trust anything you get from the KGB because they're completely unreliable and dishonest." On a later occasion he said that if I thought it would be of any use, he supposed I should go ahead, but he repeated his doubts.

In the end the RIS turned down my request,[5] but the remarkable thing was Halperin's initial response to my proposal. Here was a man who says he has lived under a cloud of false accusation for a half-century. He should have leaped at the opportunity to get into the KGB files and show the world at last that a terrible wrong had been done to him. He should have gone to the rooftops and shouted, "Now you'll see. I told you all along that I was innocent, and now you'll have to believe me." Not Maurice—his response was to warn me not to believe what he was afraid I *might* find. But this is absurd. How could KGB files implicate him in espionage if he was never involved in it? Why would the Soviets have bothered? This was not the response I would have expected from an innocent man, and it did not surprise me at all. And yet. . . .

Postscript to an Epilogue

There is a principle in logic known as "Occam's razor," which says, in effect, that when there are two or more possible solutions to a problem we should choose the simplest. Or, to put it in terms of my earlier framework, we have to look for the most probable explanation. Hayden Peake, for example, applied that principle in

---

5. See the Note on Sources.

testing the credibility of Elizabeth Bentley. To be sure, the course of human affairs is complex, and sometimes the simplest explanation turns out to be the wrong explanation. In any case, I have followed this principle throughout, and it has been a distressing exercise for me, for it has led me to indict someone I am fond of and admire in many ways. I don't know if Halperin was a party member or not, but I don't think that is really important. I don't have any idea what the degree of his complicity was, and I don't think that is important either. What matters is that, in the essentials of the story, I believe the lady, not the tiger.

Still, for me it is difficult to stand in judgment against Maurice. If I had come along ten or fifteen years earlier, I might have found myself ideologically at home in the Popular Front, too, perhaps even in the party. And from there who can say? A little inside information nudged out of me by a pleasant, intelligent woman, then a piece of paper slipped to her, and then who knows what more? When I put myself in that position it seems as easy to fall into such a pattern almost accidentally as to plunge into it deliberately. And why not? The enemy was evil, and the situation was urgent.

But I didn't come along in the 1930s. I came of age politically after the war, when it was no longer fashionable to be pro-Soviet. By then the Soviet Union was a curse, not a cause in America. For me it was easy.

Note on Sources

The basic source for this book is Maurice Halperin himself. I have had to rely primarily on what he told me in the several dozen hours of our taped interviews. Conducting the interviews was, in itself, a delightful experience, for Halperin is an accomplished raconteur with a lifetime worth of stories about famous, non-famous, and infamous people, places, and events. Unfortunately, there was often no way I could verify his account. Most of the people I would like to have interviewed or written to are either dead or unavailable to me in foreign countries. Please note also that my interviews with him were all taped before Gorbachev fell from power, which will explain why Halperin refers to Gorbachev as if he were still the Soviet leader.

Halperin's own publications sprawl over more than fifty years, and provide insights into his shifting ideas, attitudes, and moods. In some cases what he did not write was as significant as what he did. Personnel at the Oklahoma University library were especially helpful in locating his early writings, and with steering me toward newspaper accounts of his troubles at the university in 1941.

For the OSS years, Woodrow Borah was kind enough to tape two interviews with me. David Bushnell, another eminent Latin American historian, who was a very junior member of the OSS during the war, generously responded to my enquiry, but he was not able to add to what I already knew. Letters to Robert Rogers, Halperin's administrative assistant at the OSS, and to Karl Deutsch, one of Halperin's prize recruits to the outfit, went unanswered. Maurice had already cautioned me that both men were quite infirm. Arthur Schlesinger, Jr., added information about the OSS years. I spent some time at the National Archives in Washington poring over declassified OSS material, and regretting the fact that I was not permitted to pore over the mountain of recently declassified, but still unindexed and inaccessible, documents from that outfit.

I was able to track down Nathaniel Weyl, who had a revealing encounter with Halperin in the 1930s, which he testified about before the Senate Internal Security Subcommittee in the 1950s; Weyl added vital information to that given in testimony in the 1990s. On the other hand, James Lamphere, who was put in charge of the FBI's Bentley files in the 1950s, responded at some length to my inquiry but was unable to add to what I already knew about the woman.

I received copies of the FBI files on both Maurice and David Halperin and the relevant part of Bentley's 1945 deposition to the FBI. All three of these sources proved to be extremely important.

After the collapse of the Soviet Union, I contacted the Russian Intelligence Service (the former KGB) by fax to see if they would allow me to search their files for information on Halperin. An affirmative response would have had me on the next plane to Moscow, but they replied that "in accordance with the practice established by intelligence services throughout the world the RIS does not comment on allegations about this or that person cooperating or having cooperated with it."

I had more success with my inquiries into Halperin's departure from Boston in 1953. I received illuminating replies from several former faculty colleagues of Halperin's, and, with the very competent assistance of Elizabeth McCrank, was able to get important information from university and local press sources.

Many of these sources corroborated Halperin's accounts, but in a few telling instances they contradicted his version. Where there was no contrary evidence, I generally accepted his word, but, in view of what was at stake for him, I did so without great enthusiasm. For all I know he has been lying through his teeth to me from the beginning. That is not a comforting thought, but I had to proceed with it in mind; so should the reader.

Index